MONUMENTAL
MOBILITY

MONUMENTAL MOBILITY

The Memory Work of Massasoit

Lisa Blee &
Jean M. O'Brien

THE UNIVERSITY OF NORTH CAROLINA PRESS

Chapel Hill

Designed by Jamison Cockerham
Set in Arno, Sorts Mill Goudy, and Scala Sans
by Tseng Information Systems, Inc.

Manufactured in the United States of America

The University of North Carolina Press has been a member
of the Green Press Initiative since 2003.

Cover illustration: Cyrus E. Dallin's statue of Massasoit,
courtesy Robbins Library, Arlington, Mass.

LIBRARY OF CONGRESS CATALOGING-IN-PUBLICATION DATA
Names: Blee, Lisa, author. | O'Brien, Jean M., author.
Title: Monumental mobility : the memory work of Massasoit /
Lisa Blee and Jean M. O'Brien.
Description: Chapel Hill : University of North Carolina Press, [2019] |
Includes bibliographical references and index.
Identifiers: LCCN 2018029696 | ISBN 9781469648392 (cloth : alk. paper) |
ISBN 9781469648408 (pbk : alk. paper) | ISBN 9781469648415 (ebook)
Subjects: LCSH: Massasoit, 1580–1661—Monuments—Massachusetts—
Plymouth. | Wampanoag Indians—Monuments—History. | Monuments—
Social aspects—United States. | Monuments—Political aspects—United
States. | Collective memory—United States.
Classification: LCC E99.W2 B58 2019 | DDC 974.4004/973480092—dc23
LC record available at https://lccn.loc.gov/2018029696

Portions of chapters 1 and 2 appeared earlier in somewhat different form in Jean M. O'Brien and Lisa M. Blee, "What Is a Monument of Massasoit Doing in Kansas City? The Memory Work of Monuments and Place," in "Unexpected Ethnohistories: In, of, and out of Place," special section, *Ethnohistory* 61, no. 4 (Fall 2014): 635–53.

We dedicate this book to

Indigenous public intellectuals in New England,

whose vitally important work enriches us all.

Contents

MONUMENTAL MOBILITY

PROLOGUE

Surprise and Mobility

In spring 2017, news leaked out that Wampanoag people had organized the reburial of funerary and cultural material and skeletal remains identified as 8sâmeeqan (more commonly known as "Massasoit") at Burr's Hill in Warren, Rhode Island.[1] These remains had been repatriated from seven institutions for compliance with federal law, following years of activism spearheaded by Ramona Peters, Wampanoag tribal historic preservation officer and Native American graves protection and repatriation director.[2] Nearly 350 years after his death, a ceremony honoring the Wampanoag leader, who attained fame in his lifetime for negotiating a treaty with the Pilgrims in 1621, finally occurred at his home. Peters remarked that the seventeenth-century leader "is a significant figure in our shared history. . . . He stands at the crossroad between the Indigenous people of this land and the origins of what would eventually become the United States of America."[3] The return of these human remains seemed especially noteworthy, given the long stretch of time since this important leader's demise. The repatriation truly represented a triumph on behalf of his Wampanoag descendants.

These events occurred just as we were concluding work on this book, a study of the remarkable mobility of a statue of this seventeenth-century leader, originally installed on Cole's Hill in Plymouth, Massachusetts, in 1921 to mark the tercentenary of the landing of the Pilgrims. The book's origins, however, are connected to an entirely different place. One fall day in 2000, as Jeani was walking to a professional meeting near the Country Club Plaza in Kansas City, Missouri, she was stopped dead in her tracks by a full-scale replica of the *Massasoit* monument she knew stood (more appropriately) in Plymouth. Her response, "What's a Monument to Massasoit Doing in Kansas City?," became the genesis of this book, as she filed away this nagging question to take up later on.[4] That "later on" came to be 2008, when Lisa took on the initial research to get to the bottom of the story of the seemingly misplaced monument.[5] Neither one of us could have imagined the places this story of monumental mobility would take us.

This book has involved one surprise after another. For Jeani, one jolt occurred when she realized the sculptor of *Massasoit* also created *Appeal to the Great Spirit*, a ubiquitous image she attempted to reproduce in Conté crayon from a box of greeting cards she found somewhere while an idealistic teen and wannabe artist. As we struggled to get a handle on this intriguing story, tapping into internet search engines aided many of our discoveries. That is how we found *Massasoit* not just in Plymouth and Kansas City, but all over eBay, with countless versions of the statue and its imagery circulating via the internet. The internet tipped us off to *Massasoit* in Salt Lake City, Springville, and Provo, Utah, and to the museum dedicated to the statue's creator, Cyrus E. Dallin, in Arlington, Massachusetts. Most recently (in summer 2016), Lisa discovered on Wikipedia the location of a statue in Dayton, Ohio, that had eluded us for years. Another moment of surprise came to us at the end of one of our trips to Plymouth, when we learned that the Improved Order of Red Men, the fraternal organization responsible for the statue's original installation, still existed (and is headquartered in Waco, Texas), and its research library became a valuable resource.

Plotting on-the-ground research, Lisa stumbled onto a particularly surprising gold mine: she contacted the campus police at Brigham Young University in Provo, Utah (where yet another replica of *Massasoit* stands), to alert them she would be interviewing people passing by the statue on campus, and police detective Arnold Lemmon happened to pick up the phone. Lemmon had been in charge of the massive police investigation regarding art fraud and unauthorized reproductions of the statue in the 1970s at BYU, and Lisa connected with him just two years before he retired—a near miss of a critical link to our work. Lemmon generously shared his time, his thoughts, and reports on the investigation itself, which allowed us to crack the case for much of the monumental mobility we had set out to understand. Interviews of passersby in Salt Lake City took surprisingly personal turns as well: Lisa was invited to the home of a Navajo couple and into the legislative office of a man who wished to share both a draft bill offering an apology for the state's role in violence toward Indigenous peoples and his family's story of adopting Native children. During one trip to Utah, we stumbled onto Plymouth, Utah, one of more than two dozen communities across the United States connected to the original Plymouth in Massachusetts where this story is anchored.[6] These fortuitous discoveries drove home something important for us: this was a place-based project that required boots on the ground. We had to go to these places and talk to people. In the case of Plymouth, Massachusetts, and in particular the Indigenous people who spoke with us (especially Darius Coombs, Linda Coombs, Paula Peters, and Ramona Peters), this place-based research is deeply connected to a place-based people. But it also set in motion our effort to understand the mobility of messages attached to monuments in time and space: while a particular set of circumstances unleashed this statue from its initial place of installation on Cole's Hill in Plymouth, we wondered about the mobility of the meanings intended by this monument, and our investigations involved grappling with that knotty problem.

Wampanoag and Indigenous people in New England more generally have always been mobile, as well as connected to particular places in their homelands. One striking connection to the monumental mobility we assess here came through to us in a conversation with Aquinnah Wampanoag Linda Coombs, program coordinator of the Aquinnah Cultural Center on Martha's Vineyard. As we explained our project about monumental mobility in April 2017, she initially expressed surprise at our story but then pointed out the longstanding mobility of Wampanoag people that included their heavy involvement in the whaling industry: "We have relatives in . . . New Zealand, in Hawaii . . . in the Arctic, literally blood relatives. . . . And last March . . . we had a man [visit] from . . . the Maori people—he and his wife are both Maori, but he's a Gay Head descendant." She told us of another descendant who had visited the cultural center several years before that, and of 600 descendants, possibly more, who had sprung from the decision of those whalers to put down roots in New Zealand.[7] "And you know," she said, "I'm thinking, yeah, we just went around the world and just 'Wamped' it up. So he's just finding his way around. . . . There's not that many of us left here, but at least we're getting around." Wampanoag people have been mobile through time and space, which in some ways opposes the impulse to fix the Massasoit in place in Plymouth. The narrative stemming from the statue also became mobile. All of this Indigenous mobility is connected to the people's experience under settler colonialism, just as the *Massasoit* monument itself originated as a tribute to that history. But what is truly striking in this story is the remarkable durability of this connection to homeland. Other stories of New England Indian mobility stretch to the

Caribbean and beyond, with New England–connected communities in places like Bermuda, where there is a legacy of the English practice of selling Indians into slavery, particularly after the Pequot War (1637) and King Philip's War (1675 76).[8] Indigenous mobility must be linked to homelands and their survival, as it is in the surprise ending to "The Messanger Runner," a short video portraying a historical reenactment, produced by Mashpee Wampanoag Paula Peters in connection with the 400th anniversary of Plymouth. In the video, the runner completes the forty-mile run from Marshpaug (Mashpee) to Patuxet (Plymouth) and pulls out of a fringed buckskin bag the important message to the people: "WE ARE STILL HERE," directed at the viewer as a text message displayed on a smartphone.[9]

Indeed, the reenactment (and embodiment) of Native history involves a significant degree of mobility. Darius Coombs and eleven other Native people paddled two mishoonash (dugout canoes) from Wood's Hole to Martha's Vineyard in an August 2002 event when, he states, "we even beat the ferry! It was amazing. The last trip like that was made more than 250 years ago. It was a chance to reconnect with the ancestors."[10] The mobility of the mishoonash (and of the Wampanoag carvers and paddlers) works to enhance the public visibility of the Wampanoag nation, assert its resilience and survival, close the distance between the past and the present, and challenge myth-laden U.S. origin stories. The momentum has picked up in recent years; mishoonash carved by Wampanoag Indigenous Program staff at Plimoth Plantation with traditional burning techniques serve as a hands-on educational demonstration in the Wampanoag Homesite there.[11] A short documentary on New England Indian canoes, *Paddling through History*, featured the program's mishoon and won a 2015 Telly Award.[12] In 2014, the program's canoe was gifted to the National Museum of the American Indian in a ceremony in Suitland, Maryland. Director Kevin Gover accepted the gift on behalf of the museum, stating: "We are pleased to welcome a creation like this one that represents a living tradition among the Wampanoag. The museum has worked closely with Plimoth Plantation to collaborate on several projects that help to dispel stereotypes about the first Thanksgiving and expand the history to include the American Indian perspective on this famous gathering."[13] As Darius Coombs explained at the ceremony, "Our culture is passed down from generation to generation. . . . You have to put yourself back in time to create one of these boats, but our work shows that the Indigenous people are still here."[14]

This project began in 2000 with the surprise of our discovery of *Massasoit* in Kansas City, but as we complete the writing of this book, the United States is passionately and explosively confronting the place and meaning of monuments to racism and white supremacy erected during the Jim Crow era. Our book is connected to that volatile debate, suggesting that monuments to settler colonialism ought to be part of the conversation about the place and meaning of historical monuments in general. This is beginning to happen around the commemorative practices embedded in monuments, marches, holidays, place-names, and more that evoke supremacist pasts of all varieties with no clear resolution in sight, as the monumental landscape is seemingly up for debate everywhere.[15] For our purposes, it is happening in a particularly evocative way in activism around monuments to Christopher Columbus, who might be imagined in connection to a figure such as 8sâmeeqan as commemorated in *Massasoit*; even though Columbus signifies "discoverer" rather than "Indigenous," both figures have been imagined as having laid the foundations for the emergence of the nation. In September 2017, New York City mayor Bill de Blasio appointed a commission to advise him regarding "how the City should address monuments seen as oppressive and inconsistent with the values of New York City," including the monument to Columbus at Columbus Circle.[16] This prompted a breathless response from the *New York Post* characterizing this development as "the most terrifying news out of City Hall since the cornerstone was laid in 1908. . . . Goodbye, hundreds of years of history, tradition, and respect for our shared past. Hello, a Communist/Fascist-style imposition of cultural martial law. Good luck, Chris Columbus!"[17] Why the emotional attachment to Columbus as a symbol of a "shared past"? A *New York Times* poll revealed that, when asked which statues might be taken down, about three-quarters of respondents pointed to Confederate leaders and the founder of the Ku Klux Klan. Christopher Columbus fell toward the lower end of the spectrum (in the company of several U.S. presidents), with 30 percent of respondents supporting removal.[18] Columbus, revered especially by Italian Americans as a badge of ethnic pride and other Americans as the "heroic discoverer" of America, signifies the unleashing of genocide and dispossession for Indigenous peoples. As the emotional response to the mere suggestion of removing Columbus monuments reveals, challenging narratives of possession of the nation is a deeply unsettling prospect for most. Even gestures toward undoing settler colonialism stand as a substantial threat to many Americans.

Why do some monuments carry the emotional weight that they do? Why do controversies over memory in monuments erupt how and when they do? We now look to monumental mobility in the guise of *Massasoit*, but we will return to these vital questions and contests over the place of disputed monumental practices here as well. Taken together, these passionate arguments demonstrate in no uncertain terms that monuments are not simply mute and static objects cast in metal, marble, or stone. Their meanings are mobile and mobilized across a spectrum of views, and these meanings are deeply felt on a monumental scale.

INTRODUCTION

Historical monuments perform a complex array of memory work. What we mean by "memory work" is the myriad ways in which monuments imbedded in a social fabric play a role in how individuals and collectivities make meaning of the past as distinct from the concrete matter of what actually happened.[1] Monuments are erected in the hopes of fixing existing memories about the past so that the individual, group, or event commemorated is not forgotten and, frequently, with the desire to convey a larger message. Indeed, in some ways, monuments signal a sort of desperation, in that the fear of forgetting lurks not very far from the surface in the urge to commemorate. A monument that draws no human engagement threatens to become a mere object in the landscape, devoid of tangible meaning. Even the placement of plaques informing the public of the purpose of monuments is an idle exercise absent the willingness of passersby to read and reflect on them. It is this process of engagement with monuments—from the emergence of the urge to commemorate, through the process of designing and installing them, the personal experience of encountering and thinking about what they are meant to convey, and even the impulse to possess replicas of them—that interests us in thinking about the memory work of monuments. In all of these dimensions in the creation and consumption of monumental landscapes and figures, how does memory attach to the personal experience of engagement with monuments?

Monuments encourage the viewer to imagine how the past shaped the present, while drawing a personal connection to a historical figure or event. Unlike reading a book or watching a screen, viewing a public monument grounds a story in place and psychically binds individuals to a larger collective. Monuments are the sites in which the imagined community is materialized and the existence of the nation is confirmed.[2] In this book we interrogate the process of creating, provoking, and/or reinforcing historical memory by examining the remarkable set of circumstances surrounding a particularly evocative monument. The Cyrus E. Dallin statue *Massasoit* was meant by the parties responsible for its creation and installation in 1921 to commemorate the moment of encounter and treaty between English Pilgrims and welcoming Native people in 1621, which ushered in nearly fifty years of peace between these two peoples. Located in Plymouth, Massachusetts, *Massasoit* is also connected to the mythology-steeped first Thanksgiving and has become caught up in an annual ritual that conjures up Plymouth in the originary narrative of the nation.

Though this story begins with a seemingly straightforward demonstration of patriotism by early twentieth-century members of the fraternal organization the Improved Order of Red Men (IORM) who commissioned the work, as is generally the case in the relationship between history and memory, the meaning that attaches to *Massasoit* became richly multivalent and dynamic. The statue is a public history phenomenon that offers a window into the complexity of how monuments relate to historical narratives and, in particular, into the question of how national narratives "travel" along with monuments that seek to "freeze" vital origin stories in time and place.[3] At the same time, in this particular case, the allure of the story, one that elevates imaginings about a particular historical moment to national significance, renders it temporally, geographically, and imaginatively portable. The story, evoked by *Massasoit* as the signifier, connects people in the present to the past no matter where they are located geographically within the United States, and the power of the generic story of peaceable encounter resonates on multiple scales. Consumers of the story see parallels in their own locales that make them relate to the narrative and elide the dangerous dissonance in precisely located historical accounts of encounter in Plymouth and elsewhere.

Installed on Cole's Hill overlooking Plymouth Harbor in 1921 to mark the 300th anniversary of this moment, *Massasoit* became mobile in complex and unexpected ways after its unveiling (fig. 1). The plaster model for the statue was donated to the artist's home state of Utah for display in the capitol rotunda in Salt Lake City. Half a century later, the model was caught up in an astounding case of fraud in the art market that resulted in four (or more) reproductions. *Massasoit* now stands on the campus of Brigham Young University in Provo, Utah; near the Country Club Plaza shopping center in Kansas City, Missouri; and in the Dayton Art Institute, with other reproductions swept up in the anonymous world of private ownership. These three known installations join the original Plymouth statue, one cast in Salt Lake City in the late 1950s for the

FIGURE 1. *Massasoit* on Cole's Hill, Plymouth, Massachusetts.
Photograph by Jean O'Brien.

capitol grounds, and the original plaster model now residing in the Springville Museum of Art in Utah. Their presence in these far-flung locations prompts us to ask how the Massasoit / *Massasoit* is understood in relation to time and place, locality and nation, past and present. A dizzying story of replication of *Massasoit* statuettes and tourist kitsch extends and redoubles the story of mobility and memory in connection to the statue, sending *Massasoit* into private collections and homes with an unknowable reach and density.

The replication and mobility of *Massasoit* challenges much of what we expect of and from a monument. As scholar Kirk Savage asserts, monuments "acquire authority by affixing certain words and images to particular places meant to be distinctive and permanent."[4] Does the authoritative power of a monument increase or diminish when it is reproduced and geographically unmoored? As the statue was recast and sold as fine art or a souvenir, *Massasoit* became a commodity; the sculpture's value derived from machinations of the market, popular associations with classical sculpture, or the personal memories of the buyer. Memorials, once uprooted from specific sites and contexts and replicated en masse, seem to cleave away from, rather than extend, historical memory. But people affixed new meanings to the statue as it became mobile, pointing to its dynamic power and continuing relevance. The statue may not exert one authoritative message from a singular location, but it does reveal otherwise obscured dimensions of American memorial culture: a certain elasticity of historical imagination; a tight-knit relationship between consumption, experience, and commemoration; and the twinned urge to sanitize and grapple with the meaning of settler colonialism.

The *Massasoit* monument — in its diverse contemporary locations — also offers a fascinating vantage point on public history and how it functions in relationship to Indigeneity and Indigenous people. This book asks a cluster of questions surrounding the problem of "What is the place of *Massasoit* in local and national narratives of encounter?" Before we can address the question, however, we must consider Wampanoag terminology, historical memory, and homelands. "Massasoit," the subject of commemoration, is the Wampanoag term for "leader" or "chief," and thus we place it in scare quotes here. The actual name of the historical figure is 8sâmeeqan. We thus use "the Massasoit" when referring to the title or descriptive role and "8sâmeeqan" to denote the historical figure, although there are times when they could be used fairly interchangeably.[5] Descendant Wampanoag communities of course understand what is meant when "Massasoit" is used as a name, but we have endeavored throughout this book to distinguish between the historical figure (8sâmeeqan/the Massasoit) and Dallin's statue by italicizing "Massasoit" when referring to the statue.

8sâmeeqan is remembered in ambivalent ways in Wampanoag communities, where he is certainly accorded a place of significance. A permanent exhibit of tribal leadership on display in the Mashpee Wampanoag Indian Museum focuses on the ongoing *role* of the Massasoit, or Supreme Sachem, and other leadership positions within the Mashpee Nation, featuring its continuity in the twentieth century and beyond (fig. 2). But 8sâmeeqan is also a complex touchstone for the history that follows the arrival of English colonists. A powerful leader in his time, but only one of many, 8sâmeeqan became legendary as a principal in the first treaty struck with the English in 1621. This leading edge of settler colonialism carried dire consequences for Indigenous people, a harsh reality and point of struggle over his memory in descendant communities. Aquinnah Wampanoag Linda Coombs observed to us that "by and large Massasoit is seen very positively. I've heard [some people] complaining about him making the alliance with the English because that set the stage for everything that came after. But . . . look at the position he was in. We can . . . look back at that and judge him, but we weren't there."[6]

The enduring impacts of settler colonialism, and contested understandings about history and place related to 8sâmeeqan, can be seen across Wampanoag homelands as well. English place-naming practices, for example, distorted history and violated Native understandings of their geography and ways of marking place. The Wampanoag homelands during 8sâmeeqan's lifetime included sixty-nine villages connected by footpaths and dotted with countless places of significance.[7] While the Massasoit encountered English colonists in the vicinity of Patuxet (what the English came to call Plymouth), he did so after traveling through Pokanoket territory from his home village in Sowams. While "Sowams" marked the principal village for 8sâmeeqan in his own language, English place-naming practices in the service of settler colonialism sought to eliminate Indigenous geographical realities. Anglo-Americans often understood his principal village in relation to English town names that came later, such as Warren and Barrington. Local historians at the turn of the twentieth century even battled over the location of 8sâmeeqan's principal village because of the interest it would bring to their respective town's history. Warren claimed a kind of victory by installing a plaque siting "Massasoit's Spring" on a residential road in the town, although the spring itself was paved over.[8] These practices placed 8sâmeeqan within a rhetorical English geography, rather than the other way around. Thus, English place-names that often come along with narratives about the Massasoit distorted the complexity of Native geographies that sustained the Pokanoket, relating more to later New English claims about possession than to Native understandings of place and belonging. These English place-names aimed to erase Indigenous peoples and geographies. Such claims of disappearance find ready refutation in the many surviving Wampanoag communities throughout southeastern New England. Not only are there the federally recognized Wampanoag tribes of Gay Head (Aquinnah) and the Mashpee Wampanoag Tribe, but also numerous other communities such as

FIGURE 2. *Leaders of the Wampanoag Nation and Mashpee Tribe, Mashpee Wampanoag Indian Museum. Courtesy of Ramona Peters.*

Herring Pond, Seekonk, Assonet, and Pocasset. Descendants of the Mitchell family (and thus 8sâmeeqan) still call Watuppa home.

Massasoit stands in a commemorative landscape in Plymouth that prioritizes English origins and seeks to place Indigeneity in the past. It is the quintessential replacement narrative, whereby English peoples, institutions, and cultures are asserted by replacing Indigenous peoples and ways of life, relegating them to the past by modernity in the guise of the American nation.[9] Seeing 8sâmeeqan (the historical figure) through *Massasoit* (the monument) is a necessary part of that story of national origins, but the Indigeneity signified by the monument is asserted as a dead end.

The larger claim about modern Anglo-Americans replacing Indigenous peoples ripples across the landscape of the United States and stubbornly dominates the nation's imaginary. Most memorials in the United States, when they mention Native Americans at all, often serve to underscore frontier mythologies and celebrate the dispossession of the nation's Indigenous inhabitants as a measure of progress.[10] American memorial practices involving Indigenous history often invoke an ambivalent narrative that combines remorse with nostalgia to punch up the emotional appeal. As Andrew Denson notes of Trail of Tears commemoration beginning in the 1920s and continuing into the present, monuments, plaques, and museums stretching from North Carolina to Oklahoma demonstrate how white southerners embraced Trail of Tears as a story of regret because they read it as a story of absence.[11] There are ways, then, in which *Massasoit* signals Wampanoag historical presence but also modern absence; it freezes the Massasoit in the past, asserting the nobility and passivity of settler colonialism as a structure that denies the ongoing vitality of Indigenous peoples in the United States.[12] This relegation of Indigeneity to the past aligns with the structure of settler colonialism with its underlying logic of "elimination of the native," so aptly theorized by Patrick Wolfe.

When remembrance of a shared past emphasizes positive values and downplays conflict, it can be more widely and readily consumed. As David W. Blight notes, "The dominant mode of memory is reconciliation."[13] But precisely because monuments serve as symbols of collective memory, values, and identity, they have also become focal points for activist intervention.[14] Memorials can be important sites for expanding the definition of "American" and reshaping public memory, because they invite reflection on national narratives viewers might otherwise take for granted or paint with a nostalgic gloss.[15] Kirk Savage has noted that statues of slaves as "faithful servants" downplay the violence of slavery and silence the actual lived experiences of slaves in favor of a mythology of intimacy, dedication, comfort, and joy.[16] Public historians in the last decade have struggled with ways to publicly present troubling pasts marked by colonial subjugation and exploitation. In museums and historic sites, the "tough" or "difficult" history of slavery, dispossession, and violence is often tied up with (and directly challenges) commemorations and memorials to heroic ancestors, and thus can be met with public resistance.[17]

The controversies over monuments in public spaces, and the appropriate way to address their messages after regimes change or ideologies evolve, have played out around the world in the last half century.[18] In recent years, city councils across the country have also taken up the question of whether to remove or preserve monuments erected to honor Confederate leaders in public space. Some activists argue that public monuments erected to people, events, or entities that promoted white supremacy and racial violence continue to shape American culture and must be removed. Council members and mayors who advocated for removal were well aware of threats of violence alongside more measured objections to "erasing history." In May 2017 in New Orleans, after two years of political and legal wrangling, the city moved to dismantle four local monuments to the "lost cause of the Confederacy," which were decried as celebrating a regime "on the wrong side of humanity." City contractors, wearing flak jackets and helmets for protection from violent protesters, removed the monuments in predawn darkness. The mayor insisted that the statues celebrating white supremacy had to be dismantled as a step toward addressing inequalities in the city. "These statues are not just stone and metal," Mayor Mitch Landrieu explained in a public address. "These statues . . . were erected purposefully to send a strong message to all who walked in their shadows about who was still in charge in this city."[19] Not all city leaders agreed that removing monuments was the way to address a history of racist violence. The mayor of Charlottesville, Virginia, announced in April 2017 that, in order to "change the narrative . . . by telling the full story of race through our public spaces," he would advocate for new memorials to the black freedom movement that would transform the meaning of Jim Crow–era statues. Such memorial additions would bring full public recognition to African Americans' experiences in a society shaped by slavery and racist policies; the Confederate statues could remain standing as "teachable moments."[20] Although the funding for additional public monuments was never certain, and the mayor ultimately changed his position on removal after white supremacists rallied around the Robert E. Lee statue in Charlottesville, he is certainly not alone in considering ways to intervene in and disrupt the racist ideology embodied in Confederate monuments while also grappling with its historical legacies.[21] Some hope to move the statues to a museum where they can be properly contextualized, while others suggest that artists should creatively reinterpret the statues to emphasize the dynamic meaning of memorials. Others advocate adding plaques with differing perspectives to explain why the statues represent memory rather than history and are therefore open to reassessment.[22] The heated discussions around monuments revealed a plethora of views on how and where to engage with monuments to uncomfortable histories. If anything, controversies surrounding Confederate statues, and those on a smaller scale that erupted around *Massasoit*, serve as a reminder of the powerful narratives public memorials can exert and of the passion of people living with monuments.

At times acting with confrontational rhetoric and at others with patient calm, Native people have also challenged the celebratory basis of certain memorials and sought interpretive control over new historic markers and monuments involving their histories. Dallin's memorial to the Massasoit invokes the nation's founding myths, and prompted responses from Native peoples seeking to disrupt and complicate the settler narratives of Indigenous acquiescence and disappearance. In Plymouth, Native activists gather at the statue each year to directly confront the notion that Indigenous people welcomed and benefited from colonial settlement on their homelands. Following years of protests and then negotiations with the Town of Plymouth, activists succeeded in writing public markers of Wampanoag history for inclusion in the town's historic district. The Town of Plymouth installed a plaque beside the *Massasoit* statue in 1998 as part of a settlement with Native protesters to present the Indigenous perspective that colonialism unleashed a series of losses that still prompts mourning today. As with other cooperative memorial efforts between Indigenous people and government officials, the process and outcomes serve to underscore the varied perspectives on a shared history.[23] As Mashpee Paula Peters explained to us, the statue has become a place of significance to mount protests and to offer Wampanoag perspectives on their history, rather than necessarily a location to pay homage to 8sâmeeqan, whose memory is more complicated. The plaque invokes grief, and as Erika Doss argues, once this powerful emotion has been unleashed, it has the potential to be mobilized toward productive structural change.[24] Utilizing a strategy that parallels that of civil rights monuments in the South, the activists turned to memorial space to assert their presence and disrupt celebratory narratives about the character of the nation.[25]

Yet educating the public about the broader historical relationship between settlers and Indigenous peoples using a single site such as Plymouth or the statue installation can be a fraught process. When casts of *Massasoit* pop up outside of New England in different memorial spaces, the figure prompts discussions (and occasional controversies) about Indian representation and the nature of relations between settlers and Indigenous people, but often in general terms. As scholar Bronwyn Batten noted of a memorial at the site of a massacre that was to represent and raise awareness of all massacres across Australia, there is an inherent danger that "the general may override the specific." The historical circumstances of 8sâmeeqan's life, his individual story situated in Wampanoag geographic and historical context, are lost if the town or statue stand as representations that broadly explain a dark process and period across all of U.S. history.[26]

The efforts to commemorate such complex histories *in place*, on the other hand, bring to the fore the complicated and intertwined nature of mobility and memory. The Trail of Tears National Historical Trail, for example, literally entails mobility in the service of remembrance.[27] Ari Kelman's study of the protracted battle among Cheyenne and Arapaho descendant communities, academics, and National Park Service employees over the precise location of the Sand Creek Massacre for the historic site revealed the gulf between scientific and traditional Native American ways of knowing places and past events. It was not until it was discovered that the course of the creek changed over time that the multiple versions of the location of the massacre could be reconciled. Kelman concludes, "The story of memorializing Sand Creek suggests that history and memory are malleable, that even the land, despite its promise of permanence, can change."[28] This is an important reminder that even as *Massasoit* statues multiply and move to new sites, the landscape itself is dynamic, not a fixed and stable location that freezes time in place.

The hotly contested dimensions of meaning around monuments are obvious when an older one is reassessed, and can also become visible in and around the installations carefully crafted for public display. The intensely fraught process of producing signage to instruct viewers about what monuments mean or represent seeks to guide public understandings of the interpretation.[29] But how are the intended messages received by those who encounter monuments as history in the everyday? Of course, public reception is difficult to nail down with precision. Over the last thirty years, public history professionals and scholars have sought to understand and measure what visitors learn from exhibits, historic sites, and commemorations. Methods for evaluating visitors' experiences include focus groups, surveys, and comment books, although such studies are unscientific because of the lack of a control group and the self-selecting nature of participants.[30] Determining the "take-away" messages from public works is yet more difficult because of the environment: unlike a controlled museum space in which people encounter exhibits expecting to learn from them, people can interact with a public monument in countless ways, from driving past it every day to leaning against the pedestal to rest. The signage and landscape may be curated to produce a particular message or psychological experience that suggests consensus on values and meaning, but that is only part of the equation. Indeed, as Kirk Savage observes, "The subjectivity of memorial space, once unleashed, cannot be so easily controlled."[31] But seldom have public historians paused to ask "What does this monument mean to you?" of the general public (as opposed to intentional visitors). How do passersby actually experience the monuments and the history they are designed to evoke for them? What do they mean to them? Surely there are many who bustle by monuments on a regular basis without giving them much thought, or think of them as simply part of the local landscape. But others deliberately seek out monuments to engage in the process of memory making through experiencing and dwelling upon the monumental landscape. In an effort to probe the reception of monuments by the general public, one element of the research for this book included interviews with passersby of *Massasoit* in its various public installations. In the original Plymouth location, we found that the newer revisionist plaque installed in 1998 next to *Massasoit* as a result of Native activism prompts at least some passersby to consider conflicting historical interpretations rather than accepting straightforward instruction about what to make of historical messages. The wrestling with historical meaning that this divergent set of interpretations provoked in passersby (reinforced in some by the annual Indian protests mounted on Cole's Hill on Thanksgiving Day since 1970 that renew the dispute in calendrical time) suggests consumers of public history have an appetite for struggling with historical meaning that ought to be taken seriously.

We begin this story of monumental mobility with "Casting," which takes up the cast of characters involved in setting this story in motion: the sculptor Cyrus Dallin and his engagement with the Massasoit in fashioning and casting *Massasoit*; the Improved Order of Red Men and the Massasoit Memorial Association in their imaginings of the Massasoit's role in creating the nation; and the Pilgrim Society, which provided the site for the original installation within a curated memorial landscape. We then follow *Massasoit* west to Salt Lake City and examine how it was recast for residence in other places through nefarious means. *Massasoit*'s various locations demonstrate how malleable it is (and is not) in a dynamic process of making historical meaning in different places over time. "Staging" follows *Massasoit* through eighty years of unveilings and dedication ceremonies across diverse locations to interrogate how the national narrative originally imagined by the IORM was staged and how audiences received it in Plymouth and locations far away from New England. We pay attention to the interplay between the intended narrative of national belonging as well as regional and local ramifications of the statue's installation, including Indigenous perspectives. "Distancing" brings personal experience with history into focus by listening to passersby talk about *Massasoit* and what the statue means to them, and juxtaposes these accounts with the living history museum Plimoth Plantation and the PBS "experiential history" series *Colonial House*. We are concerned here with understanding how people experience historical distance between the past and the present, efforts to close the historical distance through consuming history as experience, and especially, the ways in which Native peoples force a reckoning with Indigenous perspectives in Plymouth-centered narratives. Finally, "Marketing" analyzes the commodification of *Massasoit* over the long history of the project to commemorate the leader. Dallin's career coincided with major technological developments in metal casting, which made it possible to reproduce sculptures faster and cheaper. Indian statuary cast in bronze was a thriving business that appealed to individuals, institutions, and especially municipalities. We begin with the fund-raising efforts of the IORM and Dallin and move through the present-day marketing of *Massasoit*, from one-inch charms to forty-inch statuettes for sale in museum gift shops, tourist stops, auction houses, and the cyberspace of eBay. All of these are imbedded in the creation of Plymouth as a popular tourist destination that peddles itself as the origins of the nation, but is a story made mobile in unexpected ways that sent *Massasoit* to unexpected places.[32]

The historical 8sâmeeqan looms large in the story of first encounters between Natives and the English in Plymouth, and the memorial thus directly relates to public history struggles over national identity and the process of settler colonialism in a way other statues do not.[33] In late winter 1621, after months of wary observation of the newcomers, 8sâmeeqan sent a pair of emissaries, Tisquantum (commonly known as Squanto) and Samoset (who, providentially, from the perspective of the colonists, spoke English), to initiate contact and set into motion the process of making a treaty of peace by informing the English that their Massasoit wished to meet them.[34] The two parties subsequently held a council that resulted in an agreement to maintain peaceful relations, provide mutual aid if attacked by another party, leave arms behind during meetings, and return anything pilfered by either side to the proper owners. These constituted reciprocal agreements, but the treaty also unilaterally called for the Pokanoket to subject violators of the terms on their side to the English for punishment, not the other way around, a signal that the English meant to be dominant. As well, William Bradford's account of the treaty (one of the few that provides documentary evidence on the events) does not mention a requirement that the English disarm themselves during meetings, which if true, also skewed the treaty in favor of English power.[35] Momentously, the Massasoit and the English pledged alliance to one another in the event either side became swept up in unjust wars. This first treaty of peace and alliance no doubt conferred a sense of security to the English, but from the Massasoit's perspective, it likely served to shore up his own diplomatic position in a world filled with peril following the uneven destruction of a deadly epidemic in 1616–19 that ripped through his confederates but left the powerful Narragansett confederacy to the south and west across Narragansett Bay untouched and even more powerful in regional Indigenous politics.[36]

To 8sâmeeqan and his people, although the English must have appeared weak and easily contained because of their times of privation and alarming death rate, still their weaponry appeared formidable.[37] Scholars note that this diplomatic event followed a tumultuous history marked by much misunderstanding, and that it by no means translated into perfect clarity in its wake. Still, these events ushered in fifty years of uneasy peace, marked by repeated instances of conflict fueled by underlying distrust and diplomatic gamesmanship from multiple Indigenous and English quarters.[38] But by no means did it constitute a real "first encounter" between Natives and Europeans, let alone the English, in northeastern North America. Nearly a century of contact up and down the New England coastline (peaceful, epidemiological, and violent) meant this encounter occurred within a world of dramatic and subtle change and created a web of acquired knowledge on both sides. The common language that facilitated the treaty is a case in point: the Abenaki Samoset, who hailed from Pemaquid to the north, learned English thanks to long-standing trade with Europeans on the Wabanaki coast, and Tisquantum, following his enslavement by Englishman Thomas Hunt in 1614 and transatlantic travels as a slave in Spain, then England, brought English language skills back with him on his return to Patuxet, which he found decimated by the 1616–19 epidemic. What the diplomatic moment in 1621 narrowly signifies, then, is the first encounter precisely between these particular individuals.[39]

In spite of the sparse documentary evidence, the circumstances and many of the details of this treaty seem pretty clear. This is especially so when placed alongside the other momentous event associated with the Massasoit in 1621 and *Massasoit* after 1921, the "first Thanksgiving." There are exactly two paragraphs of textual evidence to reconstruct this iconic event: the observations of Edward Winslow contained in *Mourt's Relation*, and those recorded by William Bradford in *Of Plymouth Plantation*.[40] Even these descriptions did not become available for public consumption until more than two centuries after they were produced; the critical passage in *Mourt's Relation* was not included in the abridged version published in 1625 and did not resurface until nearly 200 years later (1820), and Bradford's manuscript did not come to light until even later than that (1853).[41] Thus, the association of the Pilgrims, the Massasoit, and Plymouth did not receive widespread attention until after the mid-nineteenth century.[42] Instead, days of thanksgiving, steeped in a complex mix of customary and religious practices rooted in England (Calvinist days of thanksgiving, harvest festivals, plus the newer Forefathers' Day—a recognition of the arrival of the Pilgrims), were staged episodically throughout the colonies and states for diverse reasons throughout the colonial and early national periods.[43] Add to this that Indian harvest celebrations are and have been routinely observed in an annual cycle of ceremonies giving thanks for the bounties of nature, presumably for millennia. Here we have a sort of convergence of cultural traditions that have over many years produced not just what is now a national holiday, but a foundational myth for the ages. The complexity of this set of intercultural exchanges, far more intricate and contested than even mapped out here, can be extrapolated as a symbol of peaceful and welcoming embrace that becomes easily consumed and regurgitated. The mythic first Thanksgiving comes to be sited near Cole's Hill in Plymouth, and the fraught history of conflict, war, dispossession, and Indigenous survival is easily passed over in the minds of those who gather to celebrate.

The widely accepted story of Thanksgiving inculcated in childhood since the late nineteenth century, about Pilgrim survival celebrated with the welcoming Indians in the late fall, took considerable time to develop and has morphed repeatedly over time, first surfacing in print in an 1841 reprint of *Mourt's Relation*, referring to the 1621 Winslow passage: "This was the first Thanksgiving, the harvest festival of New England."[44] Nationwide observances of Thanksgiving were declared by the Continental Congress in 1777 and by George Washington in 1789, but they were not associated with the Pilgrims or the idea of the first Thanksgiving. They then petered out until Abraham Lincoln declared one in 1863 as a gesture of healing and unity, which initiated an unbroken string of Thanksgiving celebrations on that day thereafter. The holiday was shifted to the fourth Thursday (rather than the standardized last Thursday) in November at the end of 1941 (following Franklin Delano Roosevelt's decree that it be observed then in 1939 in order to extend the Christmas shopping season to spur consumerism).[45] The development of the Pilgrim association and massively commercialized imagery awaited the very end of the nineteenth century and did not come into its contemporary form until the middle of the twentieth century.[46] By then, Thanksgiving's ubiquitous iconography around encounters between Indians and Pilgrims even became one of the few instances of Indian appearances in television sitcoms, including the "Turkey Day" episode in *The Beverly Hillbillies* that featured the Massasoit and Tisquantum.[47]

What can we reconstruct of the circumstances of this "first Thanksgiving"? After a year filled with illness and physical privation, Plymouth appeared to have weathered multiple storms, including the deaths of half of the 102 who arrived on its shores weakened and fearful of Indians (with distrust remaining strong).[48] According to the version of this story widely in circulation, based mostly on Edward Winslow's account, in the fall of 1621, the Pilgrims decided to celebrate the progress made in building Plymouth and their successful harvest by mounting a feast, during which the Massasoit arrived with an additional ninety men. The Winslow passage does not indicate (contrary to the commonly told story) that the Pilgrims "invited" the Indians to this "Thanksgiving," but rather that during their celebrations, "we exercised our arms, many of the Indians coming amongst us, and among the rest their greatest King Massasoit, with some ninety men, whom for three days we entertained and feasted."[49] The fact that 8sâmeeqan arrived with men but not women and children suggests caution on his part about the possible martial intent of the English.[50] According to Ramona Peters, Mashpee Wampanoag tribal historic preservation officer, 8sâmeeqan and his men were not invited, but rather set off on a "fact-finding mission" after hearing the Pilgrims discharge their weapons in celebration of their first harvest. Upon discovering the purpose of the gathering, they decided to camp nearby and keep an eye on the scene. They hunted, and they ate together, but amid a wary atmosphere of mutual suspicion.[51] This version seems to square much more comfortably with Winslow's account than the notion of the Pilgrims extending an invitation to the Wampanoag to attend a cheerful celebration of their cordial relationship and a bountiful harvest. In fact, earlier nineteenth-century imagery of the first Thanksgiving hewed closer to the uneasy forestallment of violence that emanates from the Winslow passage and the contemporary Wampanoag interpretation of the event as well.[52] In any event, the message of peaceful embrace and celebration of bounty remains firmly in place as an iconic American holiday, with football entering the picture as early as 1876, when the Intercollegiate Football Association introduced an annual game between the best two college teams from the previous year.[53] But that mythic "first Thanksgiving," the iconic joint celebration of Indians and the English, was a "one-off," to our knowledge, not to be repeated in calendrical time like that holiday that has become so quintessentially American.

The group that commissioned and installed *Massasoit* asserted a particular meaning to both the object and the historical 8sâmeeqan. The Improved Order of Red Men, a fraternal organization limited to "physically, mentally, and morally sound" white men, united around the twin goals of mutual assistance and "self improvement by emulating North American Indian characteristics."[54] Originally established in 1834, the organization enjoyed the height of its popularity in the 1920s, with a membership of over half a million. Today the organization's museum and library are located in Waco, Texas, though its membership has declined to around 15,000.[55] According to IORM official Alvin Gardner Weeks, in addition to teaching patriotism, in 1919 the IORM "endeavored to preserve some of the customs of the aborigines, and to pay due tribute to their many manly virtues which we, as the dominant race, have been too strongly inclined to ignore."[56] To IORM members in New England, the Massasoit merited his place in this commemorative landscape, with a "memorial to the Great Chief," because he was "a historical figure and the fact that his kindly treatment of the Pilgrims, in protecting them upon their landing at Plymouth, and subsequently making a treaty with them which lasted for fifty years, made it possible for laying the foundation of this great Republic of the United States."[57]

The IORM incorporated the Massasoit Memorial Association to oversee its fund-raising efforts in the 1910s. But this was not the first Massasoit monument association that looked to install a physical marker commemorating him. A single donation made in 1880 in Warren, Rhode Island, commenced the effort of the Massasoit Monument Association there to install a fitting marker for this momentous history. After years of determined fund-raising, in 1907 the association finally managed to fix a bronze marker to a large boulder on the site of the so-called Massasoit Spring only six years before the IORM campaign.[58]

In 1913, the Red Men passed a resolution to purchase and erect a monument to the Massasoit to be dedicated at the tercentenary celebration of the Plymouth colonists' landing. The funds were solicited from among the membership by selling a souvenir pocket piece featuring a facsimile of one of Dallin's early clay models and a book published by Alvin Weeks titled *Massasoit of the Wampanoags*. A statue, the fund-raising committee asserted, was perfectly in line with the mission of the Improved Order to honor (through imitation) the noble features of Indigenous life as founding principles of the United States. The Pilgrim Society of Plymouth joined the effort by donating the tract of land on Cole's Hill for the installation.[59]

In Cyrus Dallin, the IORM found an award-winning and reputable sculptor whose studio was conveniently located in Arlington, Massachusetts, just outside of Boston. Praising his fame in Indian statuary in particular, Weeks explained that Dallin had "created a model of the proud warrior in the prime of life, bearing the peace pipe to the strangers from across the great waters." He also approvingly noted the appropriateness of the Cole's Hill location as a place for *Massasoit* to look over Plymouth Rock. His publication aimed to convince Americans to join the effort "to pay deserved but belated tribute to this great Chief, that he may forever stand guard over the gateway through which the pilgrim bearers of the torch of Liberty first entered New England, even as he kept a watchful eye over her early struggles for existence."[60] The *Massasoit* monument site "will make the statue so prominent that it can be seen for miles by passing vessels and those approaching Plymouth either by steamer or rail, and, with the face turned towards the sea, [it] will make it one of the most picturesque statues ever erected."[61]

The timing of the IORM efforts could not have been better. The Town of Plymouth, ragged around the edges because of its decaying waterfront and antiquated commercial base, took up the task of remaking itself with vigor and more in keeping with how it imagined its appearance at "first settlement" in the years preceding the tercentenary of the landing of the Pilgrims that resulted in New England (though the landing lagged thirteen years behind Jamestown's establishment in 1607, a feat generally overshadowed in New English narratives about itself). The celebration of centennials, sesquicentennials, bicentennials, and now a tercentennial of localities in New England amped up the stakes laid out in the annual Forefathers' Day commemorations begun in the immediate aftermath of U.S. independence from England.[62] Renewal efforts in Plymouth included gussying up the infrastructure around the storied and mythic Plymouth Rock, the creation of a monumental landscape commemorating the Pilgrims, and the sanctifying of Cole's Hill overlooking Plymouth Harbor, where *Massasoit* would come to reside on the location of the Pilgrims' first cemetery. Looking across Plymouth Harbor, *Massasoit* would eventually gaze out onto a full-scale replica of the *Mayflower* (the *Mayflower II*), sailed from Plymouth, England, in 1957.[63]

Securing the services of a highly acclaimed sculptor for *Massasoit* afforded the IORM an opportunity to beautify the hill overlooking Plymouth Harbor and fix a vital historical narrative in place. In commissioning a fine artist to commemorate history, the IORM facilitated and responded to the rising interest of monumental public art in the United States. Following the guiding principle of the American Renaissance—the late nineteenth- and early twentieth-century expressive style that sought to unify the arts and mixed European traditions with notions of American progress—Dallin's *Massasoit* serves as a stellar example of the artist's commitment to making monumental art that engaged public audiences in larger narratives and ideologies.[64] Monuments are predicated on communicating powerful messages in the cause of remembrance, but public art can be viewed as expressing an idea, frequently devoted to the cause of physical beauty. *Massasoit* unquestionably beautified Cole's Hill, but it also became a powerful symbol that invites individuals to process their own ideas about history and place, especially around the powerful narrative of hospitable Indians welcoming the newcomers to their homelands in peaceful coexistence.

In 1921, Dallin's *Massasoit* was typical for the time in its monumental form, even if the subject was an original. Americans were somewhat ambivalent about monuments in the early years of the republic—the European tradition of statues to great men seemed too closely aligned with monarchy—but by the mid-nineteenth century, Americans embraced the monument form. The "statue mania" that gripped the nation in the decades following the Civil War emphasized heroic men, great ideas, and significant moments, demonstrating a supposedly collective reverence for a monolithic and masculine national history. Indeed, thirty years before *Massasoit* was installed, Plymouth erected an enormous granite Pilgrim monument (now called the National Monument to the Forefathers) within walking distance of Cole's Hill. By the 1890s, monuments were increasingly dedicated to common soldiers and civil servants who represented the civic ideal.[65] Popular appreciation for public art grew alongside the professional identity of American sculptors; the 1893 World's Columbian Exposition in Chicago provided the first opportunity for a generation of European-trained American sculptors to display their works before a mass audience and fashion themselves as experts in what constituted good public art.[66]

If the number of commissioned works through the Progressive Era is any indication, public art and the cultural status of the sculptor were both on the rise—as were concerns about the future of the nation.[67] The subjects of the monuments, whether depicting a figure from the period or the distant past, were intertwined with the concerns of the time in which they were erected. The majority of monuments to the Confederacy, for example, were erected in the South between 1900 and 1920, just as these states were enacting Jim Crow laws to disenfranchise African Americans and resegregate society.[68] At times, popular tastes and those of academic sculptors clashed. In the aftermath of World War I, municipalities across the country raised funds for generic memorials, the most popular of which was the vigilant doughboy. At the height of their popularity, from 1918 through the 1930s, approximately 800 doughboy statues popped up in parks, alongside roadways, and in central squares. Professional art organizations and cultural critics dismissed the mass-produced statues as an assault on authenticity and the aesthetic principles of art itself.[69] Yet these mass-produced memorials resonated with the Red Scare and the racial ideologies of the time, which reflected (and perpetuated) widespread suspicions of immigrants. The heightened interest in generic memorials and nostalgic history pageants into the early 1920s was symptomatic of anxieties about national unity and the rapid advance of modernism, immigration, and mass culture. These generic monuments were often patriotic, tying small U.S. towns together by allowing them to rally around an identical figure, but they also oriented memorialization to local spaces and integrated the statues into everyday life.[70]

Just as U.S. cities were vying for public memorials that would cement bonds of nationalism, private and public patrons also began to favor sculptures of Indian subjects.[71] In many ways this is not surprising, given the popularity of generic Indian representations in America's literature, visual culture, and public spaces. And in the mid-nineteenth century, Indian figures became associated with commerce and consumer space; as ship builders moved from wood to metal prows, the carvers who once sold figures for ship prows were employed instead by the tobacco industry, which found the wooden "Indian chief" figures to be effective for branding and popular with customers. An Indian figure was also one of the first bronze fine art sculptures to be cast in the United States, in 1849. Managers of the American Art-Union commissioned twenty statuettes of a figure "illustrative of Indian form and character" for distribution to the organization's subscribers, which encouraged further reproductions for middle-class consumers.[72] Cities also clamored for the affordable casts. Many of the metal casts that now preside over public parks and fountains were modeled on the wooden Indian figure produced for tobacco store signs. *Tobacco*, a trade publication, estimated in 1893 the number of such carved figures to be in the tens of thousands.[73]

By the last quarter of the nineteenth century, the most favored Indian statuary usually depicted a representative racial "type" set in an unspecified past and often adapted classical statuary poses.[74] The subjects were most often male because, as William H. Truettner argues, elite white males wanted to believe that the heroic Plains Indians of the past—who had acquired a patina of nobility in popular culture—represented America's original racial stock and served as a masculine model for the present.[75] The "typical" figure of the bare-chested Indian man was particularly popular in salons and international competitions, appearing in world's fairs in Philadelphia (1876), New Orleans

(1884–85), and Chicago (1893) and garnering the gold medal in the 1889 Paris Exposition.[76]

Sculptor Cyrus E. Dallin's career as an academic expert and professional sculptor was buoyed by the popularity of Indian statuary, and his works contributed significantly to their form. Like other professional sculptors of his generation, Dallin believed in the didactic power of public art to hasten moral reform by modeling harmony—in technical skill, aesthetic sensibility, and civic-mindedness.[77] Dallin pursued this sense of unity in his Indian sculptures, and audiences, students, and critics responded positively. Dallin entered his generic Indian busts and figures into art competitions and routinely won acclaim, commissions, and artistic influence. He received a classical art education from Truman H. Bartlett in Boston and the École des Beaux-Arts in Paris in the 1880s, and he held teaching positions at Drexel University and the Massachusetts School of Art, where he emphasized technical proficiency and naturalistic forms.[78] He built a reputation in the 1890s as a master sculptor of Indian statuary, and considered himself to be a friend and advocate for Native people and histories. His most famous works are part of his four-sculpture "Indian Cycle" series: *Signal of Peace, The Medicine Man, The Protest,* and (the most widely recognized) *Appeal to the Great Spirit* (fig. 3).[79] Together, these Plains Indian figures tell a sympathetic story of Indian-settler relations in the West, in which Indian men offered friendship to settlers until they were pushed into defensive wars that they could not win and sought comfort in the Great Spirit. Although Dallin also sculpted patriots, settlers, and other commissioned works now found on public display across the country, his Indian statuary was particularly popular in a period in which sculptors explored the didactic potential of public art, and easterners lamented the supposed disappearance of Native people.[80]

Meanwhile, changing techniques for metal casting made it possible for large foundries to produce statues faster and cheaper, allowing for sale by catalog. In the 1870s foundries could produce statues of iron and zinc alloys for homeowners, businesses, institutions, and municipalities.[81] For much of his career, Dallin contracted with the Gorham Manufacturing Company of Rhode Island for bronze casting, and with the P. P. Caproni and Brother terracotta company of Boston for plaster replicas and catalog sales. Between 1916 and 1947, the Gorham Company produced 400 of Dallin's *Appeal to the Great Spirit* in three sizes, indicating the appetite for such subjects and Dallin's considerable influence over popular taste. If we expand the study to include all of Dallin's Indian statuary sold by catalog to cities and to individuals over his career, the number would likely rise closer to 1,000. Based on his 1919 royalties

FIGURE 3. *Appeal to the Great Spirit.*
Courtesy of the Cyrus E. Dallin Art Museum.

from Gorham, the best-selling bronze statues were nine-inch and twenty-inch casts—perfect for office desks and home décor. Notably, the royalties that year came exclusively from replicas of generic Indian figures rather than named memorials.[82]

One of our observations is that, regardless of specific signage informing viewers otherwise, *Massasoit* takes on a generic Indian "persona" or another identity altogether, especially when it "travels" to different locales. Catalog sales certainly propelled statues into public and private settings across the country and increased viewers' encounters (and familiarity) with the generic Indian form. In the 1970s, researcher Oliver Knapp located one generic "Indian Chief" produced by the J. L. Mott Company and sold by catalog in more than twenty towns from Maine to Georgia and as far west as Michigan. But, unexpectedly, generic statues can become specific memorials in different locales. In many of the locations in which the zinc "Indian Chief" was installed, residents interpreted the generic statue to memorialize a particular Native individual with historical ties to the place: in Cincinnati the statue was known as "Tecumseh"; two identical statues in Calhoun, Georgia, commemorate Sequoyah; and in Barberton, Ohio, it was Chief Hopocan. In other locales, the individuals identified with the statue were not actual historical figures: in Schenectady, the monument was erected to honor "a Mohawk Indian," although townspeople called it "Lawrence the Maquase" (a nod to the seventeenth-century usage of "Maquas" for Mohawks), and in Mount Kisco, New York, the statue is referred to as "Chief Kisco." In Muncie, Indiana, Dallin's *Appeal to the Great Spirit* came to be known as "Chief Muncie," a fictional character. Perhaps most commonly, the generic "Indian Chief" monuments claimed to represent the fact of historical Indigenous presence in the area.[83] As James Buss points out, the common phenomenon of American towns expropriating Indian imagery and claiming it as their own illustrates "the complex nature of settler-colonialism, whereby Native and non-Native peoples have shared a hand—if unequally—in constructing the meanings of settled places and regions."[84]

Unlike the mass-produced generic "Indian Chief" statue, *Massasoit* was sculpted by a well-known artist who cast only one original bronze in his lifetime, and Dallin endeavored to capture the likeness of a specific historical figure based on surviving written descriptions. The later heroic-sized posthumous replicas of *Massasoit* were cast in a limited edition and, following the whims of the buyers, were installed as fine art installations or as memorials. And yet the public reception of the reproductions of *Massasoit* in midwestern and western locales has been similar to those of the "Indian Chief" because viewers expect to see a generic image of a Native man. When viewers outside of Plymouth turn their attention to the subject of the statue rather than the famous sculptor, they read it as "a Ute" or a generic memorial to Indigenous presence. Americans appear conditioned to simultaneously recognize generic Indians as national figures, and claim these figures as representatives of local places, histories, and experiences.

Although *Massasoit* was originally commissioned for Plymouth to contribute to the town's memorial complex, the statue's gaze now drifts across an array of scenes in Utah, Ohio, and Missouri (and, thanks to private auction sales, additional but unknown places). When Dallin donated the original plaster model of the statue to the state of Utah, he initiated a new era of mobility for *Massasoit*. The plaster model began a process in which two kinds of "casting" took shape: the numerous bronze replicas made from the plaster model multiplied the figure, and the Massasoit was in turn cast into a number of different roles in the geographic, economic, and cultural contexts in which the bronze sculpture was placed. And just like in Plymouth, the statue's meaning shifts according to the setting.

Massasoit's aesthetic qualities, its dual national and localized meanings, and its dynamic shifts between public and private space reveal the complexities of monumental mobility. Monuments can, by virtue of their design, accomplish many kinds of memory work simultaneously. Because granite and bronze monuments appear permanent and unshifting — Kirk Savage describes them as an inherently conservative art form — they can bring a core identity to a place. But once fixed on a landscape, monuments become enmeshed in the complexities of life that are in constant change. The landscape can also subtly shift or completely transform over time, giving rise to new ideas about how and where to site collective memories.[85] While the monument form suggests solidity, *Massasoit*'s travels demonstrate its plasticity when audiences engage and grapple with its meaning. As we focus on the dynamic between the monument, the landscapes it inhabits, and the stories it produces in different spaces, we can understand the twin powers of place and narrative in forming individual, local, and national identities.[86]

Massasoit, as a monument to an Indigenous figure, reveals how settler memory is highly mobile and woven into this process of identity formation. The Indian statue, when set in memorial spaces, facilitates public engagement with the history and ongoing features of settler-Native relations. Some local places embraced Dallin's monument and made it their own by grappling with the way the national origin myth reflects or refracts local experience.[87] In private, commercial, and fine art settings, the monument fails to invite engagement and reflection; passive viewers seldom make meaning from history, yet the statue often encourages powerful associations between Indigeneity and disappearance, and consumer choice and personal identity. In the statue's mobility, we see a popular drive toward appropriation (of art, Indian figures, experience); the tourist industry and art market effectively divert or subsume conscious reflection on the history of settler-Native relations. Yet the memory work of this monument is multilayered and dynamic, exhibiting a hunger for a connection with the past that unsettles and challenges, and remakes our stories and ourselves.

Chapter One

CASTING

The heroic-sized bronze *Massasoit* stands alone on its rock pedestal in Plymouth, a solitary figure facing the bay. The monument — and its reproductions — may suggest a certain proud loneliness wherever it stands, but it embodies a plethora of ideas, influences, and desires. The *Massasoit* story in fact involves a large cast of characters beyond 8sâmeeqan. Even the statue itself had a role to play, both in staging a historical drama about national origins in Plymouth and in sparking memories, controversies, and debates there and far away from the Pokanoket leader's historical domain. The *Massasoit* story did not freeze time and space as those who sought to memorialize this history intended. Rather, the actual course of events surrounding it dramatized the ways in which the meaning of monuments is a dynamic and socially produced phenomenon rather than a way to capture history and fix it in place.

How did *Massasoit* come to take center stage in this historical drama, and what other characters deserve billing in this historical production? Some are obvious: the sculptor Cyrus Dallin who fashioned the likeness, the Improved Order of Red Men, the Massasoit Memorial Association, and the Pilgrim Society of Plymouth outlined the script by taking up the idea, raising the funds, hiring the sculptor, and selecting the original location for the drama to be staged. Dallin turned to historical research about 8sâmeeqan and his own memories of growing up in the shadow of the Wasatch Range of Utah. As a boy, he recalled playing with Native companions and observing the diplomatic performance of treaty making; as a young sculptor, he was dazzled by the pageantry of *Buffalo Bill's Wild West* show in Paris and inspired by the performers' bodies and clothing. He also employed at least one human model while working on his sculpture. All of these experiences influenced how he cast *Massasoit* for residence on Cole's Hill in Plymouth.

Indigenous people play multiple roles in this drama, even though the scripting of their roles has changed over time. While *Massasoit* is the lead actor on Cole's Hill, the non-Indian script writers of the time cast the still-present Wampanoag people in bit roles with no lines during the unveiling of *Massasoit*, even though they had plenty to say about the story, as we shall see in the next chapter. After 1970, Native people themselves rewrote the script, challenging the totalizing narratives the IORM sought to implant that denied the settler colonialism inherent in the entire project of memorializing this history as one of the welcoming embrace of English colonialism in the service of American patriotism.

This historical drama became infinitely more complicated following Dallin's decision to donate the plaster model for *Massasoit* for display in the capitol of his home state of Utah in 1922. Utah officials' seemingly benign gesture of recognition of the sculptor's fame and accomplishments resulted in a new drama in which *Massasoit*, recast as a commodity, was surrounded by an ensemble of museum managers, art dealers, and collectors hoping to make a profit. Together they mobilized the posthumous reproductions that would cast *Massasoit* in new roles in Salt Lake City, Provo, Springville, Kansas City, suburban Chicago, Spokane, and Dayton and perhaps elsewhere. In all of these ways, the Massasoit story told through various iterations of *Massasoit* continues to be rescripted and recast as a dynamic and socially produced historical drama tightly connected to the changing meanings of monuments and place over time.

THE SCULPTOR

In the 1880s and 90s, Cyrus Dallin's fame was on the rise. The sculptor began to win awards at European competitions and international expositions. His American career seemed assured when a Boston commission selected his anonymous entry for the Paul Revere memorial statue in 1884. But there was a problem. When civic leaders, competition commissioners, and the city's cultural elites discovered the design came from a young Utahan from a so-called pioneer family, the project was put on hold. On second thought, Dallin's entry began to look a little too rough to the Boston commission members. Perhaps the energy in the figure reflected Wild West lawlessness or carried the taint of Mormonism rather than the refinement one expects from a sculptor who truly understood his New England subject matter. Dallin (a Unitarian with a studio near Boston) labored for the next fifty-five years — the rest of his American career — to revise the Revere statue to the patrons' satisfaction.[1] But what ultimately vaulted Dallin's artistic reputation and made him into a significant figure in the American fine arts and commemoration movements was his turn to subjects about which he claimed personal and authentic knowledge: Native people and western sensibilities. As a western miner's son trying to succeed as a sculptor in the rarified air of eastern society, Dallin took a different tack when crafting his reputation and creative works. He cast himself as the embodiment of the authentic West and a civilized conduit of Indian aesthetics. His Indian statuary, meanwhile, embodied Dallin's notions of classic beauty and modern manliness.

Dallin often repeated in speeches and interviews that he was "born and raised in a two- room log cabin on the frontier in Utah." While such an up-bringing might have been a liability for a classically trained sculptor seeking commissions from eastern patrons, Dallin framed these humble beginnings as a strength. The log cabin was a powerful national symbol that referenced such luminaries as Abraham Lincoln, reinforced the Horatio Alger myth, and com-memorated a patriotic past.[2] Dallin's boyhood in the log cabin on the Wasatch Range in the 1860s not only meant he was fully American; it also gave him ac-cess to unmediated nature and imaginative space unsullied by the artificiality of urban modernity. "The stars were my comrades," he told one journalist in 1938. "I slept out of doors spring to late fall. In the winter the cabin seemed stuffy."[3] The domestic space of the cabin, much like modern life, confined and stifled creativity and boyish energy. Dallin found true inspiration not only in nature, but in western Indian art. In this way, Dallin appealed to popular ideas in the arts and crafts movement in which Indian culture was considered a counteracting force to the crippling effects of modernity.

In a speech before the Plymouth Women's Club in the 1890s, Dallin claimed that he had a different understanding of Indians than did most east-erners, and in fact he owed his "first awakening to art and beauty" to his Ute neighbors. While his log cabin was unadorned, simply utilitarian, in Ute crafts Dallin saw color and composition that appealed to the imagination. "I can well remember the positive ache in my little soul when I followed them about coveting their beautifully decorated trappings," Dallin mused. "They seemed to me denizens of another world, a world of beauty and romance in which I longed to enter and which the drab and prosaic hardships of frontier existence was far removed."[4] Like other artists and collectors in this period, Dallin saw a therapeutic value in proximity to another, more authentic culture.[5]

Dallin's tendency to equate Indians with nature reflected Euro-American expectations of Indians as closer to effete emotion and further from masculine intellect. To be sure, this was part of the appeal of proximity to Indianness:

Dallin said that "the Indians [*sic*] reaction to the color of nature is not esoteric or aesthetic, but a perfectly natural one."[6] Indians have an intuitive feel for beauty, but civilized Americans had the capacity to benefit from nature by following rules of composition and cultivating aesthetic appreciation. While nature is correlated with the Indigenous and feminized spheres, the truly civilized individual can translate these elements into masculine "high art."[7] Dallin credited Indigenous artists and bodies for his inspiration, yet he alone — as a western artist — could transmit an Indian sensibility into art. And how might Dallin's Indian sculptures serve the greater good as public art?

In *Massasoit* and his other Indian statuary, Dallin hoped to marry the didactic principles of public art with the careful study and sympathy required of monuments. The task of the sculptor, Dallin lectured his Boston art students, is to select the "dominant characteristics" of nature and then combine and arrange them to "express the larger, deeper, and more abiding truths."[8] This work of "elevation" is important because the products of such work — public memorials — serve a civic and didactic purpose. Dallin explained that memorials should not only celebrate heroic men and deeds, they should also add beauty to America's public squares and inspire viewers' aesthetic appreciation.[9] Dallin looked to Europe as an example of the salutary effects of public art on society, and he feared that Americans' hostility toward the genre would "leave us plunged in barbarism."[10] Dallin's answer to this threat was not only to translate Indians' intuitive sense of beauty into high art, but to also present idealized male Indian bodies as public art memorials that would inspire and cultivate the civilized mind. Although memorials were often criticized in the early twentieth century for being overly emotional, Dallin conceived of masculine Indian sculpture as a counteracting force to effete civilization. Unlike other memorials to revered individuals or a collection of soldiers, Dallin's monuments sought to recast Indian men more generally as desirable, inspiring, and educational figures.

Dallin's discussions of his artwork therefore focused on Indians' intuitive love of beauty and on Indian bodies — which struck Dallin as decidedly and idyllically manly. In the speech delivered to the Plymouth Women's Club, Dallin explained that Indians possessed "fine, manly qualities," as opposed to the image of "the blood thirsty savage" that dominates in New England. Dallin offered a corrective to New England stereotypes by asserting that the Native people he encountered in his youth in the West — apparently all men — modeled the gentlemanly virtues of honor and self-restraint. The purpose of his sculptures of Indians, then, was to convey this truth about Indian history and to create an inspiring model of manliness for non-Indian viewers. Dallin was not a cultural outlier in his obsession with male bodies at the turn of the century; although white men were considered to be at the apex of civilization, some feared that men and boys would be harmed by decadence unless taught to tap into the primitive aspects of their psyches—a primitiveness that came all too easily to nonwhites who threatened white male dominance. Dallin contributed to the construction of manhood in this period by fashioning himself as a model, and *Massasoit* as a desirable symbol, that could inspire white men to be properly civilized and savage at once.[11]

Dallin's carefully crafted artistic origin stories in the West and in proximity to real Indians were essential to the appeal of his sculptures and the work they could do as public art. In speeches and interviews, Dallin recounted those elements of his biography that proved his special importance as a civilized conduit of primitive beauty and authenticity. Notably, eastern art critics and journalists eagerly reported on Dallin's origins, perhaps adding flourishes and details along the way. As the story goes, as a boy in the Salt Lake Valley, Dallin played "warrior games" with local Indian boys, including one game in which they made balls and other shapes out of clay. Eastern sources interpreted this as his introduction to clay modeling.[12] The oft-repeated narrative of his discovery as a sculptor is set in the Tintic Mining District (named for Paiute chief Tintic), located thirty-eight miles southwest of Springville. During the summer of 1879, teenaged Dallin worked with his father at the silver mine where, on his breaks, Dallin formed an impressive bust from clay that caught the attention of a wealthy patron, who insisted he develop his talent in an eastern art academy.[13]

When his family and sponsors raised enough money to send Dallin to study with a Boston master in 1880 at the age of eighteen, he had another transformative experience. By his own telling, on the first leg of his journey east, Dallin was joined on the train by a delegation of Lakota leaders headed to Washington, D.C. "Those four days on that slow train gave me a deep and abiding respect for those fine-looking specimens of manhood," Dallin later wrote. And he observed these male bodies with particular interest: "When they took their morning ablutions, I watched with [an] artist's eye, their huge, graceful torsos, their clear bronze skin, their muscular bodies, their rippling muscles, and was fascinated with them." Although the language barrier apparently prevented an exchange of ideas, Dallin was deeply impressed by what he called "perfect specimens of athletic development and discipline." His observations of these men's bodies made such a profound impression on the artist that he claimed the experience influenced his life and art for the next half century.[14]

Despite this deep impression, Dallin did not actually sculpt an Indian figure for nearly a decade, until he once again came into contact with male Plains Indian bodies, this time in Europe. In 1889, *Buffalo Bill's Wild West* show played a six-month engagement in Paris while Dallin was studying at a Parisian art institute. The sculptor later reported that the sight of Indians and their colorful regalia conjured up vivid images from his Utah childhood. For several weeks, *Wild West* performers posed for Dallin after the shows. A man named Phillip, the son of Chief Rocky Bear, served as the preliminary study for Dallin's first major Indian equestrian, *Signal of Peace*. The *Wild West* show and resulting statue represented a complex act of cultural transference and memory blurring. The idea for the pose in *Signal of Peace* came to Dallin when he saw a *Wild West* performer lift a spear over his head. The artist claimed the vision conjured a mental image from Dallin's youth in which he saw a Ute chief lift a spear with two white feathers to signal his peaceful intent as he entered a treaty council. Dallin was so struck by the memory that he put his impressions into clay immediately.[15]

Who created the image of Indianness in this moment—Dallin's place-specific memory or the show performer in Paris? Although *Signal of Peace* was in all practicality modeled on a scene from a *Wild West* show, Dallin insisted his own cultivated western mind was the true source. And his story unintentionally lends legitimacy to the *Wild West* show performances as accurate depictions of the western past, which in turn enhanced eastern viewers' experiences of both the show and Dallin's sculptures, while cementing Indian stereotypes. Unlike other classically trained artists and audience members who formed idealized images of Indians in the 1890s, Dallin's purportedly unique strength was his ability to draw on authentic memories formed in proximity to nineteenth-century Indians to craft his figures.

As Dallin gained greater success in the fine arts world, he married into an eastern family and established a home and studio in Arlington, Massachusetts, near Boston. Nearly a decade after gaining acclaim for *Signal of Peace*, Dallin finally sculpted his next Indian figure—again for fine arts competitions in Paris. Conflicting reports claimed that Dallin's studio was either crowded with Indian art and regalia or completely devoid of props because Dallin worked from photographs of Native people rather than models.[16] In a way, it may not have mattered to his audiences whether Dallin could access Indian arts and bodies for inspiration. His origin stories meant he carried authentic Indianness within him—even embodied it. At the 1904 St. Louis Exposition, while Dallin's *The Protest* won the gold medal, the artist won the national archery competition, proving, according to a Boston newspaper, that "he retained the skill acquired as a boy, learned first-hand from his Indian playmates."[17]

Fusing his carefully crafted origin story with his sculptures was an effective strategy; one art writer claimed of Dallin, "Seldom does a painter or sculptor reproduce the psychology of a race in his work with such delicacy, fidelity, and strength." Another critic extrapolated from Dallin's work that the sculptor "must have lived very close to the heart of his subject to have vitalized and spirited it as he does."[18] Art critics even quoted Native people to confirm Dallin's authenticity. In what appears to be a review of Dallin's *Appeal to the Great Spirit*, the writer recounted a story in which "an old Indian chief" was brought to the Boston Museum of Fine Arts by his son to view the statue. The older man "declared that only an Indian could do such a piece of workmanship," because "only an Indian could understand their modes."[19] Indeed, Dallin corresponded with Native people and appeared to be respected among Native friends and admirers of his art. He approached his Indian studies with sympathy and recognized the importance of accuracy and cultural specificity.[20]

However, Dallin also seemed to be drawn to classical notions of the masculine ideal and Plains figures as quintessential models of Indianness. Market forces can partially account for this aspect of his work. The fallibility of memory and Dallin's origin stories may also play a role. Dallin's boyhood memories may have been shaped by New Englanders' expectations in ways that Dallin could not register or escape. Part of the cultural impact of the *Wild West* show was the perception that the Lakota performers represented all Native peoples. When Dallin observed the Lakota man at the 1889 Paris *Wild West* performance grounds, he may have unconsciously recast his boyhood memories among Lakotas. For example, Dallin insisted that he met a deeply impressive delegation of Lakota men on the first leg of his train ride from Salt Lake City to Boston. Although an Otoe-Missouria and a Lakota delegation arrived in Washington, D.C., in late 1880, the most efficient route to the capital would not have put them on Dallin's train.[21] A more likely possibility would have been his encounter with a predominantly Mountain Crow delegation composed of six notably younger chiefs (Plenty Coups, Two Belly, Pretty Eagle, Medicine Crow, Long Elk, and Old Crow), who left Montana for Washington, D.C., in 1880 to negotiate a land agreement.[22] Another delegation composed of leaders from several Ute groups also traveled the same route as Dallin in 1880 to testify in Washington, D.C., about the recent state of war in the region. The Ute delegation captured public attention for more than its members' physical fitness; crowds gathered at the Pueblo depot station to harangue and throw coal at the Ute men.[23] Whether it was a Crow or Ute contingent, Dallin was oblivious to his fellow passengers' political mission, as well as to the threats of violence that infused a number of late nineteenth-century interactions between white settlers and Indigenous peoples in the West. In a framing that would hold greater appeal to sympathetic easterners, Dallin insisted that the delegation on the train was composed of Lakota men who good-naturedly bantered with him in sign language. Likewise, Dallin later wrote that a *Wild West* performer's action prompted boyhood memories of a Ute treaty council. This may have been a reference to councils held between the United States and Ute representatives to sign a treaty establishing a reservation east of the Wasatch Range in 1868, when Dallin was about seven years old. Moments that could have revealed ongoing Native political concerns in Dallin's home state instead morphed into critical moments of transference that were foundational to Dallin's artistic appeal.

Dallin bridged divides between high art and primitivism, eastern and western regional cultures, and settlers and colonized subjects when he cast male Indian figures into heroic sculpture. Dallin benefited from Americans' fascination with Indian art during the Progressive Era by playing up his personal association with premodern and preindustrial simplicity without delving into the political concerns of contemporary Native people.[24] By carefully crafting an origin story in a frontier cabin surrounded by inspiring Ute neighbors, Dallin illustrated how adopting Indian aesthetics could help non-Indians advance their skills and careers.[25] In his reflections about his subjects, Dallin was careful to cast Indian artists in the past tense. Dallin distinguished the authentic Indians of his youth with those present-day peoples who had been corrupted by civilization. "I knew the Indian before he became the reservation Indian," Dallin explained, back when he "still possessed [manly] virtues and dignity."[26] In addition to conjuring the "noble savage" myth, such rhetoric also tapped into the powerful sensation of nostalgia: an emotional longing for that (or those believed to be) lost to the rapid changes of modernity and the march of progress. Queer theorist Hiram Perez argues that in the late nineteenth century, nostalgia mapped onto supposedly savage peoples, generating a desire for "brown bodies" inextricable from white privilege and U.S. empire.[27] Thus Dallin presented himself as uniquely positioned to lift Indian primitive sensibilities into fine art without suffering the crippling effects of civilization himself, while also sculpting a figure capable of eliciting both longing and satisfaction among viewers.

Although Indians served as inspiration, it was up to civilized people to revitalize American culture. Dallin built into the American art movement an understanding that western non-Indians with proximity to both western authenticity and classical European training held a social responsibility to translate their memories into didactic public artwork. Buying public art *inspired* by

Indians, rather than *created* by Indigenous artists, provided viewers with access to the redemptive qualities of primitivism without forsaking a sense of cultural superiority.

Dallin's statues conveyed a complex message about the place of Indianness in the memorial and public art movement — and American redemption more broadly. As public art, Indian figures might rescue Americans from overcivilization. As memorials, the statues rescue viewers from the guilt of colonial violence by sympathizing with Indians while promoting imperial amnesia. Although Dallin struggled to make the Paul Revere statue a reality by the end of his career, his creation of a didactic public art movement based on notions of idealized masculine Native bodies and western authenticity stand as his lasting legacy in dozens of cities across the country.

Once installed as public art in American cities, did his Indian statuary achieve the kind of civic impact Dallin hoped? Did they inspire Americans to think grander thoughts and reflect on national identity? After a 1915 interview with Dallin to discuss *The Scout*, New England travel writer Agnes Edwards wrote about how little Americans seemed to know about Indians and, by extension, their own families and place histories (fig. 4). "Historically, [the Indian] is so necessary that it is strange that we do not, as individuals, know more about him," Edwards mused. Her probing reflection on public memory and popular knowledge naturally turned back to national origin stories. By the early twentieth century, those origins had become fixed to Plymouth, Massachusetts. "Many people would be amazed to the numbers of Indians still in New England," Edwards wrote, noting that a drive through Mashpee would reveal Wampanoag faces to any alert observer. New Englanders, Edwards concluded, should take a lesson from the Indian subjects of the western sculptor. "Mr. Dallin's choice of a model is not only admirable from an artistic standpoint, but most beautifully appropriate from a national one." Like the great American novel, Dallin's sculptures provide "the study and comprehension of our own country."[28]

SCULPTING *MASSASOIT*

When Dallin received the commission for *Massasoit* in Plymouth, he spent years studying historical accounts of the man's physical description. Dallin tried to please his clients while staying true to his identity as an artist by utilizing a combination of English settlers' written descriptions and his own notions of a perfect Indian body to sculpt *Massasoit*. The president of the Pilgrim Society of Plymouth supplied Dallin with William Bradford's and Edward Wins-

FIGURE 4. *The Scout*, Kansas City, Missouri. *Photograph by Jean O'Brien.*

low's descriptions of the Pokanoket leader to aid his sculptural study. *Mourt's Relation*, first published in 1622, did not provide Dallin with much to go on. Although most of Bradford's and Winslow's descriptions of the Massasoit in *Mourt's Relation* focused on his character and diplomatic actions, physically he appeared to the writers as "a very lustie [*sic*] man, in his best years, an able body, grave of countenance, and spare of speech." 8sâmeeqan's head and face

Casting

were greased and painted red, and he appeared similar to other Pokanoket men, who allowed their hair to grow long but did not have facial hair. As for the men's clothing, Bradford and Winslow vaguely described how "some had skins on them, and some naked," and the Massasoit dressed no differently from his accompanying warriors, with the notable addition of "a great Chaine of white bone Beades about his necke, and at it behind his necke, hanges a little bagg of Tobacco." Based on these and related published notes, Dallin made sure to include the moccasins, bead necklace, and single feather in his *Massasoit* piece. In the absence of more direct observations of the seventeenth-century Wampanoag man, Dallin reached for imaginative contextual clues and elicited feedback from scholars and artists in the hope of correcting any inaccurate details. Dallin's sculptural style was known for its simplicity, but the artist certainly had an eye for details. The first prototype depicted a middle-aged man with a softer middle section and loose flowing hair. The next revised version, *Massasoit* no. 1, sported clothing appropriate to the New England winter, complete with full-length leggings and a panther skin draped over his shoulders. Dallin also added details to reflect a Wampanoag leader's status, including a badge of office and a knife strapped across the man's chest (fig. 5).[29]

In the final version of the statue we see a large cast of influences, models, and memories that can be difficult to disentangle (fig. 6). Surely Bradford and Winslow played a crucial role by supplying the basis for Dallin's visual imagery. The Pilgrim scholars and genealogists who preserved *Mourt's Relation* and other English accounts of Wampanoag people built an archive that informed the sharp-eyed artist's work. One may also consider 8sâmeeqan's own role contributing to his later memorialization. The sachem made conscious choices about self-presentation when meeting the English colonists; the beads and tobacco pouch that distinguished him as a leader would not escape the writers' and the later sculptor's notice.[30] Although descriptions of 8sâmeeqan's facial features were noticeably absent from English reports, here we might see glimpses of further Wampanoag influences in the statue. In the 1990s, Wampanoag tribal historian Russell Gardner suggested that Dallin relied upon 8sâmeeqan's descendants as models to accurately depict his physiognomy, but Dallin did not credit Wampanoag models in his surviving records.[31]

Dallin does, however, write about employing a live model in Boston to craft the body for the final version of *Massasoit*. In Dallin's words, "The model for my Massasoit was a young negro of magnificent figure. I was wanting a model, and happened to call upon John Singer Sargent, who was at work on his decoration for the [Boston] Art Museum. I spoke of the matter, 'Why not use my model.' He said, 'in the afternoon, since I use him only in the forenoon?' So

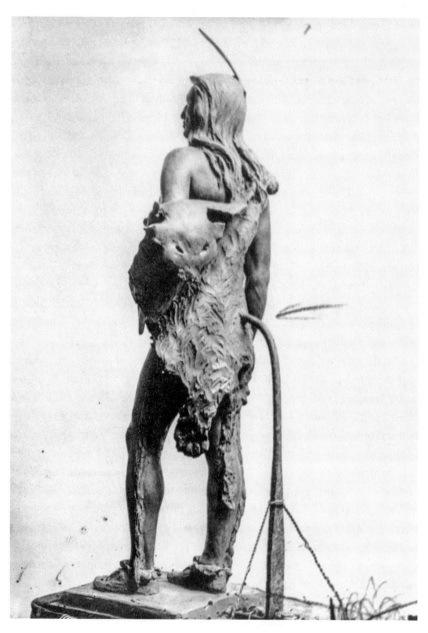

FIGURE 5. *Massasoit #1* clay model, from behind.
Courtesy of the Cyrus E. Dallin Art Museum.

FIGURE 6. Cyrus E. Dallin posing in his studio with *Massasoit.*
Used by permission, Utah State Historical Society.

that is what we did. The model was Apollo in the forenoon and Massasoit in the afternoon."[32] Considering the tight connection Dallin drew in his autobiography between Native bodies, the masculine ideal, and artistic inspiration, it is notable that he reported to a friend that he hired an African American model, Thomas McKeller, for his detailed design work. Dallin's use of Sargent's model may have signaled his entry into elite East Coast art circles while contributing to a larger American art movement that embraced the Other as a subject in public art (and consequently considered nonwhite bodies as interchangeable). In the context of the period's racial, gender, and artistic conventions, in which nude nonwhite bodies became objects of desire and black manliness was defined in relation to white norms but also separated from its social implications through aesthetic rendering, Thomas McKeller gave substance to Dallin's notion of perfect manly physique; he certainly helped Dallin to define the figure's chiseled chest and prominent abdominal muscles in the final version (fig. 7).[33] One wonders how McKeller, who worked for Sargent for years (serving as the model for nearly all of the figures in Sargent's murals in Boston library rotundas), sculpted his own body according to the white male gaze in order to secure paid work as a model of the perfect male form in the height of Jim Crow. The model certainly helped Dallin to transform his first version of *Massasoit* no. 1 from a slender figure (the manly ideal of Dallin's childhood) to a final version with a muscular frame one imagined to be shaped by strenuous outdoor activity that pulsed with virility (the 1890s ideal).[34]

In addition to capturing the physical ideal at the turn of the century, Dallin was attuned to his audiences' popular associations with Indian figures. Dallin's Indian statuary contained cultural markers that popular audiences had come to expect in Indian statuary—perhaps the same markers that attracted Dallin to the *Wild West* show performers in the first place.[35] Consequently, some details not mentioned in *Mourt's Relation* but associated with Plains Indians made their way into the revised version of *Massasoit*, most notably the braided hair and peace pipe. The fur cape and leggings, which would have surely been more appropriate for a New England winter, were thrown off to emphasize the muscular bare chest and thighs. Dallin's curated origin story in Utah also encouraged audiences to see frontier references in the figure. On the final *Massasoit* statue, for example, Dallin altered the pipe to reflect Wampanoag designs, and included the details of two small bears playing on the pipe (fig. 8). This whimsical addition, art critics gleaned, was meant to recall Dallin's fond memories of playing games with Ute children as a boy.[36] Dallin's origin story certainly encouraged such an interpretation, but few critics knew that a pipe with a bear effigy (a powerful clan symbol) had recently been transported to the Museum of the American Indian in New York alongside items removed from a Pokanoket burial ground. Just as Dallin was crafting *Massasoit*, several items (and human remains) assumed to belong to the Massasoit were removed from Burr's Hill in Warren and, along with other assembled materials, cataloged in New York for study and display. Local newspapers announced the

FIGURE 7. *Nude Study of Thomas E. McKeller*, ca. 1917–20.
John Singer Sargent, via Wikimedia Commons.

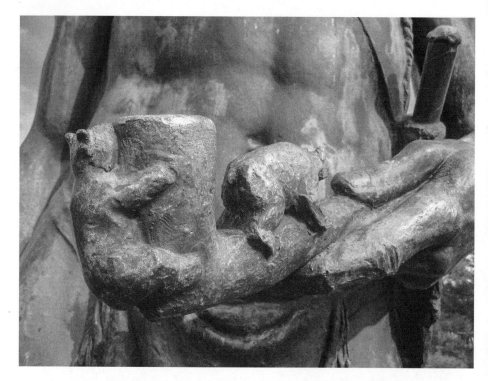

FIGURE 8. Detail of *Massasoit* pipe, Kansas City. *Photograph by Lisa Blee.*

findings, and the Improved Order of Red Men sent news about the possible discovery of the Massasoit's burial site and descriptions of its contents to its members in 1915. Whether Dallin knew about and incorporated the pipe or the plundered items from the Burr's Hill site into the statue model is not known; Dallin's choice to depict bears playing along the peace pipe in the final version was either deeply informed or coincidental, but the artist himself offered no explanation.[37] *Massasoit*'s casting involved the input of many people and emerged at the confluence of several processes — all filtered through the artist's imagination, experiences, and beliefs. As a work of public art and a monument to an individual, the statue is masterful, while also revealing non-Indian values on matters ranging from the primacy of written documents to cultural authenticity, manliness, colonial violence, and racial ideology.

SITING/SIGHTING *MASSASOIT*

Once given a solid form, *Massasoit* was then cast in a new dramatic origin story on the New England shore. According to many interpretations of the installation, the statue re-creates the moment when the Massasoit first caught sight of the *Mayflower* entering the harbor. In fact, 8sâmeeqan was in his home village forty miles to the south when the settlers arrived, and the passengers on the *Mayflower* first encountered a deserted village decimated by European diseases. As indicated on a map from James Thatcher's *History of the Town of Plymouth, from Its First Settlement in 1620 to the Present Time* (1846), the site of first encounter was to be found inland and to the south, on "Watson's Hill" (labeled as the place of the "first interview of Massasoit with the Pilgrims").[38] But the actual site of the storied first encounter was too remotely located from the central drama of English colonialism in which vulnerable settlers clung to the coastline and faced an uncertain fate. The placement of the statue on the site of Cole's Hill overlooking Plymouth Rock was meant to evoke a particular fantasy of first contact and what this moment made possible for the settlers.[39]

Furthermore, 8sâmeeqan's role in forging an alliance with the English is central to the statue's memorializing function, despite (or because of) the rarity of this bond of interdependence in colonial New England. And because the memory inscribed on the statue comes from a settler perspective and is stripped of its Indigenous political context, there is no clear motive for 8sâmeeqan's peace treaty. Viewers of this didactic public art may then conclude that *Massasoit* represents the universal values of friendliness and charity and that the leader's true greatness comes from recognizing the importance of the English colonizing mission. The *Massasoit* memorial installed near Plymouth Rock for the tercentenary is a testament to what Kevin Bruyneel calls "the habit-memory of conquest: a commemoration that re-marks that threshold of conquest in the present." The statue became a recurring "marker of white Euro-American authority in and over this territory." Long after the anniversary year of 1620, the statue would continue to refound the settler society in the moment of the viewer.[40]

In addition to his role in the nation's first contact story, the Massasoit was also cast as the ultimate saintly patriot to punch up the Christian dynamics of the Pilgrims' mission. The Massasoit Memorial Association appealed to the IORM membership to contribute to the commission of a memorial that could "atone" for the shameful neglect of the Massasoit's memory. The planned monument would cast "his saintly figure in enduring bronze, in a place overshadowing, as if still protecting the rock where the Pilgrims landed."[41] In 1915, John Converse, the Massachusetts IORM leader and historian of the Massasoit, published an essay in *News from Headquarters* comparing the Massasoit's aid to Roger Williams to that of the good Samaritan who offered relief to the Israelite. Converse pushed the comparison further, boldly arguing that the Massasoit—though aiding Williams and his religious project "in ignorance"—consequently had a hand in the making of the Constitution and forming the ideal of religious liberty in the United States.[42] *Massasoit*'s role—as a figure on the Plymouth shoreline and encased in a Pilgrim story—was to confirm an Anglo-Christian national identity framed by a modest, peaceful, yet vulnerable, Puritan settlement.

The Massasoit Memorial Association also argued with alarmist rhetoric that the statue was imperative for the maintenance of national memory that included the Massasoit. Without a bronze monument, even patriotic souls would struggle to remember the Massasoit's role in saving the colonial project in New England. Despite the numerous New England histories featuring 8sâmeeqan, the association's own assertion that every public school pupil learned about the Massasoit, and the fact that Wampanoag people continued to honor and tell their children about this ancestor, the Memorial Association members claimed it was their solemn responsibility to keep his name alive.[43] The purchase of a certificate, the fund-raising association insisted, would signal to the world that "the Improved Order of Red Men is determined to hand down the name of Massasoit to posterity, to generations yet unborn, to rescue this great Chief from oblivion and the tongueless silence of an unmarked grave." (Note that the IORM thus contributed to erasing 8sâmeeqan's actual name in favor of his role as political leader—the Massasoit.) Such lofty rhetoric was taken as a literal challenge to one reader, who reported to the newsletter that excavations at Burr's Hill had uncovered a grave containing items that were described as belonging to the Massasoit. The archaeological dig—and widespread looting—in the Wampanoag burial site had only recently begun, after a 1913 gravel mining operation revealed the remains.[44] But just as 8sâmeeqan's historic home was not considered for the memorial placement, the Massasoit's actual grave site was not really the point.

Massasoit, when fixed into a national narrative, came with the added benefit of placing the nation's true origins in New England and nudging the memorial compass to the northeastern shore. As Michael Kammen points out, southerners knew that Jamestown predated the Plymouth colony and, in the context of a growing memorial movement in the early twentieth century, expressed resentment toward New Englanders' claim that the nation began in Plymouth. The fund-raising records for *Massasoit* bear out this regional competition: the majority of the donations came from the "New England Reservations" (in keeping with the appropriation of Indians, the IORM used "reservations" to denote local/regional chapters of the national organization), and an accounting from a few months in early 1921 confirmed that only 1 percent of the receipts came from organization members from the former Confederacy.[45] When finally erected in Plymouth, *Massasoit* was cast into a role promoting a story of national origins told from a New England– and Puritan-centered perspective. *Massasoit* embodied peaceful encounter, lending material form (and the weight of bronze) to a narrative that glorifies colonial settlement.

CASTING IN PLASTER AND BRONZE

While the Plymouth *Massasoit* has remained rooted on Cole's Hill since 1921, the plaster model had legs. Shortly after *Massasoit* was unveiled in Plymouth, Dallin was convinced to donate the plaster original to the state of Utah in 1922. Dallin chose not to make reproductions from this model during his lifetime, but Utah political elites had other plans.[46] The plaster original stood in the center of the capitol rotunda for thirty-five years, where it delighted visitors but rankled those who wished to see a memorial to Mormon "pilgrims" instead. Twelve years after Dallin's death, a donor pledged the funds necessary to cast *Massasoit* in bronze and move the monument outside. The Utah secretary of state's 1957 decision to use the plaster original to cast a bronze meant that *Massasoit* was posthumously reproduced for the first time. It would, of course, not be the last. Dallin's generous gift initiated a series of events that (quite literally) cast *Massasoit* in new dramas. As an art commodity rather than just a monument, replicas of the statue came to embody clashing ideas of ownership and reveal deep levels of appropriation in the art market. If the Plymouth statue translated a story into solid form, its replications became vessels for profit when surrounded by a cast of politicians, museum managers, art dealers, and collectors.

The meaning of sculpture reproduction, and particularly posthumous copies cast without the artist's input, has evolved over time and is now fraught with legal, ethical, and artistic concerns. Sculpture reproduction was relatively common in the nineteenth century, and unlimited reproductions met a high demand in France and across Europe. Many sculptors arranged for foundries to cast reproductions—larger or smaller, marble or bronze—according to demand. Some artists remained involved in the entire casting process to ensure the quality of the finished product, but not all sculptors insisted on this level of control.[47] But during Dallin's career—and continuing through the life of the plaster model of *Massasoit*—anxieties about authenticity, modernity, and the commercial art market shifted the meaning of sculpture reproductions significantly.

Just as Dallin began his formal art education in the 1880s in Boston and

Paris, art dealers and critics began to develop the concept of the limited edition and the notion of originality. This change in thinking about the value of originals emerged from postmodern critiques of the mechanical process of art reproduction. During the late nineteenth century the belief emerged that an original bears the direct mark of the artist's hand on the material and is therefore highly prized. Statues replicated in unlimited series and sold by catalog (as Dallin's smaller works were) did not fetch the higher prices of an original. And, of course, posthumous reproductions cannot meet the definition of an original.[48] The artist plays an important role in guiding the bronze reproduction process to achieve the desired results. The wax mold can vary in thickness and must be carefully formed to transfer small details to the bronze reproduction, and the resulting cast must be shaped and corrected by hand (in a process called "chasing") and colored with solutions of salts and acids to achieve a specific patina. The College Art Association notes that the process of casting, chasing, and patinating a bronze reproduction from a plaster model is difficult, even with highly skilled technicians who are well versed in the original artist's standards of quality. When the artist's standards are not known, which is often the case in posthumous casting, the bronze reproductions likely carry small changes or distortions. It is then up to the buyers to determine whether the reproduction is of high quality and reflects the artist's original vision. Many art experts consider posthumous bronze reproductions not only undesirable, but also inauthentic and unethical.[49]

This focus on "authenticity" was wrapped up in early twentieth-century concerns about the cultural and moral ramifications of mechanical reproduction. Postmodern sculpture critics expressed anxiety over "artistic integrity and commercial exploitation" associated with posthumous reproductions but, according to art historians Anthony Hughes and Erich Rannft, such concerns place a "faintly sensational" spin on formerly unremarkable practices that had been going on for a long time.[50] After all, the historic process of sculpture reproduction had the effect of exposing larger numbers of people to such artwork and driving demand for the form.

Dallin's career was deeply impacted by the principle of limited reproduction and the ubiquitous process of mechanical reproduction—both of which offer rewards in the commercial art market even as they operate at cross-purposes. Once a foundry has a model, it is in the artist's, dealer's, and foundry's interest to cast few copies in order to maintain a high value for each piece, yet each party also profits by selling reproductions.[51] For Dallin, as for any other artist, the economic promise of one's career depended upon maintaining direct control over the casting process and preventing the other parties from brokering separate deals that cut the artist out of the proceeds. In his lifetime, Dallin fought against poor reproductions and unauthorized copies of his statues, which reveals how he may have thought of the *Massasoit* reproductions.

In 1897 Dallin wrote from Paris to Utah governor Heber Wells to protest the city council's plan to dedicate one of his statues in downtown Salt Lake City. He considered the work unfinished because he had not yet completed the design for the pedestal. Without Dallin's own input on the final casting and pedestal, the artist asserted the memorial would tarnish "my own reputation, pride in my work, and the desire to be fittingly represented in my own state."[52] The state of Utah soon tested Dallin's authority over the display of his work once again. That same year, the program committee for Utah's fifty-year jubilee celebration asked Dallin for a copy of his famous *Signal of Peace* for display at the occasion. Dallin secured permission for a plaster copy from the authorities in Chicago who owned the bronze on the condition that the plaster would be destroyed following the Utah festival. The plaster replica was apparently poorly made, but nevertheless shipped to Salt Lake City for the jubilee. After the event, state officials stored the statue in a government building rather than destroying it as agreed. When the capitol building was completed in 1916, the plaster copy was reportedly given a bronze patina and displayed in the rotunda for several years (just as the plaster model of *Massasoit* would be).[53]

Out of concern for his professional contacts in Chicago and his artistic reputation, Dallin lodged complaints with Utah officials in 1918, but the governor responded that "it would take an act of the legislature to remove the statue."[54] On a return trip to Utah, Dallin went to the capitol to inspect the replica with Chief Justice William McCarty, an "experienced horseman," who reported that the horse suffered from "spavins and ring bones" on the legs and feet — imperfections resulting from poor casting. According to Dallin, the critique prompted him to action: "I broke the left leg off the Indian rider and knocked all four legs off the pony, completely breaking it." Indeed, the custodian charged with attending to the mess reported that "Mr. C. E. Dallin willfully with malice did break the leg from off [*sic*] the Signal of Peace."[55] According to Dallin, the judge who accompanied him on this nefarious mission only jokingly threatened to arrest him for destroying state property. But the replica was, in fact, state property. Capitol officials repaired the statue for continued display and ignored Dallin's protests. The state only moved the replica from the rotunda to make room for Dallin's donation of *Massasoit* in 1922.[56] These episodes suggest Dallin's relationship with his home state was exceedingly fraught, with Dallin both craving the attention and recognition he received from Utah and violently reacting to its cavalier disregard of his rights as an artist. He regularly suffered from the excesses of capitalism even while he gained fame as an artist.

Dallin also entered into a legal battle in 1924 against "pirates" selling photographic prints of his *Appeal to the Great Spirit* without permission or furnishing royalties. This copyright case was complicated by questions of ownership and technology; Dallin had sold the equestrian statue to the Boston Museum of Fine Arts in 1912, which then contracted with publishing companies for photographs or pictorial reproductions of the piece for marketing purposes. Dallin retained casting rights to the statue and could reproduce smaller copies, but it appears as though his copyright did not extend to photographic representations of his work.[57] Dallin ultimately dropped the suit and acknowledged that he would not receive royalties for the pictorial reproductions. In the end, Dallin made a plea to the publishers to credit him as the artist on future pictorial representations, although they were under no legal obligation to do so.[58] The publishers profited from the sales and the museum likely benefited from increased visitation as a result of the advertising, but the vexing case revealed to Dallin how little control he maintained over the fate of his sculptures in the commercial art world.

RECASTING *MASSASOIT*

The bronze casting of *Massasoit* at the Utah State Capitol in 1957 was the first posthumous reproduction of Dallin's work, but far from the last. The plaster model, which was dismantled and shipped to a foundry in New York, presumably returned to Utah with the bronze cast in 1958, where it then sat in storage in an unknown location for nearly a decade. Although there is no clear title of ownership or surviving loan documents, possession of the plaster model was apparently transferred to Brigham Young University by 1968.[59] How and why was the plaster *Massasoit* sent to Provo? The statue's provenance is murky because the sizable sculpture collections at BYU were in a state of disarray. It is likely that the plaster *Massasoit* was sent to BYU around 1959 — the same year the university acquired the estate of Mahonri M. Young (another Utah sculptor and contemporary of Dallin's), which included more than 10,000 objects.[60] The BYU Art Department was put in charge of managing the windfall, and the faculty formed the Art Acquisition Committee in the early 1960s to oversee the collection. After years in storage, the sculptures were moved to the newly constructed Harris Fine Arts Center on campus in 1965 but only partially unpacked.[61] The gallery director recalled that the collections were neglected and unorganized in 1968, when he began sifting through the storage boxes; it was only by shelving the sculptures that "Massasoit appeared" during that time and the documentary trail picks up again.[62] A number of art dealers eyed the sculptures when they attended the unpacking and began angling for ways to acquire the works by advising and influencing the collections managers.[63] The temptation to profit from the sculptures held in the disorganized BYU collections proved overwhelming.

Fraud and unauthorized reproductions have been a problem in sculpture for much of the twentieth century. Dealers and museums have established formal policies directing sales and reproductions in an attempt to protect the artist, buyer, collector, and public. The management of collections at BYU was largely governed by university policy, which required the approval of the dean and president for larger art sales.[64] In the early 1970s scholars and art museums made an effort to draft standards to guide sculpture reproductions and prevent unethical bronze casting. Although the scholars who drafted the professional ethical standards in 1974 hoped their advised practices would eventually gain recognition by the courts, the state of Utah did not pass laws specifically regulating the reproduction of bronze sculpture.[65] In this context, BYU art professor and art acquisition director Wesley Burnside, working in cooperation with dealers and galleries, entered into a number of unauthorized deals involving the BYU sculpture collections. A criminal investigation into these deals resulted in charges of unlawful sales, forgery, counterfeiting, and tax fraud against a few of the individuals involved.[66] While such schemes have been documented at other museums, "few were as extensive as the one operating at Brigham Young University in the 1970s and early 1980s." The case was of such notable scale (with 1,000 pieces lost from the art museum's collection) that, for the first time, the International Foundation for Art Research devoted a special issue of its art fraud publication entirely to one story.[67]

Starting in the 1970s, Wesley Burnside organized and operated a tax shelter program in which artworks were overvalued so that buyers who intended to donate the object to a charitable organization could claim substantial tax deductions. This "high-low" scheme worked in different ways. In some cases, a dealer could buy a cheap knock-off at auction and acquire an altered provenance through BYU so the piece could be resold as an original. Dealers solicited art in the university's collection to buyers — typically doctors, lawyers, and developers with little art knowledge — who were offered a low sales price but supplied with grossly inflated appraisals. The buyer could donate the art to BYU or other institutions and receive a tax deduction based on the appraisal rather than the purchase price. By simply creating fake documentation and inflated appraisals, the same sculpture could even be "donated" back to BYU repeatedly without leaving the museum's archives (or existing in the collections at all). Several of Dallin's sculptures were used in the tax shelter scheme. *Chief Washakie* was posthumously cast and marketed to buyers with a fraudulent claim of authenticity, and the Art Acquisition Committee accepted counterfeit bronze casts of *Chief Washakie* and *Appeal to the Great Spirit* as donations of authentic lifetime works in an effort to launder them through BYU.[68]

According to Arnold Lemmon, one of the police detectives on the case, BYU was known to dealers as "the laughingstock of the art world." Crooked gallery owners and bedroom art dealers went on a "feeding frenzy" at the university. Reflecting on the size and scope of the fraudulent dealings, Lemmon remarked that *Massasoit* "was just a very small sliver, but some of our key players were involved in it."[69] It was at the height of this free-for-all in 1976 that a notorious Santa Fe dealer named Forrest Fenn entered into a "verbal business arrangement" with Roy Anderson, a BYU alum and private art dealer with Brand Galleries, to make reproductions of *Massasoit* for sale. Not long after, Anderson solicited Wesley Burnside with a deal to make two bronze casts from the *Massasoit* plaster model. Burnside dutifully inquired into the copyright status of the statue in the BYU collection in the summer of 1976. The university's legal counsel notified Burnside that although there was no title, it was his opinion that the university could proceed with casting without violating copyright.[70] The details of the verbal agreement between Burnside and Anderson were never made clear, although the police investigation revealed that Burnside was "wined and dined" and blackmailed by Anderson; the curator "would sign anything."[71]

On the surface, the deal looked typical: the owner of the original (BYU) would receive a free bronze in exchange for providing the plaster model, and the dealer (Anderson/Brand Galleries) or the foundry would sell other reproductions in a limited series to recover the costs of casting. When the Art Acquisition Committee learned of Anderson's proposal, they even toyed with expanding the series to five bronzes to "[use] this work to make money for the university," although one member raised questions about BYU's legal right to do so. Did the university have a clear title to the piece? Did Dallin's family retain rights? Regardless of the murky provenance, committee members warmed to the idea of numerous posthumous bronze casts and began discussing sale price ($30,000–$40,000) and soliciting a potential buyer (Massasoit College in Massachusetts) for its free bronze.[72] Based on the verbal agreement between Anderson and Burnside, Brand Galleries then increased its planned series from two casts to six in January 1977. The BYU Art Acquisition Committee pushed for a compromise at four casts and tried to pass the buck on possible copyright issues stemming from the murky title; although the dealer would be making a larger profit from sales than BYU in the deal, the committee decided to add a clause that Brand Galleries assume legal responsibility for proof of possession when selling the bronzes.[73] Once Anderson of Brand Galleries received the plaster model from Burnside, he quickly made arrangements with Richard Young Fine Art Casting in Salt Lake City to begin the casting process.[74] Meanwhile, members of the Art Acquisition Committee and university legal counsel spent months trying to reconcile the terms of the verbal agreement (in which Brand Galleries claimed unlimited casting rights) with an acceptable contract for a limited edition of four bronze reproductions to retain the highest market value for each piece.

MOBILIZING *MASSASOIT*

For a few months in 1977, Brand Galleries and Young Fine Art Casting apparently operated on the assumption that they held unlimited rights to make reproductions from the plaster model in their possession. Because of the size of the statue and complexity of the casting process, Young Fine Art Casting took several months to make the bronze reproductions.[75] But how many reproductions of *Massasoit* were ultimately cast, and what happened to them? The owner of the foundry reported to police investigators that he cast four bronzes for Anderson and delivered them to Ken Garff in Utah, the J. C. Nichols Company in Kansas City, the Evergreen Plaza in Illinois, and Forrest Fenn in Santa Fe.[76] However, at least one of the 1977 buyers was under the impression that there were five casts in the edition.[77] And the foundry may not have stopped at full-sized casts. Members of the BYU Art Acquisition Committee visited Fenn Galleries in Santa Fe in 1980 and found out that the gallery had already sold "one or two heads" and was offering for sale "parts of the statue."[78] The rampant abuse of the model meant that unknown numbers of consumers could literally get a piece of *Massasoit* (just like in the years before Plymouth Rock gained its protective canopy, souvenir seekers took pieces of the rock away with them).[79] A few months later, Roy Anderson ordered at least one more bust of *Massasoit* delivered to Fenn Galleries, and a foundry employee recalled that "extra Massasoit heads were also cast."[80] The composite figure that Dallin had labored for a decade to craft was thoroughly dissected in the art market. In 1981, one committee member suggested the committee take whatever steps necessary to regain control of the reproductions: "Go right to the foundry if need be and put a restraining order on the Massasoit."[81]

Because of the preponderance of fraudulent documentation attached to BYU statues and the secretive verbal agreements made between the involved parties, the provenance of the reproductions is confused and unreliable. Clearly a private dealer had taken control of the process with no apparent limits or oversight. It was not until 1985 that BYU attorneys followed up with the foundry to confirm that the mold had been destroyed, but even then, the confusion over whether the contract allowed for four or six reproductions persisted. By that time several bronze reproductions popped up around the country as charitable donations from buyers.[82] The statue grab at BYU was clearly responding to, and further driving, an appetite for Indian sculptures in the commercial art market. The mobility of Massasoit replicas is deeply intertwined with consumer demand, further demonstrating the challenge for any single person or entity hoping to control the visibility of Native figures (and representations more broadly) in American culture.

Notably, the foundry did not deliver one free bronze cast to BYU as directed in the contract, and so BYU was stung by its own shady dealings. Working without the knowledge of the university and the Art Acquisition Committee, Burnside and Anderson arranged for BYU to receive a bronze cast as a donation from a buyer rather than directly from the foundry. The dean of the College of Fine Arts accepted the statue on loan without concurrence with the BYU legal office. The buyer, Ken Garff, a local car dealership owner and member of the BYU Advisory Council, only said that he intended to donate the statue at some point in the future. A monumental-sized bronze Massasoit was delivered to campus in 1978 and only later would investigators learn that BYU did not hold title to the reproduction; it remained on long-term loan from Garff until the investigation revealed the improper deal and prompted the owner to make the donation official.[83]

Although the members of the Art Acquisition Committee had approved the reproductions of Massasoit, they had failed to make a plan for the bronze when it arrived on campus. The committee considered two options: selling it or installing it on campus.[84] The committee's early solicitation to Massasoit College to purchase the bronze seemed promising, although the small Brockton, Massachusetts, college struggled to meet BYU's asking price. In late 1976 the assistant to the president of the college wrote to the BYU gallery director to explain, "You could never realize how much we want that statue here on our campus." The commissioner of the Wampanoag Indians of Massachusetts even joined the effort. "I hope," wrote the college administrator, "that [with] the efforts on our part combined with the interests of the Wampanoag Indians and your latest offer, we will eventually end up with an appropriate honor for the great Sachem at our college."[85] Despite the fervent wishes of Massasoit College and the Wampanoag commissioner, *Massasoit* remained on the BYU campus. When Massasoit College requested a bronze reproduction or the plaster model in 1980 for a bicentennial celebration, the Art Acquisition Committee finally admitted, "We do not have the right to cast the Massasoit. We cannot negotiate with Massasoit College as there are problems. . . . The rights to Massasoit are in question and we are not able to move at this time."[86] And so the statue would stand on campus as the legal issues were sorted out, despite the fact that the statue and the man it memorialized meant practically nothing to BYU students and Provo history. But no matter; members of the committee reasoned that the statue was "an acquisition that would grow rapidly in value and that in five years it could be traded or sold" once the provenance was cleared up.[87]

According to the foundry owner and collaborating documents, the second bronze reproduction of *Massasoit* was delivered to the J. C. Nichols Company of Kansas City, Missouri, in 1977. The path for this cast followed many others in the BYU tax fraud scheme. Miller Nichols, the J. C. Nichols Company board chairman and inheritor of his father's vast real estate company in Kansas City, visited Fenn Galleries while on vacation in Santa Fe in the summer of 1977. Here Forrest Fenn propositioned him with the purchase of a bronze cast of *Massasoit*, although it was not physically in the gallery. Nichols could not personally inspect the bronze to determine its quality, but he nevertheless considered purchasing it for donation to Kansas City after looking into some financial matters.[88] Nichols inquired with legal counsel whether he could "acquire an art object for $35,000 and make it a charitable gift two years later, using a fair market value of $100,000." According to the lawyer, such a donation was perfectly fine as long as the gift was made to a public charity and "you could obtain a valid appraisal of $100,000."[89] The next day Nichols wrote to Fenn to agree on the purchase price of $35,800, and Nichols received an appraisal of $130,000 from Brand Galleries at the time of sale.[90] And, six months after donating *Massasoit* to the Kansas City Parks and Recreation Department in 1979, Nichols received an updated appraisal from both Roy Anderson of Brand Galleries and Forrest Fenn of Fenn Galleries for the identical amount of $145,000.[91] The Fenn Galleries appraisal was apparently based on the recent sale price of another of Dallin's monumental Indian sculptures. The crucial distinction between the *Massasoit* cast sold to Nichols and the comparison piece, however, was that the other piece had been cast with a clear provenance and installed under Dallin's direct supervision. An appraisal based on a comparison between a lifetime original and a posthumous replica is highly questionable.[92]

The J. C. Nichols Company spent $21,033 on the boulder pedestal for the public installation, which prompted Nichols to quote the value of the donation to the city of Kansas City at $166,000.[93] The bronze reproduction was treated in this exchange as though it held the value of a lifetime cast, and no one seemed to be looking too closely. A few years later, the Parks and Recreation Department proudly featured *Massasoit* in its publication *Historic and Dedicatory Monuments of Kansas City* and identified the piece as "one of five originals" — effectively playing into the tax scheme and obscuring the machinations of the commercial art market that explained *Massasoit*'s presence in the city.[94]

In addition to a hefty tax deduction for the donor, this bronze *Massasoit* was also good for business. The city's parks department supplied the space for the statue at the intersection of Forty-Seventh Avenue and J. C. Nichols Parkway, which was on the edge of the Country Club Plaza — a shopping center developed and owned by the J. C. Nichols Company. Although installed on city property, *Massasoit* could be folded into the company's Art & Architecture Walking Tour featuring other sculptures installed in the private shopping center.[95]

This bronze *Massasoit* welcomed shoppers to Kansas City's Country Club Plaza for over a decade, until the statue had to be relocated to make room for new tennis courts. Nichols suggested a spot south of the K.C. Masterpiece restaurant in the plaza, but Parks and Recreation decided on a new location a block away, at the newly expanded intersection of Main Street and Forty-Seventh Avenue. Although outside of the Plaza, *Massasoit* continued to be connected to commercial space. The city worked with the owners of Winstead's restaurant group to create a new landscaped area and parking lot at the busy intersection, and *Massasoit* would be included in the sixty-foot circular flower bed.[96] *Massasoit*'s main viewers are shoppers coming from the Plaza, residents waiting at the bus stop on the corner, or patrons of Winstead's Drive-In — a classic Kansas City burger joint.[97] Every now and then a visitor or East Coast transplant will stumble upon the statue and recognize the figure — and once again a Massachusetts college inquired into buying the cast for a fitting memorial on campus — but the statue garners little attention otherwise.[98] All in all, *Massasoit* was arguably a poor deal for the citizens of Kansas City, who lost out on tax payments from one of the city's wealthiest companies and received a posthumous cast (of uncertain quality and questionable provenance) of a historical subject that made little sense for the location. The fate of this *Massasoit* cast reveals how the proliferation of Indian statues in cities across the country can be explained in large part by pursuit of profit (which was encouraged by tax codes), rather than any coherent popular understanding of the role of Indian representations in American culture.

The third bronze *Massasoit* cast in the 1977 series was also purchased by a developer and art collector. Much like J. C. Nichols and his son Miller in Kansas City, real estate magnate Arthur Rubloff made a fortune by reshaping and expanding the urban and suburban commercial landscape: he was a driving force behind the marketing of Chicago's Magnificent Mile and the development of Chicago suburbs. Rubloff began to purchase bronze sculptures to adorn his Chicago-area shopping mall, Evergreen Plaza, in the 1970s. He kept an eye out for Dallin's Indian statuary in particular. In late 1975, Rubloff acquired a sizable collection of twenty-seven bronzes, including one of Dallin's equestrian statues, from a New York auction.[99] Although the single largest bidder at the auction, Rubloff nevertheless lamented that one nine-foot Dallin bronze, *The Passing of the Buffalo*, went to a higher bidder from Muncie, Indiana (who would donate the statue to the city for a public park, where it would stand just down the road from a copy of Dallin's *Appeal to the Great Spirit*—clearly Nichols and Rubloff were not alone in their statuary quests).[100] Rubloff was reportedly "thirsting for the Indian" to add to his shopping center bronze collection, and so he may have jumped at the chance to acquire additional copies of Dallin's heroic-sized Indian bronzes when the opportunity arose a year later.[101] In April 1977, Rubloff announced that *Massasoit* was among a number of Dallin's statues to be added to the collection at Evergreen Plaza.[102] We do not know the details of how Arthur Rubloff came to find and purchase *Massasoit*. However, the four other statues Rubloff acquired with *Massasoit* had all been named in the BYU art investigation as counterfeit bronzes created and used in the tax shelter program. Most were cast in the same Salt Lake City foundry as *Massasoit*, and all were accepted at BYU as donations of authentic lifetime works; the art acquisition director Wesley Burnside was involved in marketing them to potential buyers with fraudulent papers of authenticity and inflated appraisals.[103]

Might Burnside have profiled Miller Nichols and Arthur Rubloff and, in collusion with dealers and the foundry, solicited their interest in bronze casts from the BYU collections? The similarities between Nichols and Rubloff are indeed notable: both commercial real estate developers in the Midwest; both major philanthropic givers in their respective cities—cities which already owned Dallin sculptures in public parks; and both searching for a statue to adorn their shopping centers. As art scholars have noted, dealers try to sell counterfeit bronzes and unauthorized casts in areas of the country where there are few original pieces in public collections, thereby making it difficult for buyers to make comparisons. And if a purchaser unwittingly buys a counterfeit and cannot resell it — "the value would be estimated by some as no more than a commercial souvenir paperweight" — the buyer may resort to charitable giving to recover the investment.[104]

Rubloff donated portions of his sizable bronze sculpture collection to the Art Institute of Chicago in the years immediately before his death in 1986.[105] Although the museum acquired six Dallin statues as part of Rubloff's donations, *Massasoit* was not among them. We do not know whether Rubloff offered to donate *Massasoit*, but the art institute accepted several other Dallin bronze sculptures from Rubloff for resale only and immediately deaccessioned the pieces believed to be posthumous casts. The only one of Dallin's bronzes to remain in the institute's collections is a cast of *Chief Washakie*.[106] Although Rubloff did not receive a tax deduction for a charitable donation on this piece (nor the social capital gained from a plaque identifying him as a philanthropist), Rubloff had used Dallin's work to successfully build a reputation as a collector and taste maker, and may have profited more directly in increased foot traffic to the mall to view his bronze collection.

Massasoit, meanwhile, remained in the Evergreen Plaza for a decade as the shopping center deteriorated around it; after Rubloff's death, a development firm acquired the mall with plans to eventually rebuild. Finally, in late 1996, the Chicago auction house commissioned to sell the posthumous *Massasoit* cast from the Arthur Rubloff Collection found a buyer. A private collector from Ohio purchased the statue and donated it to the Dayton Art Institute. The donor mentioned that the statue was saved from a shopping mall slated for demolition, but offered the Dayton museum no further information on the provenance of the piece.[107]

A fourth full-sized *Massasoit* bronze was delivered to Fenn Galleries in late 1977, where Fenn once again found a buyer in the Midwest. The owner, Denver Haase of Geneseo, Illinois, retired from his feed mill business in 1977 and presumably purchased the cast directly from Fenn Galleries without shipping it first to Geneseo. In fact, Mr. and Mrs. Haase arranged for the statue to go to the Museum of Native American Culture at Gonzaga University in Spokane, Washington. The statue, apparently initially transferred as a permanent loan, was installed outside the museum by early 1978. The *Spokane Chronicle* reported the value of the statue at $155,000, which aligned closely with the appraised replacement value Fenn Galleries produced for Miller Nichols for the Kansas City donation.[108] Why would a retired Illinois businessman purchase a statue sight unseen for display in another state? This buyer's motivations cannot be discerned from available records, although the practice of purchasing art and then loaning it for use in a different state than the buyer's place of residence was a maneuver utilized by some collectors to avoid taxes on the transaction.[109] Museums benefit by being able to display valuable works of art without any financial outlay, and supporters defend the practice because it provides public access to art before it disappears into private collections. This little-known tax maneuver has produced, according to one *New York Times* investigation, "a startling pipeline of art moving across the United States."[110] *Massasoit* was not the only sculpture on the move.

And the Spokane *Massasoit*, just like its mate in the Evergreen Plaza, would also be moved from its initial installation after the owner's death. In the early 1990s, the Museum of Native American Culture became defunct and the collections fell to the stewardship of the Eastern Washington State Historical Society. Soon after Denver Haase died in 2000, the historical society (which acquired ownership at some point), deaccessioned the piece in 2001 and sold it at auction to an unnamed buyer.[111] Where is the statue? For now, it exists in the liminal space of a private collection within the commercial art market, where it may be "hidden" in a home or storage facility only to surface in public records at auction or as a charitable donation.

Beyond these four bronze reproductions reported by the Utah foundry, the trail of *Massasoit* reproductions grows cold. What happened to the busts and "body parts" of *Massasoit* up for sale in Santa Fe? Could Brand Galleries, Fenn Galleries, or other dealers have ordered additional monumental-sized bronzes from the foundry before the mold was destroyed? In the 1977 newspaper story announcing the bronze collection on display at Evergreen Plaza, the *Massasoit* statue is described as one of *five* statues cast in the same edition.[112] Not surprisingly, the BYU Art Acquisition Committee members who visited Fenn Galleries in 1980 found that the gallery was offering for sale a full-sized bronze reproduction of *Massasoit*—a year after the Spokane Museum of Native American Culture acquired the fourth cast.[113]

As for the original plaster model of *Massasoit*—which is usually destroyed by the artist to prevent posthumous reproductions—the foundry returned the piece to BYU, which had little interest in keeping it. The Art Acquisition Committee hoped to loan or trade the model to the Springville Museum of Art, but the museum initially declined the offer in 1977. Within a couple of years, the museum apparently changed its position and received the original plaster in a "gentleman's agreement" for a long-term loan in 1980.[114] The piece found a fitting home in the Springville Museum of Art in Cyrus Dallin's birthplace, but the statue poses some preservation and ethical problems. When the museum received a request from the former mayor of Springville to cast an additional

FIGURE 9. *Massasoit* statue in the Springville Museum of Art, Springville, Utah. *Photograph by Lisa Blee.*

bronze from the plaster model (to be donated to Springville as public art), it had to deny the request on the grounds that the museum did not own the piece (since it was on loan from BYU), the museum opposes posthumous casts on principle, and the plaster is now too fragile to survive another cast. Currently the Springville Museum faces the challenge of preserving the stained, repaired, and oft-reconstructed and recast original model (fig. 9).[115]

What can the casting of the Massasoit through *Massasoit* tell us? The initial act of appropriating an Indigenous man's image helps to draw the connection between colonial dispossession and a capitalist system. The African American body and Native American histories and cultures—the elements that made this statuary object possible and desirable—were incorporated into a system that rewards ongoing cycles of appropriation. As those who commissioned the statue understood, patriotism demands Indians; American popular culture needs an innocent and innocuous reframing for the founding principles of taking and profiting. The moment of national founding and its naturalization as an ongoing fact is embodied in the *Massasoit* memorial. It is a national founding premised on the transfer of land from Indigenous people to colonists, which can only be justified with the belief that honorable Native leaders promoted this process. The same cultural act of appropriation persisted within the machinations of the art market. When the statue became a commodity, it was alienated from place and time, making the process of appropriation at the heart of the colonial project all the more visible. The art market (and charitable tax loopholes) allows for personal gain while obscuring bad behavior in principled guise of a "public good," which is another expression of the colonial order first established with the statue's commission.

And yet Indigenous people have also found ways to appropriate the commodity, reclaiming the statue back to the realm of social and political meaning, as we shall see in subsequent chapters. Though cast as foundational figures subsumed to the lofty notion of making the nation through *Massasoit* and made mobile through the machinations of the commercial art market, Indigenous people continued to find ways to mobilize their own messages through the statue after its original casting and subsequent replication. Perhaps this is the stage at which, in Kevin Bruyneel's terms, the collective memory that structures the perpetual refounding of the settler state may be disassembled. Native people—as subjects and viewers of art—are central to the statue and the significance of appropriation in American culture. As with monumental landscapes everywhere, the meanings to be made through *Massasoit* are dynamic and rich with potential reimagining.

Chapter Two

STAGING

The dominant narrative of the Massasoit and the Puritans — of peaceful colonization by freedom-seeking Pilgrims — is often understood as an illustration of the roots of American identity (of innocence) and American history (as English and freedom loving). Yet at the level of lived experience, national identity and national memory can be remote concepts, largely the construction of political elites, city boosters, and scholars. As Christine DeLucia argues in her study of New England Indigenous memoryscapes, most people form their identities and memories in specific sites.[1] As we follow *Massasoit* through over eighty years of unveilings and dedication ceremonies, we can see the interplay between the national narrative and its reception by audiences in diverse locations and settings. These somewhat formulaic ceremonies reveal the role of cultural and political elites in attaching the dominant national story to *Massasoit*, as well as the way *Massasoit* was incorporated (or not) into local communities and historical memories by residents. At each unveiling and dedication ceremony, *Massasoit* took center stage but was surrounded by props and a cast that worked to communicate a story — whether a narrative of national belonging, regional consciousness, or Indigenous perspective. While these narratives work at cross-purposes, they were often staged together, simultaneously, and legible through the figure of *Massasoit*. After the pomp and ceremony faded, the monuments continued to accumulate meaning, serving as stages for public discussions over cultural appropriation and the place of Native people in national and local historical consciousness.

When the Improved Order of Red Men incorporated its fund-raising committee to commission the memorial, the organization had a vision for *Massasoit* as the lead actor on the stage of Plymouth in the 1921 tercentenary. The memorial would bring together the story of the first meeting between Natives and newcomers—the setting for the first encounter and the first Thanksgiving—and cement the supposedly shared values of friendship and patriotism upon hallowed ground shared with Plymouth Rock. These two memorial anchors—the rock on the shore and the Indian on the hill—would create a narrative of peaceful colonization with national appeal. However, the artist, 8sâmeeqan's descendants, and tercentenary planners had a different vision for the staging, the actors, and the story the memorial could tell. Although the IORM's fund-raising efforts were a success, the group's intention with the statue did not always match the outcome, because the staging in Plymouth was (and is) complex, layered, and contested.

In Utah, the plaster original and bronze cast (no. 2) were set upon stages far removed from Plymouth's memorial landscape and tercentenary context. In Salt Lake City's state capitol building, the plaster Massasoit was simultaneously downstage and far off in the wings. Some political elites appreciated the monument for telling a story of Utah's cultural sophistication, while other Utahans came to see Massasoit as a major contributor to their sense of place within the community's social fabric. But dissenters abounded in the audience, leading to the creation of cast no. 2 to stand outside the capitol in Salt Lake City. Cyrus Dallin was apprehensive about setting Massasoit on a Utah stage, and political and cultural elites in the 1950s saw Massasoit as an intrusive force, upstaging the true heroes in a story of the state's historical development. The decision to remove Massasoit from the capitol set off a chain of events that would place cast no. 6 in the awkward setting of the Brigham Young University campus, where Massasoit stood in perpetual defiance of the school's honor code and in questionable allegiance to the university's rival sports teams.

The staging for casts no. 3–5—in Kansas City, a Chicago suburb, and Spokane, respectively—was further removed from the IORM's vision and the national narrative it hoped to construct. In fact, the initial staging for casts no. 3 and 4 was commercial rather than memorial, the stories they told (when discernable at all) circling around civic pride and abstract cultural appreciation. Cast no. 5 in Spokane (1978–2001) and cast no. 4 (when moved to Dayton in 1996) both came to represent timeless and priceless fine art by virtue of their museum staging, yet both settings stripped the monument of identifying information and context. However, some elements of the stage set around Massasoit remained remarkably consistent from place to place and over time. Certain associations between an Indian figure and nature, the past, and nobility persisted. And Native people interacted with and sometimes responded to the memorial in public ways that defied non-Indians' intentions and expectations. The national narrative of Thanksgiving may break down around Massasoit as the casts multiplied and the staging evolved, but the memorial remained front and center to larger debates about the place of Indians (real and imagined) in local and national historical consciousness.

VISUALIZING THE INSTALLATION

When Cyrus Dallin received the commission to sculpt a memorial to the Massasoit, he spent years refining his vision. What would the Massasoit wear and hold? What message should his posture communicate? And not least important: How should he be staged? Dallin made specific choices for the Plymouth installation—the size and appearance of the stone pedestal and the statue's orientation—that supported his vision for properly conveying the sachem's significance. Yet Dallin could not control other aspects of the stage. Many elements that helped to produce a narrative about the memorial's meaning were in others' hands. The Pilgrim Society of Plymouth, working closely with the IORM fund-raising committee, donated the land atop Cole's Hill for the installation and thus determined the memorial site.[2] The hill rises from the channel of Plymouth Harbor and, on a clear day, provides a view of the surrounding bays and the distant hills of Roxbury up the coast (fig. 10). It is also fixed within a web of memorials spread across Pilgrim Memorial State Park, which is currently managed by the Massachusetts Department of Conservation and Recreation. Cole's Hill is interpreted as the site of the first cemetery used by the English colonists, standing adjacent to Brewster Gardens where the first Thanksgiving took place, and across the road from a statue of William Bradford (also sculpted by Dallin, but in much diminished stature compared to *Massasoit*) and Plymouth Rock. In Memorial Park, visitors are encouraged to imagine the moment of English colonists' arrival at a sacred place where American settlement—and history—began.[3] The site became instrumental to the narrative of peaceful encounter that reinforced the perception of Plymouth as a sacred colonial site.

When *Massasoit* was unveiled atop Cole's Hill, reporters and art critics fashioned a celebratory story of colonization around the statue that did not exactly reflect what Dallin hoped to communicate based on his research. One art writer explained that Dallin was to "represent Massasoit stepping out of the woods to meet the Pilgrims with his peace pipe in his hand. He sees the white man for the first time, but though he himself is lord of the demesne he is willing to share it with the white man."[4] Another art writer in 1937 described how the bronze *Massasoit* "stands looking out to sea as if watching the white man land on these American shores. Welcome is in his eyes, but also fear and

FIGURE 10. *Massasoit* on Cole's Hill overlooking Plymouth Rock.
Photograph by Jean O'Brien.

anxiety." The writer noted of the statue's orientation: "Mr. Dallin has Massasoit watching the 'Mayflower' approaching. He has him gazing down an old channel through which the ship bearing the Pilgrims neared the harbor." In the same publication, Dallin is quoted as correcting such historical inaccuracies. Dallin noted that the Pilgrims who came ashore at Patuxet did not see Indians for the first three months after landing, until the day that Samoset walked into the settlement to inform the English of the Massasoit's power and peaceful intentions.[5]

Journalists and art critics interpreted the statue's orientation and the land on which it was installed, and thus directed the public meaning of the monument and cemented *Massasoit* within a Pilgrimcentric narrative. The cultural landscape of Plymouth Harbor, and the historical memory drawn from its monuments, was restored to reference the first year of Pilgrim settlement. In this aspect, Plymouth Harbor fits within the preservationist approach of "freezing," which encourages visitors to imagine they can step back in time and experience the lives of past people. This is a common interpretive choice to draw tourists to sites of national heritage and memory, such as Colonial Williamsburg, Mystic Seaport, and Civil War battle sites. But, as several scholars have pointed out, "freezing the landscape . . . could result in a form of purposeful amnesia, a way of returning to a past in which we remember only the golden times."[6] In proximity to a place in which visitors are told the first Thanksgiving took place, visitors to Plymouth might be primed to think about peaceful contact and exchange, rather than imagine a dynamic Wampanoag world under stress from disease and enemies.

Furthermore, a precious few clues around the harbor point to precolonial histories or the devastating divides exemplified in King Philip's War. The interpretive and memorial focus on Pilgrims in Plymouth Harbor in 1620–21 obscures a great deal of cultural history. How was Patuxet laid out and how did the community incorporate elements of the landscape and their belief system into contacts with newcomers from across the Atlantic? How did the men and women of Patuxet use the shoreline, and how were they connected to other villages across the region? The colonial landscape that provides visitors with only select memories and a snapshot in time suffers from what Michael Kammen describes as "heritage syndrome," resulting in the "warping and whitewashing" of a more complicated past.[7] The interpretation of this landscape encourages a veneration of the harbor as sacred, fitting all of the criteria Kenneth Foote identified as the elements of sanctified place.[8] Thus any challenge to the narrative or physical layout can be seen as not only controversial, but veering into the realm of defilement and heresy (as the United American Indians of New England found out in the 1970s).[9] Whether Dallin was consciously aware or not, his sculpture worked to cement a single-sided narrative that even his own comments at the unveiling could not penetrate. The Plymouth stage was set for *Massasoit*, and the monument would play a role in a Pilgrim-centered production.

PLYMOUTH UNVEILING, 5 SEPTEMBER 1921

For the formal unveiling ceremony on Memorial Day in 1921 (which took place over a year before the official dedication), a small platform was built next to the flag-draped statue on Cole's Hill.[10] The nine-and-a-half-foot bronze figure was installed atop a nine-ton boulder, with brass bolts drilled into the underside of the feet. The boulder had its own pilgrimage story, for this town appreciates storied rocks. Rather than emerge from the rocky shore a few yards away as may be expected, *Massasoit*'s pedestal was "one of many glacial drift boulders found on the Manomet Hills about five miles from the centre of the town." Ac-

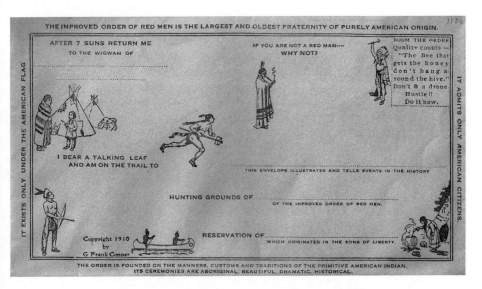

FIGURE 11. Front of envelope showing organization symbolism, Improved Order of Red Men. *Courtesy of Leominster Public Library, Leominster, Massachusetts, Municipal Building Time Capsule, 1915.*

cording to the newspaper coverage of the unveiling ceremony, the rock pedestal helped to tell the story that viewers were to glean from the statue. The description of the antiquity of the boulder pedestal distinguishes it from the rock on the shore upon which the English once stood (thus marking the beginning of history). This boulder fixes *Massasoit* in backwoods and the past, even as the venerated rock on the shore became the center of a civilization that ushered the English into modernity. This pedestal helped build associations between Indigenous people and primordial nature, a trope often repeated in *Massasoit* installations. Furthermore, *Massasoit*'s stance atop the boulder was a staged setting meant to be read as a snapshot of a moment, fixed in place and time. The Massasoit stepped up on the rock for a better view of the approaching ship, which he realizes in this instant is "bringing white men here to the lands over which he is a ruler." The statue's face is to be read in this moment of contingency as belonging to "one who would make a staunch friend or a good enemy."[11] The unveiling ceremony was not ambiguous on the Massasoit's position with the colonists, however, and maintained a consistent narrative of friendship.

The idea for the *Massasoit* memorial originated with a past IORM local president, or "Great Sachem," John W. Converse, although he would not live to see the unveiling (figs. 11 and 12). Along with his prominent national role

FIGURE 12. Back of envelope showing organization symbolism, Improved Order of Red Men. *Courtesy of Leominster Public Library, Leominster, Massachusetts, Municipal Building Time Capsule, 1915.*

in the organization, Converse was also a lawyer residing in the Boston suburb of Somerville and a lay historian who consulted with scholars familiar with 8sâmeeqan's descendants and Wampanoag places.[12] In his 1915 appeal for a memorial, he introduced the Massasoit to the organization members as "Woosamekuin or Osamekin, and these names mean 'Yellow Feather.'" Converse quoted scholar Virginia Baker, who identified Sowams as the principal village for the Pokanoket in the densely populated southern portion of their homeland, and the place where the Massasoit spent the majority of his lifetime.[13] Sowams, which Baker noted was located about forty miles west of Patuxet, near present-day Barrington, Rhode Island, was where the English settlers met with the Massasoit to discuss their strategic alliance and Edward Winslow administered medical care to the sachem.[14] After describing Wampanoag geography and the political organization ("[Massasoit] had jurisdiction over some thirty villages"), Converse delved into 8sâmeeqan's kinship relations and character, notably dispelling the "noble savage" image of the Massasoit that was otherwise pervasive in Puritan-focused histories. "Massasoit had no sympathy with the white man's religion or civilization," Converse declared. "The relations between him and the Plymouth Colony were purely political on both sides." The resulting treaty, an agreement drawn up to help the Massasoit shore up his weakening power, only lasted as long as it did because the Massasoit "was a loyal ally to the Plymouth Colony." Therefore, Converse concluded, the Mas-

Staging

sasoit "and his fidelity to the treaty ought to be commemorated by a suitable memorial." By the 1921 unveiling and soon after Converse's death, the history lesson of the treaty memorial would be condensed, simplified, and not surprisingly, framed within a non-Indian perspective that emphasized friendship rather than political strategy.

In his 1915 article, Converse laid out his vision for an appropriate dedication ceremony for the memorial: "Descendants of Massasoit are now living in Abington and Middleboro [sic]. . . . One of them, a woman, still wears only Indian costume and is known by the Indian name of Teweeleema. One has been a teacher in a Boston private school. All are well-educated. One of these living descendants should unveil the memorial while the others are grouped around it at the time. They should all be given prominence in our dedicatory exercises. The burden of speech and song should be fidelity to duty and obligations and to promises, for that is what Massasoit represents."[15] Although Teweeleema (or Melinda Mitchell) died in 1919, only a few months before Converse passed away, other IORM members agreed that the Massasoit's descendants should be part of the unveiling (figs. 13, 14, and 15). Ultimately, the unveiling ceremony resembled Converse's vision on the surface, if not in spirit.

According to the IORM newsletter, "Princess Wootonekanuskee [sic], the last living descendant of Massasoit, was the central figure on the platform." Wootonekanuske, or Charlotte L. Mitchell, had informed IORM president Alvin Weeks years earlier that she could trace her lineage directly to the Massasoit's daughter Amie. But she was not the only one. Just four years earlier, the General Court of Massachusetts identified Wootonekanuske and her two sisters Teweeleema and Zeriah Robinson, as the Massasoit's descendants in a resolution. Charlotte also informed Weeks of the whereabouts of two other surviving siblings, Helen and Alonzo, who lived nearby although they were in poor health. In fact, the family's home near Lakeville in Plymouth County had garnered journalistic attention for over twenty years, and published photographs and stories of the family members were readily available. Charlotte's younger sister, Emma Safford of Ipswich, Massachusetts, fielded invitations to speak to collectors and scholars through the 1920s.[16] In addition, Weeks speculated, based on his own genealogy research, that there were a handful of other possible descendants.[17] Despite the fact that the current and former IORM presidents had published information on the Massasoit's numerous living descendants, the newsletter offered its members a representative of the "last" of an Indigenous lineage in order to tell the more popular and romantic story of Indian disappearance from New England.[18] The trope of the "last Indian" was apparently inescapable for this family; one journalist described the matriarch,

FIGURE 13. Group portrait of the Mitchells.
Courtesy of Gerry Biron.

FIGURE 14. Postcard, Teweeleema (Melinda Mitchell).
Courtesy of Gerry Biron.

FIGURE 15. Wootonekanuske (Charlotte Mitchell). *Courtesy of Jean O'Brien.*

Zerviah Gould Mitchell, in 1891 as "the last of her ... family" and "the only type of a race which has now almost vanished from New England," and some Red Men in attendance could have purchased a postcard depicting Charlotte's sister Melinda and identifying *her* as "the last living descendant of Massasoit." Not surprisingly, Charlotte's 1930 obituary described her as the last of her tribe, despite the fact that she was survived by two siblings.[19]

In what was by 1921 a time-honored New England memorial tradition, Charlotte Mitchell shared a crowded stage with non-Indian men dressed in regalia and prepared to speak on her and her family's behalf. Notably, Charlotte was introduced to the membership by her Algonquian name in order to emphasize her Indigenous identity.[20] Reflecting to a reporter two years after the event, Charlotte recalled that it was only "by dint of much urging" that she was persuaded to attend the unveiling, where she "resentfully" played her part.[21] Charlotte and her sisters were well known among their Lakeville neighbors for their pride in their ancestry, the miniature plaited and dyed rye-straw baskets they sold for income, and their distinctive Wampanoag dress.[22] A visitor to Charlotte's lakeside home in 1913 recalled that the sisters spoke of "their glorious heritage from Massasoit" with an attendant sense of outrage at the "irresistible wrong done them by the alien in the land of their forefathers."[23] Did Charlotte use the occasion of the unveiling to don her best Wampanoag regalia and challenge the viewers' perception of a harmonious friendship? Charlotte was reportedly "garbed in full ceremonial dress" with a "vivid head-dress of feathers" — which may not have stood out as she hoped among the 1,500 "Brothers and Sisters" wearing their version of Indian regalia — when she began the ceremony by laying down a bouquet of dahlias at the foot of the veiled statue.[24] But Charlotte admitted later to feeling "heartily ashamed of myself" for "helping celebrate the killing of my own people."[25]

Charlotte was surrounded on stage by a number of other notable actors: Alvin Weeks, the clerk of the Massasoit Memorial Association, the leaders of the Red Men and Degree of Pocahontas Massachusetts chapters, the president of the Pilgrim Society, and Cyrus Dallin (presumably the only person on stage without Indian regalia). Following an "invocation to the Great Spirit" by a former IORM president, Charlotte was silently escorted to the statue to remove the flag; as the figure was revealed the crowd erupted in "cheers and whoops" while the band played "The Star-Spangled Banner."[26] In this moment of jubilation, Charlotte pointedly turned away from the cameras trained on her face.[27] It was Alvin Weeks who was allotted the most time on stage for his "Long Talk" and concluded the formal ceremony by placing the monument under the care of the Pilgrim Society until the formal dedication the following year. The theatrical production completed, the crowd walked downhill to the Pilgrim pageant stage for photographs, and then proceeded to Stephens Field where they were treated to a clambake and fireworks display.[28]

The audience in attendance (mainly IORM members and tourists in town for the tercentenary) witnessed a production in which *Massasoit* was literally surrounded by symbols of U.S. patriotism. The bronze figure served as a visual aid for regalia-clad non-Indians as they told a story of America's veneration for freedom and welcoming Indians. Charlotte's role could be seen as affirming this story, lending yet greater satisfaction to the crowd as they witnessed the persistence of friendly and cooperative relations between settlers and Indigenous people. If Charlotte, who was in her seventies at the time, expressed her thoughts about the statue or her ancestor during the ceremony, her words were not recorded. On other occasions Charlotte was known to say that the Massasoit had been mistaken for signing a peace treaty with colonists, and the Massasoit's son Pometacomet (sometimes referred to as Metacom or Metacomet) had only tried to correct his father's error.[29] Given Charlotte's insistence on this narrative of Wampanoag resistance, it is not surprising that she served as a voiceless visual element in the IORM ceremony—not unlike the likeness of her ancestor she unveiled on that day.

This was not the first time she had silently participated in a public memorial celebration as a representative of the dwindling number of 8sâmeeqan's descendants and "prehistoric men" more generally. In the Rochester, Massachusetts, bicentennial celebration in 1879, Charlotte, Melinda, and their mother, Zerviah, stood on stage while non-Indian speakers made toasts and offered a prayer for "the few relics here to-day of those primal lords of these ancient forests."[30] Of course, Charlotte's participation in these memorial ceremonies does not mean she acquiesced to the problematic narratives of Indigenous decline the orators promoted. If anything, the events provided an opportunity to heighten the visibility of her family and her Wampanoag relatives to directly challenge such narratives.[31] Even if she had not been allowed to speak, her role announced and confirmed her Indigenous identity in public—an identity often contested and seldom affirmed for New England Natives. Her participation also strategically cemented a relationship with the local IORM chapter, which took a particular interest in her welfare after the unveiling. In 1927 the "Nunkaset Tribe" sponsored a fund-raising effort among the Massachusetts members to provide Charlotte with a pension after the state legislature denied her request to increase her annuity. The member-funded appropriation for the elderly woman's care was initiated after non-Indian friends learned that "the tribe of Massasoit never has been maintained" as wards of the Bureau of Indian Affairs, and the government "is powerless to help descendants of the Indian friend of the Pilgrims."[32] Even if the federal government failed to recognize Charlotte's tribal identity and any responsibility toward her, local IORM members were invested in advocating for the importance of her lineage.

Indeed, the statue and the narrative of friendly cooperation surrounding it became useful tools in Wampanoag people's long struggles to retain and reclaim their reserved lands near 8sâmeeqan's historic home. The Watuppa reservation, established shortly after King Philip's War on either side of Watuppa Ponds near Fall River, was intended for the "use and occupation of Indians." Zerviah Mitchell held a claim on the reservation for a time in the 1850s before a disagreement with her appointed "guardian" over timber sales convinced her to relinquish her lots and move to Abington. Hers was not the last of the Wampanoag families pushed from the reservation. In 1907 the state used eminent domain to acquire 100 acres of the eastern waterfront reserve.[33] The city of Fall River petitioned the state legislature to take the tract based on the contradictory arguments that "there are apparently no Indians left" (with the very notable exception of Fanny Perry and her family) and that the Perry family's dwellings should be condemned "for the protection and purity of [the city's] water supply."[34] The city's petition hedged around the illegal seizure of reserved Indian lands by questioning Fanny Perry's Indigenous identity; the petition described her as an "occupant" who had received poor relief from the city, and claimed that "no one is absolutely certain that any of [the Native land-owners'] true lineal descendants are in existence to-day."[35] The Wampanoag people removed from Fall River were not compensated for their loss.[36]

In 1938, a newspaper byline announcing "Massasoit's kin ask legislature to return Fall River property" was accompanied by a large photograph of *Massasoit*. Josephus Perry sponsored a Senate resolution to establish the rights of the Wampanoag Tribe to the 100-acre Fall River tract. Although Perry did not claim to be directly descended from 8sâmeeqan, the legendary figure could be called to the task of establishing Perry's Indian identity and reminding senators of the lessons the sachem was to impart to non-Indians. "The historic magnanimity of Chief Massasoit of the mighty Wampanoags was recalled by his descendants," the newspaper announced, alongside the appeal to return tribal lands.[37] Perry's claim was eventually successful. Under pressure from federal officials in 1939, the state reverted 277 acres in Freetown to the Watuppa reservation in compensation for the lands taken by Fall River officials in 1907.[38]

The staging for bronze cast no. 1 was dominated by trappings and symbols of a Pilgrim-centered narrative that anticipated English colonization while placing Indigenous peoples in the past. The actors on stage largely celebrated the values of freedom and Native cooperation, although only non-Indians could speak. For many audience members in Plymouth, the unveiling confirmed what they believed to be a story of national origins, marking the spot where two peoples met in peace and the English built a modern nation. Yet we see other interpretations were also possible: the artist hoped the memorial might convey the distinct greatness and unique qualities of an Indigenous political leader; the former IORM president and lay historian John Converse hoped to acknowledge the persistent place of the Massasoit's descendants in the region; and Charlotte Mitchell and the "Fall River Indians" could point to the statue to confirm Indigenous identities and make moral claims to rights owed to New England Natives for their role in building the nation. The meaning of the statue and the story conveyed at the unveiling was neither fully national nor regional. Likewise, it never presented a convincing case for Indigenous disappearance, nor publicly affirmed Indigenous persistence.

SALT LAKE CITY DEDICATION, 31 JULY 1922

As bronze *Massasoit* statue no. 1 was unveiled at what the Improved Order of Red Men hoped would be the center of Plymouth, the plaster model became a placeholder on another stage 2,400 miles away. Even as Dallin loaded his wife and two of their sons into the family car for the cross-country drive from Boston to Salt Lake City in the summer of 1922, he wished he were speaking at the unveiling of a different statue.[39] Dallin had long hoped to sculpt a memorial specifically for the Utah State Capitol, where stories of the state's development and civic values could be communicated to residents and visitors alike. Dallin's home state completed a major renovation and rebuilding project for the capitol building in 1916, and the Capitol Commission and other political and cultural elites were looking for art to adorn the marble interior. But what was the narrative of Utah history to be presented within the government building? For a state with a history of Native communities, French fur trading, Mormon settlement, and extractive industry, the answer to this question was both complex and contested. But Dallin's answer seemed clear: relations with Indigenous people in the state had made all of the other developments possible. The most fitting sculpture for the capitol must include a memorial to a notable Native person in Utah in order to tell this story. Unfortunately, the artist's home state lacked the funding or the will (or both).

Just as Dallin was beginning to sculpt *Massasoit* in 1913, he was putting his final touches on a small clay model of Chief Washakie, a memorial to a Shoshone leader who passed away in 1900 (fig. 16). *Chief Washakie* had not been commissioned; it was the artist's idea to honor a leader whom he strongly associated with Utah history. Washakie was born around 1800 to Salish and Shoshone parents and experienced many of the major changes wrought by white settlement in the region over the nineteenth century (fig. 17). As a young man, Washakie was deeply involved in the fur trade in present-day southwestern Wyoming. He established close ties with non-Indian traders while also participating in battles against Blackfoot and Crow enemies. By the 1840s, just as thousands of migrants began traveling through the Great Basin on the Ore-

FIGURE 16. *Chief Washakie*, 1914. *Courtesy of Springville Museum of Art.*

gon Trail, Washakie emerged as a leader among the Eastern Shoshone. In 1847 members of the Church of Jesus Christ of Latter-day Saints entered Shoshone territory and settled near the Great Salt Lake. Washakie, like most other Native leaders, was friendly to these newcomers and formed a relationship with Brigham Young. But by the 1850s tensions between the colonists (settlers and miners) and Shoshone people rose as they competed for precious resources, and regular skirmishes broke out in the territory. On 29 January 1863, nearly 300 California volunteers departed Camp Douglas and attacked a group of 450 Shoshone people encamped on Bear River, about 140 miles north of Salt Lake City near present-day Preston, Idaho. The armed volunteers murdered about 350 men, women, and children in one of the largest Indian massacres in

FIGURE 17. Chief Washakie portrait.
Used by permission, Utah State Historical Society.

U.S. history.[40] Many of the survivors of the Bear River Massacre escaped to Washakie's camp in Wind River. Devastated by the massacre and under pressure from federal authorities to keep peace between overland migrants and Shoshone people, Washakie entered into a treaty at Fort Bridger with several other Indigenous leaders in 1863. Yet the settlers continued to arrive and challenge Shoshone people's access to land and crucial resources. In response, Washakie and the Indian agent requested that the Wind River valley be reserved for Shoshones, and in 1868 he signed a second treaty at Fort Bridger securing those lands. Although Washakie did not convert to Mormonism, many members of his band joined the Church of Jesus Christ of Latter-day Saints. Together with non-Indian Mormon families, Shoshone families took homesteads in northern Utah and built agricultural communities in the 1880s — one of which bears Washakie's name (and happens to be eight miles from the town of Plymouth, Utah, which was founded at about the same time and named for Plymouth Rock). A few years before Washakie's death, the federal government enacted the General Allotment Act that would strip the Wind River reservation of thousands of acres for the benefit of white settlers.[41] Washakie played a significant role in securing a Shoshone homeland and fostering a peaceful relationship between his band and newcomers in the face of unprecedented immigration and violence.

In recognition of Washakie's prominent role in Utah's past, Dallin labored on his own time to craft a fitting memorial to the leader. In 1914 Dallin sent Utah governor William Spry photographs of the model with a plea to commission a large statue for the front of the capitol grounds. "Washakie was a man of peace" and the Shoshone "were always friendly to the whiteman," Dallin explained, and these qualities were captured in the statue's gestures.[42] The equestrian figure dons an elaborate feather headdress and cradles a buckskin-covered scroll—perhaps representing the 1863 peace treaty. He lifts his right arm to offer the unmistakable sign of peace: his pointer and middle finger form a *v* held high above his head.

Dallin had good reason to believe Governor Spry might engage the sculptor in a large public art project. As the celebrated local kid who achieved international fame, Dallin's sculptures dotted the Salt Lake Valley. Although not a member of the Church of Jesus Christ of Latter-day Saints himself (Dallin's parents separated from the church when he was a child), LDS leaders had previously commissioned Dallin to sculpt the Angel Moroni atop the Salt Lake Temple (1892) and the Brigham Young Monument (1893). Considering how important and supportive church members in Salt Lake City had been in developing Dallin's early career, the sculptor logically assumed future joint projects would be a possibility. The Utah Capitol Building Commission apparently approved the Washakie monument and used Dallin's small model in a modest fund-raising effort. The model was placed atop a collection box in the capitol where visitors could drop contributions. Just like the IORM fund-raising campaign for *Massasoit* that flagged during the Great War, public donations for a Washakie memorial in the 1910s ultimately came to naught.[43]

If not for the fact that the cash-strapped Capitol Commission could not afford the statue, this may have been fertile ground for Dallin's vision. But it is also true that Utah's political and cultural elite more fervently pursued other options for decorating the capitol and staging the state's history. In 1915, accomplished local artists and brothers Avard and J. Leo Fairbanks proposed a "sculptured frieze" for the capitol dome that included depictions of "the primitive Indian life in Utah, or Desolation of the Desert," and "Friendly Relations With the Indians." Notably, the image of peaceful exchange with Native people was to be followed by the "bounteous harvest" in the pictorial narrative. The proposed sculptural depiction of the "miracle of this transformation of the desert into a great state" included Native people to justify colonial settlement as both necessary and welcomed in order to make the land productive.[44]

The narrative of Utah settlement proposed by the Fairbanks brothers bears a striking resemblance to the contours of the Pilgrim story, despite the thousands of miles and hundreds of years between them. This story of American progress was not unique to Plymouth and Salt Lake City, although the regions of New England and the West both experienced a flurry of memorialization activity at this time. Artwork depicting Indian-settler relations in the West (both friendly and confrontational) reached the height of popularity in the 1920s, just as the Tercentenary Commission printed guidebooks leading Plymouth's visitors to the site of the first Thanksgiving. Certainly, the regional movements relied upon the same tropes of peaceful settlement and friendly Native assistance for colonial success in their presentation of the past.[45]

In any case, the Fairbanks brothers advanced to the final stages of approval, but ultimately did not receive the commission. The capitol building renovations went over budget, and the commission had to rely on donations to adorn the interior. A few elites who were familiar with Dallin's local works and international reputation—including former governor Spry—hoped the famous native son might be willing to help. Thus, the Salt Lake Commercial Club, composed of the city's prominent businessmen (and Spry), convinced Dallin to donate the plaster model of *Massasoit* to the state in early 1922.[46] It was not *Chief Washakie*, with all of the attendant connections to the history of relations between settlers and Shoshone people, but it was a free statue by a Utah artist. The Commercial Club likely hoped that featuring one of Dallin's statues would increase visitor interest and build the city's reputation as a refined cultural center.

Although Utah's Indigenous history is rich and complex, the staging for the *Massasoit* plaster was rather simple. Surrounded by unadorned rotunda walls, the plaster pieces of *Massasoit* were unpacked from their shipping crates and reassembled atop a hollow wood base situated in the center of the grand capitol rotunda.[47] The formal dedication ceremony on 31 July 1922 was reportedly "impressive" but brief: Dallin gave a short speech and Governor Charles R. Mabey accepted the statue on behalf of the state. If numerous members of the public attended the ceremony besides writers from the women's Relief Society (an auxiliary of the Church of Jesus Christ of Latter-day Saints) and the *Deseret News*, their large presence was not recorded. *Massasoit*, however, was surely outnumbered by references to Dallin's other sculptures. A poor-quality plaster replica of Dallin's equestrian figure *Signal of Peace* had been installed at the center of the capitol rotunda for years, although Dallin had repeatedly asked the state to remove it (fig. 18). In fact, as we noted in chapter 1, Dallin was so embarrassed by the sight of the inferior cast that he had tried to destroy it with his cane a few years earlier.[48] Apparently oblivious to the insult to the artist, state officials simply moved *Signal of Peace* to the rear of the rotunda during the dedication ceremony for *Massasoit*. This statuary placement was intended to provide visitors with a side view of the mounted Plains Indian figure when they looked at *Massasoit* straight on—an odd cultural and directional orientation for visitors who may not have known where to look and how to make sense of what they saw (fig. 19).[49]

Although *Signal of Peace* visually competed with *Massasoit* in the rotunda, it was the absence of *Chief Washakie* that preoccupied Dallin. The artist admitted to feeling "mixed emotions" about placing *Massasoit*, rather than *Chief Washakie*, in the place of honor in the Utah capitol. In Dallin's eyes, the distinct landscape of the intermountain West formed the bedrock of his and other Utahans' identity and historical consciousness. "These mountains are linked with the story of the Indian," Dallin explained at the unveiling ceremony, and the figure of Washakie would more appropriately memorialize this unique place story.[50] What stories could *Massasoit* tell so far from its subject's southeastern New England context?

Dallin chose to use the ceremonial occasion to honor Washakie and continue to advocate for a commission by pointing out the parallels, in his mind, between the two Native leaders. Washakie, Dallin said, "bears the same re-

FIGURE 18. *Signal of Peace* in the Utah capitol rotunda.
Used by permission, Utah State Historical Society.

lation to the pioneers of the Great Salt Lake valley as does Massasoit to the
original Pilgrim Fathers." 8sâmeeqan "saved the Plymouth Colony" just as
Washakie "preserved the life of the early settlements in Utah." Dallin soberly
concluded the ceremony with his hope "to see the day when a statue of Washakie should overlook the valley, as the bronze original . . . now overlooks the
Plymouth Rock."[51] Dallin left out a few other parallels to be drawn from a comparison between 8sâmeeqan and Washakie, including the changes and stresses

FIGURE 19. *Massasoit* in the Utah capitol rotunda, ca. 1916–22.
Used by permission, Utah State Historical Society.

European settler-colonists brought to Wampanoag and Shoshone homelands and the enormous scale of violence that followed the respective peace treaties (not to mention that each watched settlers erect a town called Plymouth in his lands). Of course, one crucial disjuncture between the two Native leaders comes down to a major power imbalance with settlers; the organized (and armed) power of the nineteenth-century U.S. state pushed Washakie into a peace accord in a way the Puritan colony was unable to muster when meeting with the Massasoit. But such comparisons would present a critical (and embarrassing) narrative of Utah history in the capitol, and Dallin was not interested in challenging his beloved state's celebratory self-image.

The governor responded to Dallin's speech with the somewhat awkward appeal to those in attendance to organize a fund-raising effort for a memorial to replace the statue Dallin had traveled across the country to unveil. A writer for the *Relief Society Magazine* claimed the unveiling itself to be so moving ("there was not a dry eye, when the Stars and Stripes fell away") that the crowd was resolute in their determination to do just that. She reasoned that if the Pilgrims had laid the foundation for a powerful nation under the protection of the Massasoit, in honoring Washakie as "the Pioneer peace patron . . . might not we, thereby, reap a realization of a greater, grander destiny?"[52] Despite the proposal to hitch Utah's future grandeur to a bronze statue of Washakie, no fund-raising campaign was launched, and Dallin's small model was not cast in heroic size in his lifetime.[53] Perhaps the setting of Salt Lake City was simply not the fertile memorial landscape of Plymouth, or the commemorative impulse in Utah was not as strong without a well-publicized anniversary like the Plymouth, Massachusetts tercentenary.

In any case, even if Utah was not ready to wrestle with one aspect of its Indigenous history, it was prepared to celebrate one of its classically trained artists. The unveiling ceremony at the capitol was modest in comparison to the reception for Dallin held a few days later in Salt Lake City. After an elaborate dinner hosted by the governor, Dallin was feted with a public reception at Liberty Park, complete with a glee club and band performance, folk music, and speeches from the mayor and governor. Cyrus Dallin answered the "tumult of applause" with a few words expressing his love for his home state.[54] If the unveiling ceremony in Plymouth had been focused on *Massasoit*, the events in Salt Lake City were focused on the miner's son who made a name for himself in the art world and brought pride to Utah.

Over time, the staging around *Massasoit* evolved and offered new interpretive possibilities for the plaster model. In 1934 the Public Works of Art Project funded the commission for a narrative mural to surround *Massasoit* in the rotunda. The four pendentives and eight cyclorama paintings offer visitors images of early non-Indian explorers and scenes of nineteenth-century Utah history (fig. 20). Two of the cyclorama paintings include depictions of Native people. The first, titled *Peace with the Indians — September 1852*, features three men in feather headdresses standing before tepees and other Native men wrapped in blankets. The lead figure gestures toward the ground and offers a peace pipe to suit-clad Brigham Young, who stands in front of two trappers and reaches gently for the offering. Notably, this event was not the 1863 treaty with Washakie that ensured a peaceful right-of-way for immigrants. The "peace with the Indians" may be a reference to Brigham Young's own report of a meeting with Ute and Shoshone tribes, in which the tribes requested Mormons settle on their lands. The "meeting" could be more fairly described as a conversion event than a peace treaty (which was never reviewed by Congress and could not be confirmed by witnesses outside of the church), and it was quickly followed by protests from Indian agents, a string of wars, and the Bear River

FIGURE 20. *Peace with the Indians—September 1852*, 1933–34.
Cyclorama in the Utah capitol rotunda. *Photograph by Lisa Blee.*

Massacre. The mural image was clearly intended to justify and honor Brigham Young's efforts to expand church settlements more than to mark a historic moment of diplomacy. Another mural in the cyclorama depicts three buckskin-clad men hiding behind trees and shrubs as a Pony Express rider arrives at a log cabin.[55] The only roles afforded Indigenous people in this narrative of state history were as potential converts or potential threats to progress. Dallin's plaster original of *Massasoit* was literally encircled by a story of peaceful colonization that closely resembled that told of the Pilgrims' in Plymouth.

PLYMOUTH DEDICATION, 13 SEPTEMBER 1922

Within weeks of his speech at the unveiling in Salt Lake City, Dallin made the long drive back to the East Coast to appear in the dedication ceremony for the bronze cast in Plymouth. A year after the unveiling on Cole's Hill, the Massasoit Memorial Association planned what it called the "real dedication" of the memorial.[56] The crowd at the 1921 unveiling had been exponentially larger, likely owing to tourist spillover from the tercentenary events. Apparently, Charlotte Mitchell was not invited for a return appearance in 1922, and no Native people participated in the ceremony. If any of 8sâmeeqan's ancestors attended the dedication, the newspapers failed to mention them. This day and this ceremony were to focus on the artist and the Improved Order of Red Men.

The ceremonies began when the membership of the IORM's national council boarded a morning train from Boston to Plymouth. They were met at the Plymouth train station by a band and delegation from the IORM's local councils and women's auxiliary. The band led the march of 600 members down the historic Leyden Street to the *Massasoit* memorial, where Cyrus Dallin was given the opportunity to address the crowd.[57] Dallin praised the Massasoit Memorial Association for its indefatigable fund-raising efforts, and the general membership of the IORM for "its generosity and public spirit" in making the statue possible. For the most part, Dallin's speech protested disparaging views of Native peoples and did not engage in the local and historical context of the Massasoit's life. "The Indian of today is essentially a peace-loving, hospitable man, courageous and loyal to the core. . . . So was his ancestor in primal days." On the statue itself, Dallin explained that he tried to convey his love for the noble character of Native peoples by sculpting "as a type" an "Indian of the age and appearance of Massasoit . . . and have clothed him as they say Massasoit was clothed."[58]

According to the Massasoit Memorial Association, the proposed wording of the plaque was likewise intended to serve as the organization's "visual protest" against the popular negative "conception of the character of the aboriginal North American Indian."[59] On the matter of the Massasoit's character, John Converse distilled the principled loyalty to the treaty as a mark of good faith. "He should be known as Massasoit 'The Faithful,'" Converse concluded in 1915. "Good faith is the corner-stone of his character."[60] The tablet first proposed in 1921[61] reads, "MASSASOIT, GREAT SACHEM OF THE WAMPANOAGS, FRIEND AND PRESERVER OF THE PILGRIMS, 1621. A GRATEFUL TRIBUTE BY THE IMPROVED ORDER OF RED MEN."

The final version of the tablet, attached to the boulder pedestal, adopted slightly altered wording that emphasized the tercentenary context and revised the description of the Massasoit: "MASSASOIT, GREAT SACHEM OF THE WAMPANOAGS, PROTECTOR AND PRESERVER OF THE PILGRIMS, 1621. ERECTED BY THE IMPROVED ORDER OF RED MEN AS A GRATEFUL TRIBUTE, 1921."

Notably, the term "protector" replaced "friend" in what is arguably a more accurate representation of the military alliance forged between the English colonists and the Massasoit in 1621. The word "friend" may have mirrored the diplomatic rhetoric the Massasoit would have used (and was in fact written in the 1621 treaty), but the word would convey a kind of camaraderie to lay viewers that Converse specifically refuted. Dallin quoted the plaque during the dedication ceremony and declared the inscription "absolutely true."[62]

Although the sculptor focused on his view of Native character as generous and way of life as beautifully simple, others at the ceremony returned repeatedly to the trope of friendship and brotherhood. The newspaper report paraphrased Dallin's main point to "give to the white man a small idea of what the red man really is—a brother."[63] Dallin's speech was followed by the song "Massasoit, There He Stands," written by an IORM member for the occasion. The lyrics describe the sachem as a "symbol of the true Red Man," and the memorial as "a beacon of light to friendship's band."[64] The final speech by the IORM's national leader, Great Incohonee Frederick O. Downes, "touched on the friendship of Massasoit" and extolled the fitting placement of the memorial in Plymouth "on the site of this mutual friendship." In an interpretive move that took him far afield from Converse's attempt to educate the membership, Downes concluded, "Massasoit loved the Pilgrims and they reciprocated the sentiment. . . . We dedicate this to the untutored child of the forest."[65]

SALT LAKE CITY REINSTALLATION, 1959

For thirty-five years following the conclusion of the small ceremony in the Utah capitol rotunda, *Massasoit* stood above a plaque that read "Massasoit: Great Sachem of the Wampanoags, Protector and Preserver of the Pilgrims." The terse interpretation, borrowed directly from the Plymouth installation, may not have meant much to viewers at the capitol. "Sachem" and "Wampanoag" were generally unfamiliar terms to western audiences; one journalist had to offer readers the correct pronunciation for "Massasoit" ("mass-a-soy-it").[66] Few visitors knew why a memorial to the Pokanoket leader was on display—according to one news story the most memorable feature was the statue's near nakedness—but the rotunda setting, journalists, and souvenirs encouraged them to make connections to Utah and the artist.[67] Visitors to the rotunda read the statue in its visual surroundings, specifically in the context of murals in which "friendly" Native men facilitated non-Indian settlement. One journalist suggested that the statue removed from its historical context would actually encourage Utahans to refine their sensibilities: "Let us get acquainted with our Massasoit. Visit him often! He will teach us, will purify our ideals of art, will enrich our impulses, and help us to understand our sculptor, Dallin."[68]

Indeed, the specific details of the Massasoit's story did not matter as much as how the statue might fit into a narrative of Utah's progress. Postcards from the capitol building gift shop in the 1920s included an image of *Massasoit* but incorrectly identified it as a replica of an original in the Boston Library (likely confusing it with *Appeal to the Great Spirit*). The postcards also pointed out another capitol mural painting depicting "the trek of the Pioneers across the Great American Desert."[69] The caption on another postcard featuring the statue and capitol building stretched time and space to make the connection more overt: "Chief Massasoit was the Indian who befriended the Mormon Pioneers in the settling of Salt Lake Valley." The sender, who evidently knew the Massasoit's history and noticed the error, quipped to his friend: "Massasoit must have been old."[70]

Despite the public confusion, the installation in the capitol rotunda was so frequently visited that *Massasoit* grew to hold a place in the civic life of Salt Lake City citizens. Far removed from the context of Plymouth and its attendant narratives, the statue served a new function as a prop attached to residents' social practices and personal memories. In addition to regular school field trips to the government building, local schools and the University of Utah held dances and the prom in the grand rotunda. Consecutive generations of Utahans encountered the capitol rotunda decorated according to an imaginative theme, and *Massasoit* stood amid a fantastically reimagined stage. Promgoers incorporated the statue into their festivities as a decorative centerpiece; in 1951 *Massasoit* was draped with robes and flanked by two winged horses to play the role of Zeus for the University of Utah's ancient Greece prom theme.[71] But years of merriment took a toll on the fragile plaster *Massasoit*. In 1953, as university students removed flowers adorning the statue for the "Orchids in the Moonlight" themed prom, the statue's arm fell off and shattered on the marble floor. According to the student who reported the incident, no one was touching the arm at the time and it was a mystery how it happened.[72] Avard Fairbanks, by then dean of the College of Fine Arts at the University of Utah, made repairs to *Massasoit* although the plaster would be permanently discolored at the break. Fairbanks reassured the distraught students that they were likely not at fault; the left arm had apparently not been firmly affixed when it was reconstructed following shipment to Utah in 1922. Thus, the festivities could continue. Two years later *Massasoit* was once again adorned to fit a "Paris under the Stars" prom theme.[73]

Although Utahans incorporated the plaster model in the rotunda into their social and personal memories, political elites grew troubled by the presence of the Massachusetts Indian, but not because it was intended to serve as a placeholder for *Chief Washakie*. Following Dallin's death in 1944, the impulse to replace the statue reemerged in the capitol, but *Washakie* was no longer the main contender. Political and cultural elites, along with a few vocal residents, believed "a Foreign Indian" was taking up a place of honor that rightly belonged to memorials to Utah settlers.[74] One writer masquerading as Paiute wrote to the local newspaper in 1948 to express faux indignation that a statue of a sachem who "never came within 2000 miles of Utah" was in the rotunda. The writer warned that "if that plastered foreigner is not soon replaced with local talent" he would "picket that wickiup on Capitol hill."[75] The letter prompted an outraged phone call from an archivist at the state historical society informing the public that the statue was intended to honor Dallin. "The identity of the Indian," she stated, "is immaterial, incompetent, and irrelevant."[76] Western writer Frank Robertson suggested putting an end to the controversy by simply changing the inscription on the plaque from "Massasoit" to "Washakie" or "Sowiette," a Ute chief, because "nobody knows what any of the three looked like anyway."[77]

But the memorial was not irrelevant or interchangeable to those who wished to project a specific interpretation of Utah history in the capitol building—one emphasizing settler fortitude, church foresight, and industrial strength rather than Indigenous people or art. Although locals had grown fond of the statue, politicians and cultural elites led the charge to replace *Massasoit* with a different monument. The president of the Brigham Young Family Association proposed a statue of Brigham Young; the president of the Utah Pioneer Memorial Foundation hoped for a memorial to the founder of copper mining operations. The secretary of state, Lamont F. Toronto, navigated through Utah's distinct political schisms by advocating for a grouping of figures that might include LDS leaders, trappers and settlers, and Catholic priests—"people who have an important place in Utah's history."[78] Although there was no consensus on which memorial should hold the place of honor in the capitol, political elites agreed that the plaster *Massasoit* had to go.

The public seemed to like the statue, so Secretary of State Toronto decided not to sell it outright. But the state legislature failed to set aside appropriations for the preservation of the statue beyond emergency repairs, and the plaster model was too fragile to endure decades of public display. The standoff with *Massasoit* finally ended in 1956, when Nicholas G. Morgan Sr., president of the Utah Pioneer Memorial Foundation, agreed to pay $6,000 for the statue to be cast in bronze so it could be moved outdoors—a "more natural habitat" for the "Indian brave," according to one journalist.[79] Similar to the decision to place *Massasoit* upon a boulder in Plymouth, Utahans drew upon associations between an Indian figure and nature in order to banish the statue from the halls of political power. The day after the Fourth of July in 1957, the statue was disassembled (with some minor damage to the pouch resting at the figure's side) for shipment to a New York foundry for casting. Scores of visitors and a smaller midholiday assemblage of staff members gathered to watch the body

FIGURE 21.
Massasoit being disassembled
in the Utah capitol rotunda.
*Used by permission, Utah
State Historical Society.*

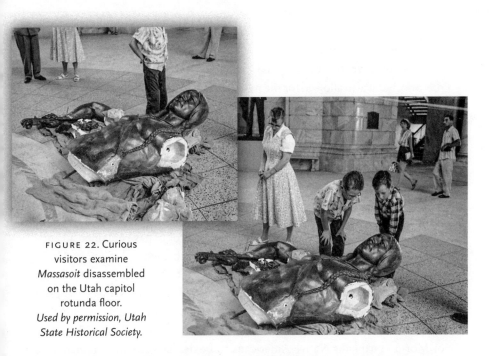

FIGURE 22. Curious
visitors examine
Massasoit disassembled
on the Utah capitol
rotunda floor.
*Used by permission, Utah
State Historical Society.*

parts separated and lowered to the ground with block and tackle (figs. 21 and 22). *Massasoit*'s departure provided an opening in the rotunda for Morgan's preferred statue: Utah Copper Company founder Daniel C. Jackling on an Italian marble base.[80]

Public outcry erupted in the newspapers after *Massasoit*'s removal; the "Thunda in the Rotunda," as a *Deseret News* columnist dubbed the controversy, gave Salt Lake citizens a forum to discuss the installation in the rotunda. Some writers were concerned about what removing the figure of an Indian from the center of the historical stage would say about the state. One citizen wondered, in reference to the Jackling statue, "Could it be that Utah places more value on wealth than it does on the historical redman who first occupied Utah?" Some citizens pointed out that Jackling made a personal fortune on the copper industry, but never lived in Utah; his statue would be akin to allowing "industrialists to rule our state." Morgan responded with his own letter to the editor stating that the criticism of Jackling hurt his feelings.[81] But even those who wished to defend *Massasoit*'s place in the rotunda were not above employing insulting stereotypes and writing letters in "Indian jargon" to make their case. And one local woman, Mrs. Patterson, applauded the removal, wondering what Indians had done to warrant a memorial when, in her estimation, they resisted schooling and caused the suffering and death of Utah settlers.[82] The public discussion in the column rarely touched on the Massasoit specifically, revealing deeper questions about the relationship between Indigenous people and narratives of Utah's past.

The controversy over the statue created space for racist views and insulting rhetoric, but it also allowed for the published thoughts and reactions of at least one Indigenous reader. A letter writer identified only as "an Indian" appealed for a return of *Massasoit* to the rotunda "as a reminder that we were once a great people, possessed of noble leaders." Furthermore, the writer took issue with the dismissive tone of Mrs. Patterson's letter. "That lady's letter really irked me," the author announced. "What have the Indians ever done indeed! First let it be remembered that we gave or surrendered this great land—our land—to those who now possess it.... We are looked down upon and shunned and have difficulty getting employment, even though many of us have obtained an education. But please tell this lady that we are not ashamed—that we are God's chosen people, and that one day we will come into our own. Meanwhile, let Massasoit be returned to his place in the Capitol."[83] The phrase "God's chosen people" was a reference to LDS church leaders' and missionaries' position that Indians had divine heritage, in common with Latter-day Saints. The Book of Mormon explains Native Americans to be descendants from Laman and Lemuel, two rebellious brothers of a family of Israelites. The Lamanites arrived in the Americas by boat in 600 BC and bear the mark of dark skin for rejecting the teachings of the gospel after Christ's visit. But according to the Book of Mormon, Lamanites "shall blossom as the rose before the Lord's coming" and could be redeemed from their "fallen" state through conversion.[84] The letter writer invoked redemptive prophesy to appeal to Latter-day Saints for support. After all, if the elders preached a shared heritage, believers should come to the defense of Native people and the statue. The letter writer, likely a convert, possibly also offered a challenge to the church's historically ambiguous positioning vis-à-vis Native people. In the nineteenth century, church leadership countered anti-Mormon charges of colluding with Indians by describing them as savages to outsiders. According to historian W. Paul Reeve, this strategy served to "position themselves as white people who were as fearful of Indians as any other Americans."[85] Based on the mixed history of relations between Latter-day Saints and Native people, the letter writer may have also asserted a principled challenge to the anti-Indian rhetoric in the newspapers and removal of the statue, which represented the continuing urge to distance Latter-day Saints from Indians. Indeed, the narrative of friendship and co-operation that enveloped the Plymouth *Massasoit* statue reemerged, but this Native writer recast the bond as emerging from within the LDS faith rather than the peace treaty and Thanksgiving story.

This was not only a fight about Utahan identity and LDS doctrine; the letter writer also used the statue to draw attention to the present-day realities facing Indigenous peoples in Utah. The letter writer may have been one of thousands of reservation Indians who moved to Salt Lake City to find jobs in the late 1940s and 1950s. In 1948 the Bureau of Indian Affairs opened a resettlement office in Salt Lake City to serve Navajo (Diné) and Hopi people, and later converted the office into a job training and assistance center open to all nations. Many Diné moved to the city to take advantage of the program, but as the letter writer pointed out, they faced employment discrimination, among other indignities. In fact, the Salt Lake City Field Relocation Office closed in 1954 because of the lack of employment opportunities. The resettled urban Indian population responded to these hardships by organizing their own support systems, which strengthened pan-Indian identity and set the stage for collective calls to address issues of land sovereignty—a topic to which the letter writer also refers.[86] The Massasoit, who was memorialized for his commitment to a treaty and, in statuary form, also came to Salt Lake City from his "homeland," could serve as a symbol for rising pan-Indian consciousness among local urban Indians. Discussion over the memorial's setting could potentially reveal contemporary Indigenous political concerns and foster non-Indian allies. This protest against bigotry and historical amnesia reached a wide public audience thanks to the controversy the memorial engendered.

After a flood of letters calling for *Massasoit*'s return, Toronto decided on a compromise in which the rotunda would remain empty of statuary and a bronze *Massasoit* would go to a prominent site on the south lawn of the building.[87] After nearly a year in storage as the legislative council worked out the funding for the installation, the newly cast bronze *Massasoit* (no. 2) was hoisted atop a granite boulder—the preferred display method for the Indian figure—in a circular concrete base flanked by planter boxes, walkways, and benches in early January 1959. The memorial faced south toward the valley and downtown Salt Lake City, and it was the first sight for motorists driving up State Street to the capitol (fig. 23). As promised, Nicholas Morgan Sr. paid for a new interpretive plaque to accompany the bronze cast. The new plaque provided a lengthy history for and explanation of the memorial in Utah, and recognized those who advocated for the statue's removal from the rotunda.[88]

STATUE OF MASSASOIT
HISTORIC INDIAN CHIEF OF MASSACHUSETTS
FRIEND OF THE PILGRIM FATHERS
SCULPTURED BY CYRUS E. DALLIN FAMOUS UTAH SCULPTOR

FIGURE 23. *Massasoit* in front of the Utah capitol.
Used by permission, Utah State Historical Society.

PLASTER CAST PRESENTED TO THE STATE OF UTAH

BY MR. DALLIN

AND ACCEPTED BY THE STATE OF UTAH

ON THE 20TH DAY OF MARCH, 1922

· CAST INTO BRONZE AND PRESENTED TO

THE STATE OF UTAH

IN THE YEAR OF 1959

BY

THE NICHOLS G. MORGAN, SR. FOUNDATION

UNDER THE DIRECTION OF THE

HONORABLE LAMONT F. TORONTO SECRETARY OF STATE UTAH

No public ceremony accompanied the January announcement of *Massasoit*'s new setting. A few grumbles about the statue continued, with the editor of the *Salt Lake Tribune* recommending the statue move to a public park to make room for a memorial to a miner or Pony Express rider.[89]

However dissatisfied some Utahans remained with the Pokanoket sachem's proximity to the center of state power, other residents continued to fold the statue into their commemorative and social practices. In this way, public discourse over the representation and continuing presence of the region's Indigenous people persisted. Six years after the bronze cast was installed on the south lawn, a local chapter of the Boy Scouts of America held its annual "camporee" behind the statue. The group pitched tepees, donned "head dress and other Indian equipment," and held competitions of "their primitive ability." Just like forty years earlier when IORM members donned regalia and took the stage for the unveiling in Plymouth, the staging at the capitol grounds drew American men to play Indian at the statue's base. In the midst of this Boy Scout performance, Diné girls from the Intermountain Indian School in Brigham City arrived to tour the capitol. These boarding school visitors reportedly showed "delight" in the Boy Scout camp and "swooped down on the village" to investigate.[90] Although filled with tongue-in-cheek phrases alluding to Indian outbreak and predation (and not unlike the image of the Indian men lurking behind shrubbery to watch and perhaps attack the Pony Express riders in the capitol rotunda mural), the newspaper was silent on the girls' thoughts on the memorial and the campers' display of Indianness. No doubt some watched silently while others offered corrections or voiced disapproval, pride, or amusement. And regardless of the pageantry on the south lawn, the girls had the opportunity to see a huge bronze memorial to a Native leader on their field trip to the capitol. Did it really matter that the Massasoit was not Diné and had never been to Utah? For these girls, too, were far from their homes and perhaps knew a little of what it was like to find a path through the challenges of settler colonialism.

As chronicled in chapter 1, the plaster model removed from the rotunda was sent into storage at Brigham Young University, where it was later disassembled once again and used to cast at least four bronze statues in 1977. The plaster was then sent to the Springville Museum of Art on long-term loan, where it remains on display with several of Dallin's other sculptures and busts. Although there was no unveiling ceremony for the plaster *Massasoit*, it is currently dramatically staged as featured artwork in the center of a semicircular exedra with northern windows framing the Wasatch Range. The backlighting from the windows gives the impression of a towering figure dominating the cozy space, but the lighting also makes it challenging for viewers to see the statue's many imperfections. The plaster is rough where the broken arm and bag needed repair; the lines for disassembly are more pronounced after so many journeys across the country for casting; an errant bird trapped inside the museum left a mess on this, the highest perch in the building. In the private space of the museum, the plaster model is unambiguously staged as a testament to Cyrus Dallin and Utah's artistic traditions. Yet, in the details of the imperfect plaster, viewers may see the evidence of other public lives and stories in other places. It is to the bronze casts created from this model—those that traveled far from Dallin's studio long after the artist's death—that we now turn.

KANSAS CITY DEDICATION, 6 MAY 1979

At exactly the same time *Massasoit* was installed atop Cole's Hill in Plymouth, the real estate company of Jesse Clyde Nichols unveiled plans for Country Club Plaza, a shopping center near the future site of *Massasoit* in Kansas City, Missouri. J. C. Nichols Company famously created the Plaza as the first planned shopping center in the country. The company established the center far from public transportation nodes but hoped to attract shoppers by automobile from quickly expanding suburban communities—particularly the neighborhoods that the J. C. Nichols Company also planned and built.[91] Nichols and his architects wanted to construct buildings in the Plaza with diverse commercial functions but connected with a shared motif; the company decided on Spanish-Mediterranean designs. The style was popularized in the 1915 Panama-California Exposition in San Diego, and designers considered Spanish motifs to be "ideal for generating a festive, slightly exotic atmosphere that could enhance merchandising efforts."[92] Nichols later told an interviewer that his goal

FIGURE 24. Country Club Plaza, Kansas City, Missouri. *Wikimedia Commons.*

was to create "the feeling of an old market place of picturesque Spain [in] Kansas City," complete with a replica of Seville's famed Giralda that became a landmark in Kansas City (fig. 24).[93] Perhaps because of this design choice, Kansas City later gifted its sister city of Seville a small replica of *The Scout* for initial display at the 1992 World's Fair.[94] In addition to providing effective branding for the city, the Country Club Plaza essentially created a new downtown around which future developments centered. Miller Nichols took over the company from his father in 1950 and vaulted the commercial landmark to new heights by adding hotels, apartments, and artwork to the Plaza landscape. By the time he acquired *Massasoit* cast no. 3, the Plaza indisputably dominated the metropolitan area.[95] As the city's most influential businessman, Miller Nichols likely recognized how *Massasoit* could enhance this neighborhood-investment in the form of public art.[96]

Nichols acquired a bronze cast of *Massasoit* (no. 3) in 1977 and, immediately after making plans for its reappraisal and donation, began to plan for its public display in Kansas City. The developer understood that presentation is everything. In an exchange with the seller, Forrest Fenn, Nichols struck on the not-so-novel idea of installing *Massasoit* atop a boulder, although he did not seem to be aware of the ubiquity of boulder bases for this statue. As he planned for the display, he only referenced his locally cultivated aesthetic sensibilities. "As you can see from the attached postcard of the Wagon Master [a public fountain in Kansas City]," Nichols wrote to Fenn, "I carried out this same philosophy of the sculpture standing on a rock just like a live horse would."[97] The comment equating the Massasoit with a horse notwithstanding, Nichols's installation mirrored those in Plymouth and Salt Lake City that also fixed *Massasoit* to a boulder pedestal. And just as the Plymouth press had provided readers with details of the boulder's journey to Cole's Hill in 1922, the Kansas City installation fixed a plaque to the boulder-pedestal with the raised-letter caption: THIS "SIOUX QUARTZITE" BOULDER WAS BROUGHT FROM MINNESOTA TO THE FARM OF RALPH DOOLEY AT BOSWORTH, MISSOURI, BY GLACIERS MORE THAN 500,000 YEARS AGO. The commemorative plaque informs the viewer that the boulder was "brought" by glaciers many millennia previously from Minnesota to the farm of Ralph Dooley (who presumably was not at home waiting for the delivery), thus collapsing some 500,000 years of history, human and otherwise. The boulder might be thought of as conveying primordial movement—a message that communicated to viewers the naturalness of *Massasoit*'s presence in a place removed from the Massasoit's own roots, a travel narrative of sorts. And one cannot help but think also about the parallels between this boulder and Plymouth Rock, that mythological icon of American origins that also embodied a narrative of purposeful, if predestined, movement.

Indeed, Miller Nichols specifically planned for *Massasoit* to stand in a "wilderness-like setting" with an emphasis on rocks. Much like the bronze cast standing on the Utah capitol grounds, the naturalistic surroundings appeared more fitting for a memorial to an Indian. In Kansas City, Nichols received permission from the city to re-landscape the grounds with a seven-foot stone wall, a sprinkler system for native grasses and yucca, and a limestone boulder imbedded with the plaque and "authentic Indian grinding stones."[98] Perhaps intended as a mute memorial to Indians in general, Nichols fixed the mortar and pestle to the limestone boulder with no interpretive plaque or contextual information.[99] One is tempted to conclude this installation was meant to underscore the premodernness of *Massasoit*, even re-creating for the viewer the novel experience of "happening upon" a scene of a generic Indigenous past world in the middle of the city.[100] One later city interpretation of the installation explains that the Massasoit introduced the Pilgrims to new foods and planting techniques (the resulting harvest thus set the occasion for the first Thanksgiving); the grinding stone could serve as a mnemonic device for Indigenous foodstuffs—one of many aspects of Indian livelihood generously and peacefully transferred to colonial settlers.[101] But perhaps also, given the fact that grinding corn constituted women's work, this association intended to feminize the Massasoit, to tame him by emasculating the warrior in favor of the passive Native who facilitated rather than resisted English invasion.

Although Miller Nichols considered himself well versed in boulders and statuary pedestals, he was not familiar with the historical subject of his acquisition. As Nichols worked with company employees to coordinate the unveiling ceremony, he tried to determine how to interpret the statue for the public and explain why it belonged in Missouri. Nichols or his employees gathered materials concerning 8sâmeeqan, including up-to-date research into Charlotte Mitchell and other descendants.[102] Meanwhile, Fenn contributed to the cause by suggesting some text for the plaque; Nichols decided to use "some if not all of the wording at Plymouth" to give the Kansas City installation "a historical tone."[103] At some point an error was made when copying the Plymouth plaque text, and shortly before the dedication ceremony a company employee pointed out to Fenn and Nichols that the spelling of the Wampanoag tribe's name on the Kansas City plaque was inconsistent with a published source. Fenn reassured the employee that "there were usually two or three ways to spell an old Indian tribe's name" but thought the spelling should be consistent with the published source. Even so, Nichols chose to keep the bronze plaque as it was, and printed dedication ceremony programs introduced the statue to the city as a monument to "'Massasoit' Great Sachem of The Wampanogas. Friend and Protector of the Pilgrims." If the price of correcting the plaque was more dear to Nichols than historical accuracy and respect for living Wampanoag people, we can see how the staging and messages elicited from the Kansas City installation might be equally muddled. The carelessness with which Nichols approached the subject of the memorial suggests that as a developer and businessman, public perception and satisfaction were to him the paramount considerations. Nichols did not correct the plaque until 1982 after he received a letter from a Kansas City resident pointing out the "goof."[104]

Indeed, the public unveiling and dedication ceremony emphasized the abstract principles of civic pride and improvement—which could be read as a celebration of local businesses and the customers who supported them—and once again surrounded *Massasoit* on stage with white men and boys wearing Indian regalia. Held in early May 1979 at the entrance to the Country Club Plaza at the intersection of J. C. Nichols Parkway and Bush Creek Boulevard, the ceremony was well publicized in the newspapers, thanks to Nichols's press bulletins. In order to capture public interest, Nichols announced, "We are combining the dedication of this piece with the Kansas City area Boy Scout

Jamboree. . . . It is my hope that this figure will become a symbol of Kansas City's Boy Scouts." Nichols received accolades for producing a ceremony for a statue that would "be a reminder of the close relationship between Boy Scouts lore and the culture of American Indians."[105] Nichols may have reasoned that the memorial might hit a more emotional register for viewers when associated with the local scouts; the combination offered audiences a nostalgic connection to premodern values seemingly missing from present-day urban American life. Like the Plymouth statue sculpted at the behest of members of the Improved Order of Red Men and the "camporee" pitched adjacent to the Salt Lake City cast no. 2, the Kansas City *Massasoit* stood as a material reminder of nostalgic American values forged from frontier struggle.

The short dedication ceremony was composed of the Pledge of Allegiance, introductory remarks by Miller Nichols, speeches and dance demonstrations, and Kansas City mayor Richard Berkley's acceptance of the gift. The components were unique, but just like at the other installations, the dedication ceremony drew white men to "play Indian" at *Massasoit*'s feet.[106] Boy and Eagle Scouts from different troops read prepared statements about the sculptor, the statue, and the city. One can only hope the speeches were more informed than the paper program, which provided a jumbled and vague account in which readers learned that the Massasoit's "extensive domain had existed in harmony and contentment," and the sachem received gifts and hospitality from the English when he visited their settlement to make a treaty that "lasted from 24 to 50 years." Following the speeches, the viewers were treated to a "Pipe Dance" and "Dance of Dedication" performed by the Warbonnet Indian Dancers of Greater Kansas City.[107] The Warbonnets, much like the IORM, were composed of mainly non-Indian Boy Scout members who organized under a "chief" and donned regalia. But rather than a charitable fraternal organization, this group was more of an entrepreneurial auxiliary; it performed dances at Boy Scout events and a local high school, as well as in Carnegie Hall and on a European tour in the 1970s. Staged images and postcards of the Warbonnets depict members posing in eye-catching Plains regalia featuring (you guessed it) enormous feather headdresses.[108]

Nichols's "philanthropy" in connection with the *Massasoit* statue promoted a spirit of civic pride and provided opportunities for other Kansas City businesses. In his opening remarks at the dedication, Nichols claimed that "a bronze figure or a fountain . . . enhances the lives of all of us," and the generous donation of statuary should serve as a model for the public to consider "what the individual might do to enhance the city."[109] Nichols suggested that the presence of public art, which he placed on or within close proximity to his private commercial holdings, would prompt viewers to high-minded civic action even as they shopped at high-end stores or indulged in luxury services. At least one of the businesses in the Plaza attempted to capitalize on the memorial by further developing this link between civic values and consumerism, as evidenced by a department store's advertisement in the *Kansas City Star* in 1979: "Massasoit Lives in Kansas City. If this statue looks familiar, it should. This bronze figure of Chief Massasoit, friend and protector of the Pilgrims, stands on the edge of the Country Club Plaza—an excellent reminder of the first Thanksgiving. On that day in 1621, the Pilgrims joined with their honored guests, Massasoit and his tribe, to celebrate their survival, which was due largely to the generosity of their Indian friends. A New England Indian in the Midwest? He may seem out of place, but we hope that the noble spirit of friendship he symbolizes is right at home here. Woolf Brothers."[110]

This civic-minded business underscored the message of generosity and good will—as well as the characterization of the Massasoit as a "friend" and symbol of Thanksgiving—as an American value that traveled across the geographical expanse from New England to Kansas City.

But not everyone bought into the feel-good celebration of civic pride and the message of friendship. C. DeClue adamantly disputed the glossing over of the actual history of encounter between the Massasoit and the English in "What's Left Out," a letter to the editor of the *Kansas City Star* published a couple of months after the dedication. Among the "unfortunate oversights" from DeClue's reading of the *Massasoit* plaque were "the epidemics brought over by the European colonizers, which killed thousands of Indian people," as well as "the land which was stolen from Indian people" and "the rape of native culture, language, and spirituality by Puritan ethics and laws. Not mentioned are the hundreds of Indian tribes who were stripped of self-determination and all rights of sovereignty." Echoing the vocal protests of the Red Power movement, this writer admonished readers to remember the devastating consequences of resistance to colonial rule, such as King Philip's War, which included the enslavement of the Massasoit's own grandson. Mincing no words, DeClue pointed out, "As far as Massasoit's dead spirit is concerned, he would hardly be pleased to learn that his tribe, which is still very much alive, has been declared extinct." Displaying a solid command of contemporary Indian affairs, DeClue referenced the 1977 land claims case lost by the Mashpee Wampanoag, when an all-white jury declared them "non-existent." In conclusion, DeClue declared, "If Massasoit and his somewhat ludicrous posture are to symbolize anything let them symbolize a struggle that is far from being dead and buried and bronzed."[111]

Beyond this potent critique and the statue's staging in close proximity to a popular commercial setting, the memorial drew little public attention. In 1993 a resident from Massachusetts read a newspaper announcement that the statue would need to be moved and wrote to Nichols to inquire. "I had no idea the statue was even there," she explained. "And being a native of Mass, I'm curious to know what the connection is and why KC would have a statue of the chief of the Wampanoags." Nichols's reply admitted the tenuous links: "You asked what connection does Massasoit have with Kansas City? The answer is none except to symbolize the noble spirit of friendship at home here."[112] Unlike the "Thunda in the Rotunda" in Salt Lake City, when the Kansas City statue was relocated from its initial installation in 1995 to a small park a block to the east at the edge of a major traffic thoroughfare, there was no public outcry. Few beyond Miller Nichols seemed to take much notice; one woman wrote to Nichols to say that she would miss seeing the statue at its original location, but she misidentified it as *The Scout*.[113]

EVERGREEN PARK, ILLINOIS, 1977–2009

As bronze *Massasoit* cast no. 3 made its way to Kansas City for its eventual unveiling, another cast (no. 4) made the trip to Illinois. Although there is no record of a public unveiling or dedication ceremony, the commercial staging in Evergreen Park, Illinois, paralleled many aspects of its mate in the Country Club Plaza. The suburban Evergreen Plaza — reportedly one of Chicago developer Arthur Rubloff's favorite developments to visit personally — was one of the largest open-air malls in the country when it opened in 1952, and remained on the cutting edge when it became one of the nation's first enclosed shopping centers in 1966.[114] Rubloff, like Miller Nichols, went on the hunt for statues to adorn his premier shopping center and was likely primarily concerned with delighting shoppers. And when *Massasoit* cast no. 4 was moved from its initial installation in the Evergreen Plaza in suburban Chicago — a year after cast no. 3 was moved from the Country Club Plaza in Kansas City — shoppers did not protest (or take much notice).

Rubloff was, first and foremost, a businessman with a knack for spotting investments and crafting good press. In April 1977, Rubloff announced to local newspapers that Cyrus Dallin's *Massasoit* would be added to the collection of nineteen statues at Evergreen Plaza. As the *Chicago Tribune* reported, Rubloff would install this and four other recent acquisitions throughout the shopping center so his customers could enjoy the art free of charge. For suburban shoppers, the presence of *Massasoit* and other bronze statues could lift the mundane act of consumerism into the realm of a cultural experience. This staging drew on an association between Native representation and commercialization, harkening back to the generic tobacco store Indian figure that signaled where shoppers could find goods for sale. As a figure elevated through classical sculpture, *Massasoit* lent a civilized air to the semipublic space, contributing to an attractive setting for those fleeing Chicago's diverse urban center for more spacious and homogeneous suburban neighborhoods. The *Southend Reporter* speculated that in total, "the exhibit is believed to be the largest collection of masterpiece statues ever assembled for public viewing outside of an art institute or museum." And, perhaps in what Miller Nichols would read as a competitive challenge for his Country Club Plaza in Kansas City, the newspaper added that the installation would be "the first time such an art collection has been installed in a shopping center in the Midwest."[115]

Within the mall, *Massasoit* was reportedly installed in front of the information booth to garner the highest visitation. As one local resident recalled, *Massasoit* appeared large and impressive despite the modest security ropes encircling it. The resident remembered that the statue stood across from the second-story entrance to the popular Montgomery Ward anchor store.[116] Indeed, even after the mall closed and cast no. 4 was removed, the commercial setting continued to be linked to the statue in viewers' memories. Apart from short newspaper reports inviting shoppers to the mall for the public art display, no pomp and ceremony accompanied *Massasoit*'s installation. Photographs from 1996—taken to document the removal rather than the dedication—indicate the statue's base was installed directly into the mall's ceramic tile flooring without a pedestal. And in the place of an interpretive plaque, a lengthy information sheet had been typed out and secured atop a small plastic stand in front of the statue. Although it is unclear how long the information sheet accompanied *Massasoit* cast no. 4 in the mall setting, the sheet does provide a wide-ranging description of the statue's subject, artist, provenance (although misleading), and connection to other statues found throughout Evergreen Plaza. The story pertaining to the historical figure of 8sâmeeqan was here more accurate than in other inscriptions associated with the monument—no doubt freed from the word length constraints of bronze plaques— and took note of the fact that the Massasoit, the chief of the Wampanoags, sent Samoset to arrange for a formal meeting with the Pilgrims rather than greeting the newcomers himself. The artistic analysis of the sculpture also hewed closely to Dallin's intent, noting that the figure's "straightforward direct presentation" was created to "emphasize the innate nobility and dignity of the American Indian." Furthermore, readers learn that Dallin was friendly with

Ute Indians, "whom he came to view as totally exploited by the United States government. His sculptures became 'protests in bronze' against the broken promises and callous indifference of the white man." Shoppers curious to see other "protest" works by Dallin could find *Appeal to the Great Spirit* in the upper level of the north mall and *The Scout* in the galleria. The text presented a national story that also referenced specific places: Thanksgiving and Plymouth, and Utes and Provo, Utah. It did not, however, reference Evergreen Park, Illinois, nor the way in which viewers may understand the statue's connection to the local place.

Did shoppers stop to read the lengthy text and reflect on its critical message? Did *Massasoit* cast no. 4 teach suburban visitors about historical Wampanoag and Ute relations with settlers, and did viewers come to think differently about the value of honoring treaties with Indian nations? Perhaps. The statue and information sheet did invite visitors to grapple with a narrative history that celebrated the Massasoit while also challenging non-Indians' tacit support for settler state policies into the twentieth century. However, no written evidence of viewers' reactions to the installation in Evergreen Plaza appears to have survived. Rubloff never donated the statue to the city of Evergreen Park (as Nichols had done for Kansas City), and the memorial remained in an enclosed, semiprivate space while in Illinois; the fact that *Massasoit* cast no. 4 was not cast in a role as public art, with a civic function, likely limited its impact.

In late 1996, the statue was cut from the tile floor, loaded onto pallets, and dragged out of the mall (fig. 25). An auction house had been hired to remove the statue and sell it to the highest bidder, and was apparently not instructed to convey the information sheet along with the bronze cast. By the time the cast was purchased by an Ohio collector and donated to the Dayton Art Institute, the statue had shed its interpretation. In the Dayton museum, the statue stands as a curious but inert fixture, without so much as an identifying label since its arrival. Currently located at one end of the museum's second-floor Great Hall, the statue appears out of place in terms of subject and material; the gray-marbled Italian villa architecture only increases the sense of disjuncture with the bronze monument to a Wampanoag leader (fig. 26). Unlike the *Massasoit* cast in the Salt Lake City capitol rotunda that became a celebrated (and thematically integrated) feature of formal dances, *Massasoit* cast no. 4 is moved or removed altogether when the Great Hall is rented out as an event space. The cast's rapid mobility—from Salt Lake City to Evergreen Plaza to Dayton—led to a loss of information and context. Because of its commercial setting or its rapid mobility, cast no. 4 did not become a part of the social life of a place.

FIGURE 25. *Massasoit* leaving the Evergreen Plaza shopping center, 1996.
Courtesy of a private collector. In the authors' possession.

SPOKANE, WASHINGTON, 1977–2001

At about the same time that Miller Nichols and Arthur Rubloff acquired *Massasoit* reproductions in late 1977, the Museum of Native American Culture on the campus of Gonzaga University received a cast on permanent loan from another midwestern owner.[117] Cast no. 5 was installed without a pedestal at the outdoor entrance to the museum—a setting the *Spokane Chronicle* interpreted as a fitting signal of welcome for visitors to the center by "the chief who greeted the Pilgrims at Plymouth Rock." In the absence of an interpretive plaque (no plaque is visible in surviving photographs, although the curator of the present collection is confident there must have been one),[118] visitors would be ill equipped to see the statue as more than a vessel for this vague notion of welcome. Indeed, the only newspaper feature on the statue printed a photograph with a staff member standing beside the statue—ostensibly "measuring [its] height"—to emphasize the enormous size of the sculpture more than any other aspect (fig. 27).[119] It was certainly eye-catching and memorable: Cyrus Dallin's great-niece recalled seeing the statue on display in this location at some point in the 1990s.[120] In any case, the staff at the Museum of Native

FIGURE 26. *Massasoit* in the Dayton Art Institute.
The Dayton Art Institute, gift of the James F. Dicke Family.

American Culture apparently did not make interpretive choices overtly connecting *Massasoit* to Spokane and its history. Once the museum collections
came under the stewardship of the Eastern Washington State Historical Society, the curators determined that *Massasoit* did not fit their mission to "actively engage all people in the appreciation of arts and culture" and deaccessioned the piece in 2001.[121]

FIGURE 27. *Massasoit* at
the Museum of Native
American Culture,
Spokane, Washington.
Courtesy of Lisa Blee.

Massasoit cast no. 6 was somewhat grudgingly placed on display on the Brigham Young University campus (fig. 28). The "general agreement" among the Art Acquisition Committee (which approved the reproductions of the plaster model in 1976) was that a bronze *Massasoit* "could not be placed outside on the campus because of the connection with the University of Utah symbols" (the rival university's sports teams are officially known as the "Utes").[122] When a potential sale fell through and the provenance of the cast raised too many questions, the statue (on long-term loan) was installed near a patio outside of the Harris Fine Arts Center on campus. Here it would wait until the title cleared and the piece gained enough value to be sold to a more appropriate setting. As predicted, campus officials noted that vandalism was an issue because of the rival university's team nickname. In 1982 students sprayed shaving cream on the statue, which remained for several days and discolored the bronze patina.[123] One alum recalled that the statue was wrapped in bubble wrap before games with the University of Utah football team to prevent more substantial damage.[124] Although occasionally mistaken for a symbol of the Utes, the memorial continued to be incorporated into BYU student life and interpreted within the university's LDS-inspired honor code over time. Now, official campus tours feature the statue among other campus artworks and interpret the memorial as a reinforcement of LDS values (to be addressed in the next chapter).

When the art museum reopened after renovation in 1993, the statue was reinstalled on an unremarkable grass lawn on the west side of the Harold B. Lee Library. Standing atop a roughly hewn stone pedestal (the origins of which are not revealed in the installation), *Massasoit* "remained unmarked and a mystery to students until June 1994," when the Intercollegiate Knights and the Native American student organization Tribe of Many Feathers added an informative plaque.[125] Despite the plaque detailing the Massasoit's significance and Utah's links to the artist (and the clear presence of enrolled Native students who cared about accurate representation), many students crafted a different message from its campus staging. Its location near the heart of campus prompted generations of students to identify it as an immediately recognizable reference and meeting point: "the naked Indian." Despite campus tours, the unmistakable presence of the plaque, and school newspaper stories that remind students of the name "Massasoit," the generic moniker has become a sort of campus tradition fixated on the statue's dress (or lack thereof).

FIGURE 28. *Massasoit* on the Brigham Young University campus.
Photograph by Lisa Blee.

The small eruptions of controversy surrounding the statue on campus focus on the physicality of the figure, but harken back to the problem of "fit" so prominent in the capitol rotunda installation. As one student wrote in the BYU school newspaper in 1997, the statue "doesn't seem to belong." *Massasoit*'s clothing and the conflict it represents with the students' dress code is the most remarkable aspect of the statue's Mormon school setting. Campus attire must be modest, meaning it cannot be "tight, sheer, or revealing in any manner. Men and women should . . . avoid being extreme or inappropriately casual in clothing." For men in particular, "hairstyles should be clean and neat, avoiding extreme styles or colors, and trimmed above the collar."[126] Although *Massasoit* does appear to follow the guidelines regarding facial hair, tattoos, and piercings, it exhibits flagrant violations with long braids, a bare chest, and exposed legs.

The physicality of the statue seems to overshadow nearly any other reading for the memorial in this setting. As the student writer pointed out, while other memorials and artworks on campus appear closely related to their location, "the muscular Massasoit in his loin cloth [creates] an odd contrast" to modestly clad students. Rather than maintaining it in proximity to the cerebral library setting, the student suggested relocating *Massasoit* to the outside of the gym to align with student-athletes "in their sometimes-skimpy BYU-issued gym shorts." Never mind how the move would strengthen the association between Indian bodies and savagery and remove the historical figure from the context of diplomacy often associated exclusively with white Americans. In a more troubling quip, the student noted that the relocated statue could be interpreted as the rival university's "Ute" mascot and serve as target practice for shot-putters, javelin throwers, and discus hurlers.[127] In a setting in which playing Indian around *Massasoit* would be considered an honor code violation and Native figures are reduced to mascots, many students saw the statue as a quirky aberration at best, and a threat to the community's morality and cohesion at worst.

SALT LAKE CITY RE-REINSTALLATION, 5 NOVEMBER 2009

One of the notable features of the *Massasoit* casts (with the exception of cast no. 1 in Plymouth) is their micromobility; the statues have been regularly moved since the 1970s. Whether reinstalled a few feet away or in another state, the casts seem anything but rooted to specific places. And yet the same responses and controversies erupt at each new installation. These patterns help to illustrate persistent concerns and associations, as well as the shifting power dynamics in public discourse on the place of Indians in "modern" public spaces (shopping centers, university campuses, government grounds).[128]

The re-reinstallation of *Massasoit* bronze cast no. 2 on the Utah capitol grounds in 2009 is a telling example of how public art and its placement pro-

FIGURE 29. *Massasoit* at the Utah capitol east entrance. *Photograph by Lisa Blee.*

vokes debate. After nearly fifty years greeting visitors to the capitol from a prominent place on the south lawn, the bronze statue was removed from beside the planter boxes. The ninety-year-old capitol underwent extensive renovation and preservation in 2004 when a study found the building to be vulnerable to earthquake damage. In addition to seismic upgrades, the Capitol Preservation Board turned to the artwork in the building and scattered around the grounds. Older bronzes such as *Massasoit* would be restored, and newly commissioned artwork and memorials would be added to the reorganized setting.[129] The capitol building was officially reopened in January 2008, and nearly two years later, on a chilly November morning in 2009, a crane lowered *Massasoit* onto a granite pedestal with the same bronze plaque attached to the base. *Massasoit* now faces east, toward the Wasatch Range and the Wampanoag homeland beyond (fig. 29). The boulder pedestal had been removed, and the new setting—on a landscaped island in a circular paved driveway—is situated at the side entrance to the capitol building. *Massasoit* has received a location demotion; the statue previously stood on a hill overlooking the downtown valley, and motorists on the busy State Street corridor faced it as they ascended the foothills. Now the

Staging   113

memorial is most visible from a side road mainly in the winter months, when the young cherry trees planted around the memorial have lost their leaves. Although once a prominent fixture that was incorporated into Salt Lake City citizens' social events and everyday vistas, now it is mainly capitol employees and visitors who arrive by school, tour, or city bus who see the memorial before anything else.

Despite the move, the memorial still garnered public interest and some controversy. The press conference held at the occasion of the reinstallation was composed of journalists, capitol employees, 8sâmeeqan descendants, and a relative of Cyrus Dallin. The public dialog surrounding the reinstallation of the bronze cast once again delved into the place of the Wampanoag figure in Utah, but the voices were no longer limited to newsprint. According to the capitol blog's coverage of the event, tenth-generation 8sâmeeqan descendant Glenn Baldwin of Salt Lake City, eleventh-generation 8sâmeeqan descendant Mary Hilliard of Ogden, and Hilliard's daughter Joni Crane of Vernal posed for photographs with the statue, and reportedly "were able to relate some history of Massasoit."[130] Dallin's great-niece, Denice Wheeler, represented the artist's family and recalled that a "big group came in" for the rededication ceremony, with seven or eight of 8sâmeeqan's descendants in attendance. "They were very, very interested and willing to share. They were just excited. . . . It was a very successful day." She particularly recalled that the descendants "loved the statue and they had great respect for Cyrus E. Dallin. They thought he had retained their legacy."[131]

Despite the splendid day for those who traveled from around the region for the reunion, blogs and online reader comments on the *Deseret News* report of the November 5 event renewed the controversy over the statue. A few readers maintained that *Massasoit* had no ties to Utah and should have been replaced with a memorial to local tribes. One blogger brought up the first dedication ceremony in the rotunda to make a point about the sculptor's intent: "According to Dallin, Chief Washakie of the Shoshones was similar to Chief Massasoit of the Wampanoags. In other words, all Indians are basically the same and it doesn't matter which one we honor." He pointed out that the bronze was a copy of the original plaster, thus proving "Utahns weren't preserving a great work of art despite it [sic] stereotypical nature. They created a duplicate statue because they were proud of its stereotypical nature." Ironically, this message was exactly the one Dallin feared when he reluctantly donated the plaster model of *Massasoit* to his home state. Although the blogger was well informed of the statue's history of replication, he was not aware of the artist's concern for accuracy and cultural specificity. But it is hard to argue with the charge that the statue's staging in Utah fostered the perception of generic Indianness, given the Boy Scout camporee and prom-theme attire in the statue's history. The blogger concluded that to put the "half-naked stand-in for Washakie" on display showed Utahans to be insensitive to Native people and the damaging impacts of stereotypes. Reinstalling *Massasoit* on the capitol grounds sends the message that "our pride in Dallin's stupid stereotypes is more important than your desire for cultural accuracy. We'd rather honor a white man's fantasy about Natives than Utah's actual Natives."[132] For her part, the capitol curator, Judith McConkle, defended the statue with the argument that Dallin's artistic genius and accomplishment were worthy of honor. And the "actual Natives" from the region who visited the statue for the re-rededication event saw the statue as a memorial to a specific ancestor.

How is the popular perception that *Massasoit* depicts a stereotypical or generic Indian connected to the memorial's mobility (and micromobility)? Is the fate of reproduced memorials, and Indian statuary in particular, a kind of flattening and generalizing out of existence? If Indian statuary is everywhere (or at least part of any respectable midwestern bronze collection) and not overtly connected to a local place, viewers might be forgiven for their confusion or indifference. But we can also understand the charge of Indian stereotyping as a valid critique of a long history of appropriation. As a point of entry into a dialog about the fraught history of settler-Native relations, *Massasoit* serves as a particularly powerful actor on a public stage. The memorial's mobility meant that critics and Native people far from Massachusetts could engage with it and see their own experiences in the displaced but dignified figure. After the publication of the 2009 story, one anonymous online commenter claimed the Massasoit as a "13th great grandfather" and made the point that the Massasoit "does have historical ties to Utah" because his direct descendants "joined the LDS church in Nauvoo and moved west with the Saints." Another reader recounted a friend's story of falling in love with and marrying the man who stood as Dallin's model for *Massasoit*.[133] Just as replicas of *Massasoit* moved and multiplied across the country over the twentieth century, so did those who claimed attachment to *Massasoit* and the stories that traveled with it. And along the way, Native people found ways to use the central prop to shift perception of the stage itself.

Chapter Three

DISTANCING

The nine-and-a-half-foot monument to the Massasoit makes him literally larger than life, and there are many ways in which the statue is narratively larger than life as well. *Massasoit* sets up a complex push-and-pull dynamic around the problem of historical memory: the Improved Order of Red Men erected it as a manifestation of their own historical distancing (shedding the violence of the colonial encounter in favor of a narrative of Indigenous acquiescence and peaceable encounter), yet as with all monuments, meaning comes from individual engagement with the statue. How effective has the IORM project been in the long run? What is the "place" of the Massasoit—in time, in space, and in narratives of the nation? Does the statue secure the distance intended by the IORM in the historical memory of this imaged foundational moment? These turn out to be evocative questions involving not just stories about the original encounter between the Massasoit and English Pilgrims, but also about the creation of a memorial landscape intended to elevate this moment to one of national significance, thus making it a story that is temporally, geographically, and imaginatively portable. Making the Massasoit central to the story of national origins was a deliberate project of those involved in erecting the statue. While this project achieved physical fruition in 1921 in attaching history to a particular place, events later in the twentieth century mobilized *Massasoit* in multiple ways, including the appearance of replicas in Salt Lake City, Provo, Kansas City, Chicago, Spokane, and Dayton, thus extending the memorial landscape beyond Plymouth. This physical distancing of *Massasoit* from its home complicated the relationship between the origin story intended by the IORM and the reception of the statue. What meaning do people make of the history in those distant locations where *Massasoit* came to be mounted? To what extent do observers hold on tightly to the historical distancing implicit in the IORM narrative of the Massasoit that so profoundly elides the violence of settler colonialism of the nation? What we found illustrates how multivalent historical meaning making can be in divergent places.

In part because of the particular mobility of this monument and its attachment to the idea of origins, the Massasoit story is fascinating for the ways it mediates local and national history. But it also helps us address important questions about public history and how it functions. A common refrain supporting the erection of monuments is some iteration of "We must not forget!" But how does the complex process of creating, provoking, and/or reinforcing historical memory through monuments really operate? What, if anything, about 8sâmee-qan and the historical narratives constructed around him travel along with the statue casts? How do passersby of *Massasoit* imagine him and what he/it might stand for in far-flung places? How do the locations of these public *Massasoits* condition and/or affect the experiences of those who encounter him? Did the claims of the Improved Order of Red Men about the vital importance of the Massasoit to the national narrative pan out in places far removed from Plymouth? How is historical memory mobilized in these distant locations?

As suggested earlier, almost by definition, the memory work surrounding monuments involves distance: temporal in particular, but also geographical, and imaginative, as a monumental landscape in the United States (and elsewhere) is imbedded in a touristic impulse sometimes characterized by the "checklist" or "bucket list" approach to experiencing the world, perhaps nowhere more performatively than on the national mall in Washington, D.C.[1] There is a tension in experiencing monumental landscapes on the local and national level as well (and on other scales such as regional and global, for example). One can think of the world as a densely marked memorial landscape with historical actors and events commemorated in particular places but their significance resonating on different scales, depending on their attachment to narratives that travel imaginatively and in other ways (including through the market in replicas, memorabilia, and kitsch).[2]

This particular set of monuments to the Massasoit and other cultural locations where this historical memory is invoked (particularly for our purposes at Plimoth Plantation and in *Colonial House*) open a fascinating window onto the process of historical memory formation, or the crucial work that physical location and cognitive distance perform on historical memory.[3] In this chapter, we focus on how passersby in different sites experience the relationship between history and place through this monumental moment and the stories attached to it: in sum, how it mediates local and national history through personal experience. In the context of the statue on Cole's Hill, we analyze how the erection of a revisionary marker to the Plymouth *Massasoit* demonstrates the possibility of disrupting viewers' perceptions of history. This Indigenous intervention reveals a deep contrast with the statues installed far from Plymouth, where the free play for historical ignorance enables cognitive distance from settler colonialism. It shows how closing that distance between understandings of the past and their reverberation in the present means considering context and a deep personal level of empathy alongside some very strong guidance from Indigenous teachers. We then turn to two venues that seek to close the distance between the seventeenth-century founding moment of Plymouth and the present through experiential reenactment: the popular living history museum Plimoth Plantation and the 2004 PBS series *Colonial House*. In both of these venues, Indigenous people insist on a reckoning with the past and the present that refuses narratives of frozen Indians in a place sanitized of the violence of settler colonialism. In all of these locations that engage with the history—whether the *Massasoit* casts, a revisionary marker, or living history set within 8sâmeeqan's world—vehicles for closing this historical distance are contested rather than resolved once and for all. These sites of memory reveal historical meaning making as dynamic, interactive, unsettled, open to interpretation. Active engagement with monuments and reenactment of historical moments demonstrates that when hailed to do so, people will (and should) struggle with time-space dynamics as they articulate them through historical memory.

For non-Indians, constructing Indians as frozen in the era of first encounter relegates them to the past and relieves colonizers of the need to confront guilt over the inheritance of Indigenous places and the history that unfolded from that moment: Americans tend to think of settler colonialism (when they think of it at all) as confined to a particular period of time in the distant past rather than an ongoing process with countless iterations across the country. This tendency can be cemented in some ways in living history venues through reenactment as a technique of historical reconstruction. But Indigenous people reject the project of freezing them in place and instead use the statue as well as locations of living history to explain settler colonialism as a structure (the ongoing reverberation of Indigenous dispossession set loose at that moment and continuing as a system of oppression) rather than an event (the peace treaty, from the non-Indian perspective, and the moment of alliance, from the Wampanoag perspective). In these senses, *Massasoit* opens a window not just on how to think about the distance between the historical moment and the present, but also the distance between the very different non-Indian and Indian projects of marking the commemorative landscape. For Indigenous peoples, there is a double distancing operating: the distance between the memorialized moment and now, and the distance between Indian and non-Indian willingness to embrace uncomfortable histories. They refuse to be frozen in this narrative, but instead they insist that the past be reckoned with in a way that includes their own perspective on this history and the ongoing ramifications on their lives under settler colonialism. Imagined from these multiple vantage points, *Massasoit* finds a place in a highly mobile interpretive terrain that unsettles rather than fixes historical narratives in bronze and stone.

HEADING WEST: *MASSASOIT* IN UTAH

We sought to get at the question of personal encounters with monuments as history by interviewing passersby at each of the publicly displayed bronze *Massasoit*s over the course of several months in 2014. We asked respondents six base questions: Where are you from? Have you noticed this statue? Does it make you think of history, and if so, what does it make you think? Who is depicted and why? What do you think it's doing here? How do you think it fits here? We then asked each respondent if they had anything they'd like to add.[4] This is what statisticians would call a "sample of convenience," for which we claim none of the sort of rigor that might be appropriately subjected to tests of statistical significance. Still, we conducted interviews until we felt we'd reached the point of diminishing returns: certain patterns seemed to emerge that gave us a sense of things.

Let's start at the state capitol grounds in Salt Lake City, where Dallin made the initial donation of the plaster model that ultimately spawned *Massasoit*'s mobility in the form of numerous posthumous casts.[5] After being cast in bronze in the 1950s and moved outdoors, *Massasoit* now stands alone at one eastern entrance to the capitol building but within view of a handful of other monuments on the expansive manicured capitol grounds. Many of the surrounding installations venerate Utahans who defended the Union or made contributions to state government, the economy, or social welfare. Much like the memorial landscape in Washington, D.C., the capitol grounds are dotted with installations that inspire reflection and reverence.[6] While the plaque below the *Massasoit* statue clarifies that Cyrus Dallin is the actual historical figure honored with the installation, the context in which a visitor encounters the statue on the capitol grounds conjures individual heroics and venerable deeds. A tourist to the capitol is primed to interpret the surroundings with civic-mindedness. *Massasoit* therefore becomes an individual worthy of honor by virtue of the setting, not necessarily because tourists can identify the figure and the broad strokes of 8sâmeeqan's story. The figure becomes abstract, allegorical, and distant from the historical moment it was commissioned to memorialize. In this context, the statue follows a pattern noted by James E. Young in which "American memorials seem to be anchored not so much in history as in the ideals that generated them."[7]

A number of respondents touched on at least a generic version of the helper Indian story the Massasoit represented to the IORM and so many others, and some offered interesting musings on language, such as the wife in an elderly couple who pointed out that the marker for the statue says "'Pilgrim fathers' . . . not 'pioneer fathers.'" Another respondent used "Pilgrim" and "pioneer" interchangeably, and the Mormon roots of colonialism in Utah complicate what might be commonly understood as the difference between these two categories. "Pilgrim" in U.S. history tends to refer rather restrictively to the English who arrived in Plymouth, and "pioneer" to those who rushed into the American West in the nineteenth century. But the religious persecution of Mormons in the nineteenth century unquestionably spurred their migration west and struck (and apparently strikes) parallels with the experiences of the English Pilgrims in Plymouth. But even these narratives glossed over Indigenous peoples and instead invoked narratives of non-Indian persecution and how it was overcome. A number of respondents produced a generic story about Indian cooperation with settlers that certainly fits with the generic 8sâmeeqan narrative, including an African American male from Tampa, Florida, who spun out all kinds of associations with the symbol of the peace pipe cradled in *Massasoit*'s arm. He was a go-between, an emissary of sorts, who might have served as a guide, the respondent explained, and "they [settlers] would have relied on him or his connections to ensure their safety initially." This respondent drew out a frontier story from a settler perspective that naturalized colonialism by casting the Massasoit in the role of guide in the valiant story of exploration. Here, the clear connotation of the peace pipe conveyed the notion of nobility and a comforting conciliatory history rather than one of conflict. He was pleased to see a figure such as the Massasoit honored in the statue.

Our twelve interviews at the state capitol installation consisted of seven Utahans and five visitors from out of state, reflecting the regional tourist draw of the capitol building. The respondents were mainly white, represented varying ages, and also included one young Mexican male, one middle-aged African

American male, an older Native American couple, and another elderly couple, with one of them claiming Native descent. Fully one-third of this set of interviewees identified the statue as one of "Massasoit," another one-third imagined it represented a local Ute Indian, and the final third described it in generic terms, a perfect three-way split. These respondents overwhelmingly thought it fit well in front of the Utah State Capitol, although one person—who works in the visitor services center—disagreed, stating, "I feel like we have much more relevant Indian statues in the capitol. We have a couple of Ute Indian busts and other things that are more relevant to the history of Utah, the government of Utah." This reaction echoed that of Utah Navajo Tom Lovell in response to the 2009 reinstallation of the statue when he quipped, "Why honor a Massachusetts Indian in a state named after the Utes? . . . It doesn't make any sense. It would be like having a statue of the Pope on Temple Square."[8] He continued, "It would be like having a picture of the governor of Massachusetts in the rotunda with the Utah governor." *Massasoit*'s mobility was not flying with him.

Several respondents referred to local Indian history even if they did not directly suggest the statue itself represented a Ute man, and this helps account for the large majority who thought the statue "fit" where it was. These respondents viewed the statue as a generic signifier to stand in for foundational narratives devoid of conflict that entailed Indians but not guilt over Indigenous dispossession and displacement. One nonlocal white male concurred that *Massasoit* belonged on the capitol grounds, explaining, "There's statuary all around the capitol of different people that have had . . . some role to play in the history of the state. Obviously, the Ute tribe were here long before anyone else, so . . . I think it would be . . . negligent to, to omit them from the . . . statuary and the other things that honor the people that founded the state." His comment gestures toward Indians rather flippantly as an afterthought. Indians belonged in this narrative, of course, but it seems only because they were there first and thus the starting point of Utah's origins as a state, rather than as Indigenous nations defending their homelands. An elderly white couple, who were from northern Idaho and Montana, displayed knowledge of tribes in their own proximity and puzzled over why a Massachusetts Indian would be displayed here, pointing out, "Are there tribes there? There must be Indian tribes in Utah." Another elderly couple was composed of a longtime Salt Lake Valley resident and her husband of nine years, who was newer to Salt Lake. She shared her childhood memories about the place, including that "Massasoit was just one of the important things . . . that we talked about. On field trips and so forth." *Massasoit* had become part of the identity of the place by virtue of its location as one stop on a ritualized school field trip junket. The husband, formerly of Oklahoma, pointed out his Choctaw descent from a "full-blooded grandmother" and stated that statues like this made him "feel good, you know, since I have it in my lineage." None of these observations demanded a particular accounting of Indigenous people in place or any details about the conflicted history of the Salt Lake Valley.

The Native couple interviewed hailed from Bluff, Utah, and the husband knew *Massasoit* from the time he ran the Susan G. Komen Race for the Cure in the mid-1990s, when someone stretched a Komen T-shirt over the statue. He associated *Massasoit* with the Utes and brought up the fact that "Ute" is the mascot for the University of Utah. He saw the statue as malleable, one that worked as a symbol of the Utes and belonged where it was: "If you look back ... this all belonged to the Indians before this.... The Utes and Comanches... they hunted all this area. And they ... the Pilgrims moved in here and ... everybody was moved south.... It represents something here.... Native Americans will come here, they'll see the state capitol, just another building, but for them to see a ... warrior statue in the front, it's a whole different outlook to it.... Very welcoming." Note that this observation flips the script of the nonlocal white male, casting the statue as welcoming of Native people in the present rather than settlers in the past, and it thus closes the distance for him between 8sâmeeqan and Indigenous perspectives today.

On the campus of Brigham Young University, *Massasoit* is read through a Mormon lens of moral principles and action. The campus is dotted with abstract art installations and memorials to specific university or church leaders; *Massasoit* falls somewhere in the space between these intentions. On a campus tour, visitors learn that the Massasoit welcomed the Pilgrims and thus offers a lesson about being kind to others and reinforces the personal code of conduct presented in the Book of Mormon. For many students, the statue is both too specific and too general to conjure up historical references. Set amid university classrooms and walkways, the statue stands out for its (to them) near-scandalous nakedness. Students passing by after a class or on their way to worship at the temple may consider the moral lesson to be drawn from it, but they also fixate upon the disjuncture between the bare-chested figure and the modestly dressed students bustling about.

A plaque erected beside the bronze cast in 1994 provides viewers with an introduction to the subject and sets the context for the statue. The first part of the caption freezes in place a clichéd snapshot of the Plymouth mythology stripped of a conflicted past, and the second portion nudges the viewer into imagining a local reason for the installation:

MASSASOIT

(Born 1580)

"Protector and Preserver of the Pilgrims"

Massasoit or "Yellow Feather" was a chief of the Wampanoag Tribe of Massachusetts. Known for befriending the Pilgrims who landed in Massachusetts in 1620, his people protected the English settlers from other hostile tribes and saved many from starvation by teaching them to plant corn and other crops. Massasoit remained an ally of the Pilgrims until his death in 1661.

Cyrus E. Dallin (sculptor) — Born and raised in Springville, Utah, Cyrus E. Dallin is recognized internationally for his realistic portrayals of the American Indian. He created the original "Massasoit" in 1921 which is currently located in Plymouth, Massachusetts. He is also recognized for creating the Angel Moroni statue for the Salt Lake City Temple.

—THE TRIBE OF MANY FEATHERS—

—THE INTERCOLLEGIATE KNIGHTS—

The titles on the plaque are potentially confusing, since "Massasoit" means "great sachem," not "yellow feather" (it is "8sâmeeqan" that translates to "yellow feather"). The Tribe of Many Feathers is a Native American student group at BYU, and the Intercollegiate Knights is a national service fraternity; both local and national concerns supported this installation. The plaque is unique among those attached to *Massasoit* casts because of its length and local details, which gesture toward the embrace of *Massasoit* by Native students on the BYU campus. This plaque can be read as a sincere effort to provide historical grounding for the statue and preempt the tendency to interpret it as a generic Indian, raising the question of whether or not passersby actually engage with plaques affixed to monuments.

Thirteen respondents (individuals and groups) addressed our questions in Provo, most of them students, mostly younger white males, but also a young African American female, Hispanic female, Taiwanese female, and young women who claimed mixed white and Native descent.[9] Virtually none of these observers paid much attention to the historical meaning of the statue, let alone how *Massasoit* might spur a wrestling with the settler-colonial origins of the nation. In terms of identifying the figure and in contrast to the respondents in Salt Lake City, nearly three-quarters viewed *Massasoit* as representing a generic Native American, only two suggested it was a Ute, and one (a middle-aged man) knew it depicted the Massasoit. Several respondents guessed, one venturing Yellow Feather (presumably from glancing down at the plaque), and another, stabbing wildly, came up with Geronimo. The young woman of mixed white and Native descent explained, "I have no idea. I know that people call him Squanto on campus." She added that when she sees the statue, "I think of Native Americans. I'm part Native American so it's just kinda like, oh hey, Squanto, and [I] just, like, walk by," echoing the Native man in Salt Lake City who read *Massasoit* as welcoming to Indigenous people. A middle-aged Hispanic female who described him generically as "Native American" did venture (astutely in some ways), "I think he's depicting something about Thanksgiving?" A young white man declared, "It's kind of funny that it's an Indian and our rival school's mascot is the Ute Indians" (the BYU mascot is Cosmo the Cougar). He did speculate that *Massasoit*'s presence "probably has a lot to do with the fact that the first settlers and the founders of Brigham Young University had to strike up trade route agreements with the Native Americans in order to survive when they first got here," thus invoking pacific colonialism rather than the possibility of contestation for Indigenous homelands that deeply marked Utah history. The Native history of the region included the Bear River Massacre of Shoshone (1863), the removal of Utes and Goshutes, and continual skirmishes between Mormons and Navajos and Paiutes.[10] Yet his observation paralleled the helpful emissary narrative we collected in Salt Lake City, demonstrating the powerful appeal of the welcoming embrace motif. Respondents at BYU were all over the board on whether *Massasoit* fit on campus, four responding yes, one saying not at all, seven were not sure or indifferent, another thought him "a little random," one did not respond, and one declared "I don't see a compelling reason for it, but if he's here then I guess he was welcome to stay." The young man who discussed early history and trade went on to observe, "It reminds me. . . . You look back but you don't dwell on the past and you continue to move forward and build off of what you have. . . . I also think a lot of the statues are meant to . . . serve a purpose if you take time and think about 'em. Kind of how . . . he seems like he's looking into the future and, you know, learning from history and going forth and changing the world so that we don't repeat the same mistakes." What kinds of "mistakes" he might have meant he did not specify, but this is an implicit recognition of conflict that he felt was best left in the past. This tendency to reach for the conciliatory message read tangibly through *Massasoit*'s cradled peace pipe recurred in observations, suggesting the desire to maintain conflict stories safely in the past rather than reckon with them in the present.

Massasoit evoked quite different things for those who bustled past him on the BYU campus that day, but overwhelmingly, the statue at BYU serves more as moral touchstone or landmark than a monument that evokes historical memory. Most striking is the attention paid to *Massasoit*'s state of undress. When asked what the statue made him think about, one newly arrived white male freshman stated, "I was just kind of thinking of the honor code and how . . . he's not living up to the honor code. . . . You're supposed to be groomed a certain way, you're supposed to be dressed a certain way while you're on campus, so I just thought it was funny that he wasn't," and he underscored the code's emphasis on proper dress, hair length, and (he added) facial hair. Other than that, *Massasoit* seemed just "like a standard Indian to me." For him, Indianness is frozen in the past in a particular way, in perpetual violation of the BYU honor code retroactively imposed on him. He summarily dismissed the Massasoit and this history, suggesting a vast chasm between them. A young African American female reported first seeing him on a campus tour—"They talked about it a little, but the tour guide just called it the naked Indian statue"—and still another student, a young white female, suggested *Massasoit*'s state of undress constituted a common topic of conversation on campus (fig. 30).

Distant from his homeland, *Massasoit* took on significance in local, situational ways in Provo. A middle-aged white man who works on campus pointed out the function of *Massasoit* as a meeting place, explaining, "It's a landmark; people say, 'I'll meet you by the Indian statue.'"[11] It sometimes became the object of pranks or took on the role of a mascot. A young white male observed, "I was always curious why it was here. I noticed it most when they turn it into a giant snowman." This was also recounted by a young, mixed white-Native female, who added that another time "when I came to work . . . it was covered in a yarn kilt, so I just think about the different things that happen to the statue." While *Massasoit* once sported a Susan G. Komen T-shirt in Salt Lake City, in Plymouth, a local woman told us that that *Massasoit* was adorned in a Boston Bruins jersey when the team got into the Stanley Cup play-off. (We collected no sartorial stories about the Kansas City *Massasoit*.) As noted in chapter 2, one alum of BYU remembered *Massasoit* wrapped in bubble wrap on football game days with the University of Utah as a precaution against pranks and potential damage (fig. 31).

MIDWESTERN MUSINGS

If the Provo *Massasoit* stands uncomfortably in a faith-based educational setting, in Kansas City *Massasoit* is fixed one block off from a consumerist sea of classical poses and allegorical figures. Installed in close proximity to the Country Club Plaza, a Spanish-Mediterranean themed outdoor shopping center,

FIGURE 30. As part of a high-tech treasure hunt in which silly photos were taken at various places in Provo, the "Fan Club" team jokingly attempted to help *Massasoit* better comply with BYU's standards. The clue that led the team to the statue: "Go to the permanent BYU student who does not conform to the dress code."
Courtesy of Chad Emmett.

FIGURE 31. *Massasoit* on the Brigham Young University campus with arrows and sign, published in the *Daily Universe*, 23 November 1982. *Courtesy of L. Tom Perry Special Collections of Brigham Young University.*

Massasoit joins a number of plaster and bronze installations in a sixteen-block outdoor gallery connected only by virtue of their designation as fine art. To emphasize and showcase this collection, the Country Club Plaza curated a self-guided art walking tour and hosts an annual art fair.[12] Within a few blocks of *Massasoit*, one may encounter an English fountain featuring a mounted figure of Neptune charging into battle, a small *Sleeping Child* cast in Florence, and a replica of an ornate fountain from Plaza de los Reyes in Seville. In this context, the Indian statue by an American artist loses any historical or geographic reference and is reframed within a classical art tradition; as the Plaza promotional material announces, "What a surprise to the traveler to find these magnificent European works of art in the heart of the Midwest."[13] Tourists of fine arts — or those taking a break from shopping to take an art walking tour — might take note of *Massasoit* because it offers contrasts to other statues, or appreciate the way in which the park-like installation contributes to an aesthetic experience.

Following one relocation in the 1990s, the Kansas City *Massasoit* now

FIGURE 32. *Massasoit* with mortar and pestle installation, Kansas City, Missouri.
Photograph by Lisa Blee.

stands at the intersection of a busy street two blocks from the main Country
Club Plaza shopping area (fig. 32). A bronze plaque informs the public that this
is "Massasoit, great sachem of the Wampanoag, friend and protector of the Pilgrims, 1621," and that the sculpture was "contributed to the people of Kansas
City, May 6, 1979, by Mr. and Mrs. Miller Nichols." We interviewed a total of

Distancing

thirteen men and ten women (individually and sometimes in groups), five of them locals.[14] The respondents were racially diverse, including African Americans, Latinos, whites, and one group of young Brits.

The collective response of *Massasoit*'s passersby in Kansas City was disinterest, and we had to nudge most of them to take a look at the statue before answering our queries. Its location near a busy intersection rather than in an inviting place within the rest of Country Club Plaza's statuary or an obvious stop on a tourist circuit does not exactly prepare passersby for notice and reflection. Of the four parties mainly from Kansas City, everyone had noticed the statue before, but none could report any historical details beyond generalities about Indians and Indian history. *Massasoit* in Kansas City serves more as a free-floating signifier of Indianness, sometimes romanticized but decidedly generic and devoid of engagement with a conflicted history that might demand reckoning in the present.

When we asked for thoughts on the statue, comments included: "I feel bad for the way the white man treated the Indians. He looks sad. He doesn't look happy"; "Somber, yeah"; "Native American heritage"; and "You know, someone who was here before all this developed and everything like this and—so I—I don't know who it is. I did read what the statue said one time but I forgot." This observation evokes a replacement narrative, casting Indians as at odds with modernity, residing in the past and yet inaugurating all that comes later by virtue of being here first, echoing observations we gathered from Salt Lake City. With one telling exception, we discerned no substantive engagement with the statue that connected *Massasoit* to the local place or to the IORM foundational narrative. When we posed the question of what they thought it was doing there, people replied, "I don't know" and "I mean, I would assume his tribe is from this region?" Others expressed utter ambivalence: "I don't see what else you'd put here that would—I mean, it works fine, I mean I wouldn't say you should replace it with anything." According to another respondent, the statue's lack of connection to the location may be reason enough that it belongs in Kansas City: "I think it doesn't *not* fit, I mean Kansas City has all kinds of eclectic statues and stuff scattered around, so . . . it's not like you say, 'Why is there an Indian here?' . . . I think it fits good." Remarkably, the statue (by virtue of its placement in a rich statuary landscape) actually seems to make nearly all passersby *less* curious about the Indigenous history of this location. It is as though the artistic randomness of Kansas City diverts rather than encourages engagement with monuments. One very pensive and responsive African American male told us, "It's a reminder to us all. . . . And we really don't see a lot of Native Americans and we don't pay enough attention, I believe, to the Native Americans, you know." All but one agreed that it fit where it was, and the thoughtful African American male added, "And I think if more people were — were able to really think about its presence it might just help our city.... We — we say we're a — a collective — and I think we are, a pretty collective city, but... we can always come closer together... and treat each other better." This respondent moved to empathy in an effort to close the temporal distance and struggled with how to apply historical lessons to the present, which gestures toward the conciliatory narrative observers invoked elsewhere. Yet he was also the only person who reached back to acknowledge a history of conflict.

Many of the visitors to Kansas City produced comparably (vague) accounts of Indians and Indian history that *Massasoit* evoked for them but from a safe distance that did not involve engagement with an actual narrative of Plymouth that might include contestation or a locally rooted understanding of the Indigenous history of what is now the Kansas City region. One observer noted, "You can tell that they [Native Americans] used to be here, you know, and — and I guess they are not anymore" — a succinct summation of supposed Indian disappearance. The companion added, "I see the Indian over there [and] I feel like maybe this was part of their territory. Like the place is connected to it? So ... it gives you an idea of where a tribe might [have] lived around here maybe? ... It makes me want to learn more and think about how they lived here and how they got around and what they did and stuff like that, I guess." Although this couple could not move to a deep engagement with the region's history, they made clear that this history mattered to them by wrestling with what the statue could be meant to evoke.

Of all of the respondents — including long-term residents of Kansas City — only one knew that the statue depicted the Massasoit. This middle-aged white woman lived in St. Louis, but she was originally from Massachusetts. She made her way over to the statue "to snap a picture," recognizing him, and she told us that the statue made her wonder why "a statue of Massasoit is [in] Missouri" — our one respondent who didn't think it belonged here. When asked what she thought it was doing there, she astutely guessed it had something to do with the sculpture-rich landscape of Country Club Plaza and was probably intended to "[honor] all Native Americans, not just the ones native to this area." When we asked her about the history surrounding the Massasoit — and remember, she knew who he was — she responded, "Oh, well actually — I get it confused because — who's the other one, Squanto? I get the two stories confused. Was Massasoit the one that had been to Europe?" (Oops, sorry. That was Squanto.) Her final thoughts were, "It's lovely. I wonder if people make the connection between the name Massasoit and ... Massachusetts." (We told

Distancing

her we wondered, too—but were quickly gathering the impression that they did not. In fact, many did not gather much about Indians and/or Indian history at all.) Some indicated curiosity about the statue and how it related to place, but for this woman, it was concretely about her original home. The three other respondent groups ventured guesses about whom the statue depicted and came up with Squanto, Sacagawea (twice, including the English group), and . . . Sasquatch.

WHAT'S IT DOING IN DAYTON?

Just as *Massasoit* began greeting shoppers in Kansas City, another *Massasoit* was installed at the second-floor Montgomery Ward entrance in the Evergreen Plaza. The shopping center, one of the first fully enclosed malls in the country and located in a suburb of Chicago, enticed customers with similar promises of a free European museum–like experience. In the shopping center context of Country Club Plaza and Evergreen Plaza, *Massasoit* was both the draw and the distraction from a primarily consumerist activity. The fact that the replications of *Massasoit* have become items to add to a collection—commodities in the art market—means that they weave between public view and private holdings, and become hypermobile, which further separates them from place, histories, and locals' experiences. For example, the *Massasoit* memorial in Spokane's Museum of Native American Culture was on display for twenty years before being deaccessioned in 2001 and sold at auction to an unnamed private bidder.[15] Meanwhile, the bronze cast from the Evergreen Plaza was also sold at auction when the mall gradually emptied for closure in the mid-1990s. A few years later, the Ohio-based buyer donated the cast to the Dayton Art Institute.

The statue now stands at one end of the pillared Great Hall, one among several statues in the historic building modeled on sixteenth-century Italian villas and the only bronze in a sea of gray marble.[16] In Dayton *Massasoit* is a mute piece of art without interpretation; the museum has not fixed a label for the piece on the wall nearby (perhaps because it must remain mobile for occasions when the Great Hall is rented out for weddings), and viewers receive no information about the artist, subject, year, or context. The bronze cast is out of place and a largely unknown entity to the museum staff. Here a further distancing of *Massasoit* from 8sâmeeqan is performed: What is one to make of this piece of art?

Few people seem to bother to pass by *Massasoit* at the Dayton Art Institute, which was our observation about the plaster model housed in the Springville Museum of Art in Dallin's hometown in Utah as well. But a comparison of interviews of two passersby in Dayton in late 2016 proved telling. One white woman could discern nothing of substance about *Massasoit*.[17] Indeed, when asked if she knew who was depicted, she searched in vain for any explanatory text near the statue. She did volunteer that the figure seemed to convey "strength" and that "he's just looking kind of wistfully at what's in front of him." A middle-aged white couple originally delivered a generic "noble savage" response to the question of who it might be, pointing out that as a bronze, the statue stood out from all of the other marble statues in the Great Hall. The man took a guess and identified him as Chief Joseph. But when informed that the statue depicted the Massasoit, a Wampanoag, he responded, "I know, I grew up in Massachusetts. . . . You'd freeze to death. . . . Anyways, I wouldn't have . . . dressed like that in New England. Except maybe in the summer time." As for what the statue represented, he delivered: "Well, Massasoit was one of, if I remember correctly — this is vague history — one of the Native American leaders who welcomed and helped the early Pilgrims. . . . In fact, wasn't he at Thanksgiving?" Pay dirt. He finished: "So the pipe? Is it a peace pipe? I don't know. But that's what I think of." This passerby drew deep to conjure up the Massasoit narrative the IORM had packaged for broad and enduring consumption nearly 100 years before. Here, as elsewhere, the welcoming posture enabling colonialism signified through the peace pipe is mobilized in interpreting the statue. While most commonly this story came out of respondents as shadowy and vague, occasionally passersby pulled that thread all the way through to Thanksgiving. The IORM, who devised this statuary tribute, would have been proud.

BACK TO THE SOURCE: PLYMOUTH

It turns out context means a lot. *Massasoit* in Plymouth still stands where it was erected in 1921, atop Cole's Hill, overlooking Plymouth Harbor and the mythic Plymouth Rock that is a tourist destination (even a pilgrimage site, quite literally, for many) and not far away from the *Mayflower II* replica as well as a rich statuary landscape commemorating the Pilgrims. The plaque next to the statue reads:

MASSASOIT

GREAT SACHEM

OF

THE WAMPANOAGS

PROTECTOR AND PRESERVER OF THE

PILGRIMS
1621
ERECTED BY THE
IMPROVED ORDER OF RED MEN
AS A GRATEFUL TRIBUTE
1921

In the space between the text is a relief depiction of a peace pipe and a head-dress, reinforcing the message of the conciliatory relationship between the Po-kanoket leader and the Pilgrims the IORM intended to convey and commemo-rate with such gratitude.

In 1998, the Town of Plymouth installed an additional—and larger—marker next to *Massasoit* that read:

> *National Day of Mourning*
> Since 1970, Native Americans have gathered at noon on Cole's Hill
> in Plymouth to commemorate a National Day of Mourning on the
> U.S. Thanksgiving holiday. Many Native Americans do not celebrate
> the arrival of the Pilgrims and other European settlers. To them,
> Thanksgiving Day is a reminder of the genocide of millions of their
> people, the theft of their lands, and the relentless assault on their
> culture. Participants in National Day of Mourning honor Native
> ancestors and the struggles of Native peoples to survive today. It is
> a day of remembrance and spiritual connection as well as a protest
> of the racism and oppression which Native Americans continue to
> experience.
> *Erected by the Town of Plymouth on behalf of the*
> *United American Indians of New England*

Here we have a war of words, and a starkly different message from the one the Improved Order of Red Men labored so tirelessly to display (fig. 33). What ac-counts for this historical revisionism? Fifty years after the installation of *Massa-soit* on Cole's Hill under the auspices of an organization of pretend Indians, to mark the 350th anniversary of the mythic landing at Plymouth Rock, the town invited the Wampanoag tribe to designate one of their own to deliver a speech at the banquet celebrating the occasion. The tribe selected activist Wamsutta Frank James, and the organizers solicited James's remarks for review in ad-vance of the banquet. Deeming them insufficiently "celebratory," they pro-vided him with a speech of their own, which he refused to read, prompting the organizers to uninvite him. James then made his way to Cole's Hill and

FIGURE 33. *Massasoit* on Cole's Hill with the Day of Mourning plaque in the foreground. *Photograph by Jean O'Brien.*

Massasoit and read in protest his own words to a gathering of fewer than a dozen people.[18] "This is a time of celebration for you," he stated, "celebrating an anniversary of a beginning for the white man in America. A time of looking back, reflection. It is with a heavy heart that I look back upon what happened to my People.... Massasoit, the great Sachem of the Wampanoag ... he and his

People welcomed and befriended the settlers of the Plymouth Plantation. . . . This action by Massasoit was perhaps our biggest mistake."[19] James organized the activist group United American Indians of New England (UAINE) following this incident, and the group has held a National Day of Mourning on Cole's Hill on Thanksgiving Day ever since, a counterpoint to the "Pilgrim Progress" parade that has been held annually since the 1920 tercentenary.[20] In reflecting on and assessing the legacies of 8sâmeeqan's actions, James and UAINE vehemently closed the distance between the past and the present, insisting on an unabashed reckoning with settler colonialism.

After a melee during the 1997 protest that resulted in the arrest of some two dozen protesters, the Town of Plymouth and UAINE came to a twenty-three-point agreement that included dropped charges against the protesters and the erection of the new plaque next to *Massasoit*. It resulted in the mounting of a new and very different monument to the Massasoit's son Pometacomet, more commonly known as King Philip or Metacomet, in Plymouth's Post Office Square (fig. 34). There is, one might say, quite a bit of distance between the messages these two newer plaques seek to communicate and the original *Massasoit* plaque and its permutations between different places. There is also a subtle and intriguing comparison to be made between the two sites of these plaques, with the National Day of Mourning plaque erected near an imagined Thanksgiving site and the "Metacomet" marker situated on the place Pometacomet's head stood on a pike for more than twenty years.

In fact, the interventions that came as a result of the 1998 settlement aimed at a dramatic reinterpretation of Plymouth history and moved quite beyond authorizing the annual demonstrations to occur (with a permit and within agreed-upon guidelines). The contestation around the annual Day of Mourning demonstrations and the new marker dramatically display the disjuncture between the notion of the frozen 1621 version of Plymouth the IORM and so many others wanted and the demands of Native peoples that the settler-colonial story be reckoned with and explained. Part of this involved an acknowledgement of the grieving implied in the very naming of the Day of Mourning, but Indigenous activists moved well beyond mourning in demanding reckoning. They rejected the distancing enabled by the original installation and narratives connected to it, and instead insisted on initiatives that entailed discomfort with a past too easily sanitized that freed the public from the need to wrestle with an uncomfortable history. The town agreed that there were lessons to be learned as well as educational and other initiatives that ought to be undertaken. Included among the agreements besides the erection of the two new plaques were recommendations about school curriculum reform to in-

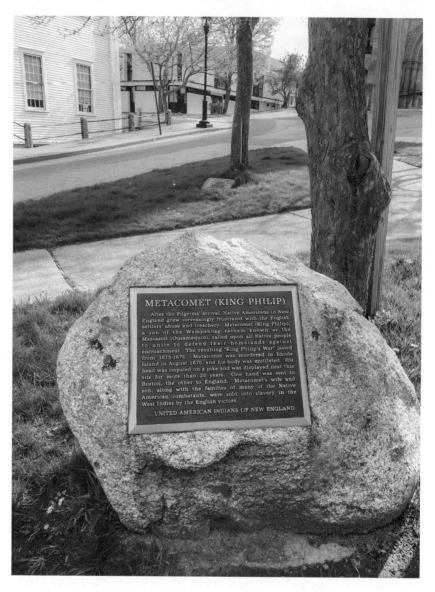

FIGURE 34. Metacomet plaque in Post Office Square, Plymouth, Massachusetts. *Photograph by Jean O'Brien.*

clude Native American perspectives and the creation of an education fund. The Town of Plymouth agreed to pay for the two new plaques and cooperate in the process to gain approval from the state and Massachusetts Historical Society for their wording and placement in the town. In the case of the plaque to Pometacomet, the agreement further stipulated that the proposed word-

Distancing

ing provided by the UAINE would be verified by the Massachusetts Historical Society, but "no higher level of accuracy for the ancient facts set forth on the plaque will be demanded than that has been required for representations that are made in the Town of Plymouth with regard to Plymouth Rock and the traditional story by the Town of Plymouth about the rock and the early history of Plymouth." In other words, the parties agreed to equal degrees of interpretive freedom in each of their versions of history.[21] The UAINE website celebrates this agreement as providing "a number of important opportunities to address the lies and inaccuracies about 'thanksgiving' and the history of Indigenous peoples that have been disseminated not only in Plymouth but throughout the country." And, with hopes for some vindication for the silencing of Wamsutta Frank James in 1970, the UAINE announced, "We are confident that this agreement represents a tremendous victory for the struggle of Native people to have our voices heard and respected." The spirit of this agreement appears to have held, with the peaceful coexistence of the parallel Thanksgiving Day commemorations — "Pilgrim Progress" and the National Day of Mourning demonstration — as ongoing events. Even the UAINE action of burying Plymouth Rock in sand on Thanksgiving Day in 1998 did not translate into arrests.[22] Locals are aware of the annual cycles of reenactments, protest marches, and especially tourist activities that take place around the *Massasoit* statue in Plymouth. *Massasoit* still stands on a boulder atop Cole's Hill, but now with the UAINE marker affixed to another boulder only a few feet away.

In early fall 2014, we interviewed eleven individuals or groups who were visitors to the city and five individuals or groups who called Plymouth home, all of them white.[23] Some of these interviews took place right next to the statue, but we pretty quickly realized few people bothered to climb the many steep stairs to the top of Cole's Hill in order to pass by *Massasoit*. At that point, we retreated below to the sidewalk near Plymouth Rock, which proved more productive. In stark contrast with the respondents in Kansas City, of the eleven who were not residents of Plymouth, six did not know who he was, but five did (some of them by virtue of reading the plaque or plaques). Interestingly, the proportion of locals who recognized the figure was comparable: two of the locals could not name him, two more could, and the fifth stated, "There's this writing and stuff on the base up there that you can read, but I don't remember now what exactly it [says]. Everybody refers to him as Massasoit, but I believe that that was the tribe? I don't think that was his real name. I'm not positive what it was. I don't remember." Recognition and frequent sightings did not necessarily bring in-depth understandings. When asked what it made her think of, that same local said, "Oh, I don't know, it's just something that's always there. You know? But if it was gone, you'd miss it. I just think of Plymouth . . . that and the rock. And the . . . *Mayflower* that's just around the corner." This local resident's nod to local landmarks in a national history narrative hints at the centrality of tourism in the harbor district. One respondent even expressed satisfaction with the statue "because . . . everything that's here for our history is here. That's why all the tourists come in — to see all the stuff."

As to the statue installation, three of the locals shared the general sentiment that *Massasoit* "fits great, this is where it all started, so . . . I guess he's welcoming the Pilgrims." Or in the words of another, "because it's where everything took place. Thanksgiving, Plymouth Rock, Indians." Two others took the question differently, assuming we meant the exact place *in* the Plymouth town landscape, and they each thought he belonged down on the waterfront near Plymouth Rock rather than up on the hill, "because that's where the tourists are." In the words of another, "One thing is you don't see many people up there. I don't know whether that's not noticeable" (to which we responded we'd noticed that too, which is why we were "down here"). When we asked a female visitor from Worcester, Massachusetts, if she was planning to go up to see *Massasoit* she lamented, "I just looked on the little pamphlet [she had picked up from the visitor center] and there are a few things on the list. Now I have to climb those stairs."

The UAINE interventions embodied in the Day of Mourning and the new plaque have effectively disrupted the older conciliatory narrative, spurring a deeper reckoning with the meaning of the past for at least some. One of our local respondents noted, "There's a big controversy, isn't there, about what truly happened? Whether they did not get along . . . or actually sit down at the table at Thanksgiving?" And although she was not sure about the details of the annual protest gathering at the statue, the respondent utilized the monument to imagine and articulate an Indigenous perspective on Thanksgiving and its popular observance: "I know Native Americans have a very different view as to whether this is something to celebrate. Which is why they protest the Thanksgiving and what he's [the Massasoit is] probably thinking is, 'Who are these people and what are they doing on my land?' . . . But it wasn't, you know, a pretty time in our history." Historical distance has collapsed between 8sâmeeqan and the protests for some, producing a more complex grappling with the past and its implications for the present and future, as a history that is not settled once and for all.

A man from Washington, D.C., and a *Mayflower* descendant also willingly engaged with the controversy signified by the contesting plaques on Cole's Hill, wrestling with the discomfort entailed in the Indigenous intervention and struggling with how to judge past actors and who should take responsibility for this history in the present:

> I used to live out on Cape Cod so I'm pretty familiar with the legacy of the Pilgrims, and I think, you know, this commemorates a national day of mourning, which I totally appreciate. I totally understand that perspective. And it's absolutely tragic—a travesty what happened. But many historians don't emphasize the fact that the Pilgrims kept a covenant with the Native Americans, I mean at least for the first fifty years. And that doesn't sound like much, but they even fought a war with the Wampanoags against other Natives because they were in covenant with the Wampanoags and therefore went to war. . . . So I do—I do know of Massasoit, and I know the Pilgrims absolutely would not have survived the first year without the generosity of the . . . Native Americans, and . . . there's been such a legacy—a modern legacy— where people say that this, the Pilgrims, you know, were responsible for the atrocities that have been perpetuated generationally with the Native Americans. And, I mean, I'm aware that with the American government, you know, I think there's 365 covenants made with the Natives and all 365 broken, which is an absolute travesty. But that was not the dream that the Pilgrims lived for.

This man demonstrated a deep familiarity with the history commemorated in the *Massasoit* monument and thoughtfully engaged with its meaning.

Three other interviewees displayed similar familiarity with the controversy, learning of it from the Day of Mourning marker, which prompted at least two of them to reflect more deeply on the meaning of historical disagreement. In this sense, the impact of the plaque might be that visitors take home with them new, deeper ideas about the meaning of Thanksgiving. A woman from Shippensburg, Pennsylvania, stated, "It could go two ways, because I was just reading what they [authors of the UAINE plaque] were saying about Thanksgiving, [that] now they mourn, because of Pilgrims, what came, and they brought disease and stole from the Indians, so they're saying it's kind of a sad situation . . . how racism and all went on way back in the 1600s." Reflecting on how the narrative on the plaque impacted her, she said, "I do see it differently now how they mourn, but we celebrate it as a Thanksgiving, but it's not to them." (Her surprise that racism is not a new thing is surprising in and of itself.) Another Pennsylvanian stated, "I understand what the—after reading the stone behind you about how things were vastly different once the white man came and settled and changed things around for their—for their benefit,

I guess you could say. You know . . . what the Indians must have gone through and are probably still going through to some degree" — a tangible recognition of the ongoing impact of settler colonialism. He related to the UAINE plaque on a personal level, revealing that "my ancestry is Armenian, so we were the victims, or subjects, of the first persecution and genocide, so I can kind of understand what the reason for this is . . . why maybe some groups may want to have this portrayed here just . . . to kind of balance things out here." (Unless he was thinking about the Armenian genocide as the first of the twentieth century, his chronology was a bit off: the Armenian genocide took place roughly 300 years after the events commemorated in Plymouth, in 1915–17.)

NARRATIVE MOBILITY

What do the impressions shared by these respondents of the various installations of *Massasoit* tell us about how the historical narratives around him travel along with the replicas? Did the assumptions made by the Improved Order of Red Men about the centrality of the Massasoit story to the national narrative bear the weight of their assertions? What can these responses tell us about the relationship between local, regional, and national narratives? Can a public history that embraces discomfort as an educational aim produce a deeper engagement with a complex history that makes room for a reckoning with the past, and a meaningful collapsing of historical distance?

It is important to remember that the version of the encounter history the IORM began with had already been stripped of complexity: the foundational narrative the order wanted to commemorate involved 8sâmeeqan's kindly embrace of the English, which translated into the treaty that ensured peace for fifty years (it is implied, with little or no conflict) and thus laid the foundation for the nation. The plaque that went up alongside the statue conveyed yet fewer details, commemorating him as "Massasoit Great Sachem of the Wampanoags Protector and Preserver of Pilgrims." To be sure, the early twentieth-century public school education about 8sâmeeqan's welcoming posture toward the Pilgrims offered few additional details (let alone contestation of the narrative) to possible observers of the monument when it was first installed. In these senses, we could conclude that the fact that the majority of passersby overall identified a generic Native American as a symbol for a long-ago history that implied passivism did indeed travel very well across time and space, even if respondents to our queries couldn't name the Massasoit or confused him for his compatriot Tisquantum, for example. Among those we interviewed, naming the Massasoit didn't necessarily bring additional details to an understanding of the history that might have been drawn from sources beyond the various plaques themselves, and even naming him is complicated around signage. (Did they read the plaques and the name stuck? Or did they bring something more substantial away with them about this history?)

Yet there are interesting comparisons to be drawn, especially between the Plymouth and Salt Lake City installations on the one hand, and the Kansas City, Dayton, and BYU installations on the other. For different reasons (but with the very interesting parallel of "pilgrims" and "persecution" as part of the local narrative in each place), the former are tourist destinations per se with similar yet still divergent contexts. Plymouth is the ultimate place of origins in this narrative, but Salt Lake City proudly claims the sculptor Cyrus Dallin. The Kansas City and BYU *Massasoits*, on the other hand, are there by virtue of commercialization of the statue in the art market. They don't "belong" where they are in the same way the other *Massasoit* casts can claim a place rooted in local narratives connected to national ones. In fact, they seem to have a place where they are as landmarks, afterthoughts, appendages to locales with different purposes (a college campus and a shopping mall), with the Kansas City *Massasoit* connected in some ways to the statuary that decorates Country Club Plaza. One could speculate that the Chicago installation in the Evergreen Plaza shopping center (before it was moved to Dayton), similarly connected to shopping and other statuary, might have been received in parallel ways to the Kansas City *Massasoit*.

Perhaps most interesting is to analyze what seems to have happened in Plymouth because of the intervention of the UAINE. There, the compromise struck between the organization and the Town of Plymouth that translates into the Day of Mourning plaque has an impact on at least some passersby, some of whom willingly engage with the historical narrative implied in the installation in more uncomfortable and conflictual ways, even relating the controversy to their own lives. There also, at least for locals, is the annual reminder of the contested interpretations of the events commemorated in *Massasoit* that likely keeps such debates alive. The UAINE interventions—spatially and calendrically—seem to deepen the historical understandings that attach to *Massasoit* and might be seen as vindication of approaches to public history that seek to provoke debate over interpretations rather than packaging singular messages for public consumption. Their interventions seem to do a different sort of memory work that reflects both past encounters and present contexts in contests over meaning.

Indigenous interventions in the construction of historical memory unleashed after the Day of Mourning protests have reverberated in Plymouth, including in connection with one of the town's venerable historical institutions: Plimoth Plantation. We turn to this living history site to take up the work of Indigenous public intellectuals there since the rupture of the inaugural Day of Mourning protest, including their connection to what was destined to become a fairly obscure historical reality television series aired by PBS, *Colonial House*. These two very different and yet intertwined instances of experiential history are a form of "time freezing" where guests (and cast members and viewers, in the case of *Colonial House*) "are invited to step back in time and experience the lives of past peoples," a particular approach to closing historical distance and making visceral connections to the past.[24] These two venues also became places where Indigenous educators pushed for contesting historical memory and forcing engagement with the violence of settler colonialism, in the case of Plimoth Plantation, in an ongoing and dynamically reimagined way. They also demonstrate the disjuncture between the impulse to freeze history, whether in 1621 (*Massasoit*), 1627/1624 (Plimoth Plantation), or 1628 (*Colonial House*), and the vital fact that Indigenous peoples are highly motivated to both embody this history and demonstrate in no uncertain terms that they are still here as modern people looking to the future.

The Plimoth Plantation pamphlet invites visitors to "have a great time in another time!" and describes how the museum staff and exhibits "tell the story of seventeenth-century Plymouth Colony and its shared history with the Pilgrims and Native people."[25] The museum's educational mission is to create an immersive historical environment where visitors "experience powerful encounters with history that spark their imaginations, delight their senses, touch their hearts and enrich their minds."[26] Besides educating its guests "in their quest for a deeper and more personal understanding of the past," Plimoth Plantation engages in historical preservation about cultural practices, including a commitment to "the re-vitalization of pre-industrial crafts, trades, domestic skills, husbandry, horticulture, and the maritime arts."[27] The transformative potential of these time-traveling encounters is further explicated on the museum website, which pronounces, "You can't change history, but it *could* change you."[28] The intent of Plimoth Plantation is to literally close the distance between the past and the present by making available opportunities for its guests to experience this history vicariously, firsthand.[29]

When it opened in 1947, Plimoth Plantation took the stage alongside other living history sites such as Henry Ford's Greenfield Village (1929), Colonial Williamsburg (1930s), and Old Sturbridge Village (1947).[30] Plimoth Plantation was incorporated with an aim to provide education about the "struggles of the early settlers" and the "expansion of that settlement and the influence of the Pilgrim Fathers throughout the world."[31] With notions about the Pilgrims steeped in decades of stereotypical fantasy, the founders devoted themselves to strict standards of historical accuracy rooted in deep and careful research.[32] Following the models for Greenfield Village and Colonial Williamsburg, the builders of Plimoth Plantation began erecting replicas of a model "first house," and "Fort-Meeting House" on Plymouth's waterfront. In 1957, plans for a reconstructed *Mayflower* came to fruition, and the outdoor museum, Plimoth Plantation, opened for its first full season in 1959 and quickly became the biggest show in town. These foundations demonstrate how the intent of the museum was to close the distance between colonial fantasies and the best available historical reconstructions.[33] The expansive programming and special events undertaken there render it a busy place year-round (the plantation itself is open from March through November), but especially during the Thanksgiving season. Indeed, Plimoth Plantation became an arbiter for those in search of the "first Thanksgiving," and Thanksgiving observances there are a peak tourist time, including coveted tickets for the elaborate Thanksgiving dinners that close the season.[34]

Plimoth Plantation has remade itself on multiple occasions since opening for full-time business. In the late 1960s, under the auspices of archaeologist James Deetz, the plantation cast aside the original mode of guides answering questions in contemporary American accents with their own points of view alongside wax mannequin figures, in search of an approach that sought a more accurate capturing of the past. Deetz and his Brown University students conducted archaeological digs and strove to pin down historical details in a drive for strict accuracy. The plantation also changed the year of interpretation in the English Village to 1627, the historical moment when the land was divided into individual plots, when the most richly descriptive accounts of the plantation were recorded, providing an abundance of detail to aid in closing the distance by adding complexity to the entire operation. The responses to Deetz's revisions to align the plantation with strict authenticity demonstrate the overall ambivalence many feel about closing historical distance versus the demands of the profit motive in historical tourism. Not everyone was pleased by the 1960s scholarly revisionism that debunked romanticism around the Pilgrims. It is risky, it turns out, to hew too closely to the actual (or revised) narrative of national origins. Still, the wax mannequins gave way to "interpreters" at this time, and although the museum planned to one day include an Indian village, through 1973 it employed non-Indian guides to interact with visitors. During the 1970s, Plimoth Plantation took the lead in the living history world by embracing active, dynamic approaches to exhibits and became a "working village."[35] Employment there as an interpreter requires deep knowledge of historically accurate information rooted in evidence from the seventeenth century.

As greater emphasis was placed upon scholarly research and historical accuracy at the museum, it soon became clear that the interpretation of Plymouth in 1627 would be incomplete without intellectual and cultural contributions from neighboring Wampanoag communities. During the 1970 Thanksgiving Day protest, activists insisted that Native peoples' experiences and perspectives should no longer be silenced or overshadowed by Pilgrim-centered narratives. During the protest, activists boarded the *Mayflower II* to tear down the English flag, tossed the shipmaster's mannequin overboard, and buried Plymouth Rock under sand before they headed to the Thanksgiving dinner at Plimoth Plantation, flipping over the tables and seizing the turkeys. Plimoth Plantation's response to the protests was to institute the Native American Program (now the Wampanoag Indigenous Program, or WIP), including bringing in local Wampanoag leaders from the community as advisers.[36] Today, the Wampanoag Homesite is where tourists begin their visit to Plimoth Plantation (fig. 35). There, they encounter Indigenous *wetu* (mat-covered houses), a bark longhouse, crops tended by Natives, a cooking site, and Native interpreters clad in period clothing (especially deerskin) engaged in a variety of daily activities. As the plantation website indicates, the interpreters "are very proud of their Native heritage, and knowledgeable of the traditions, stories, technology, pastimes, music and dance of the people who have lived in this region for more than 10,000 years. Ask lots of questions! You may be surprised what you will learn." Since its inception, the WIP has been a dynamic and changing element of Plimoth Plantation that allows viewers to construct a more complete picture of settler-Wampanoag interactions and Wampanoag lifeways.[37]

Notably, from the beginning, the Wampanoag Homesite used third-person interpretation in modern English by Native interpreters in contrast to the first-person role playing exclusively employed by interpreters in the English Village until recently.[38] The associate director of the WIP, Darius Coombs, explains that the third-person interpretation was chosen because guests would not understand Wampanoag, and because visitors are curious about "not just what happened in 1620 but what's going on today. . . . When is the next powwow going to be? What's going on with the language project?"[39] Because visitors come from across the country but may have limited contact with Native

FIGURE 35. Wampanoag Homesite welcome sign, Plimoth Plantation.
Photograph by Jean O'Brien.

people and nations, the WIP interpreters must represent both historical Wampanoag people and present-day Indigenous nations across America. Reflecting on the educational value of the program for visitors, Coombs explained that "there's not many places you're going to go and have that opportunity."[40] This interpretive approach might break the fantasy of time travel, but it also allows interpreters to close the distance between the past and the present when they answer visitors' questions. This is an opportunity for Native interpreters to challenge popular depictions of Indians as static denizens of the past and to intervene in narratives of disappearance — themes that emerged among some passersby as they reflected on the meaning of the *Massasoit* monument far from Plymouth.

Native interpreters must not only master seventeenth-century Wampanoag history and material culture, but also communicate accurate and informed portrayals of contemporary Native life, which demands a great deal of patience and emotional labor.[41] Guests sometimes engage in abusive behavior, and WIP staff must take up and take on visitors' insensitive and ignorant commentary as teachers. Guests to the Wampanoag Homesite must feel welcome to ask questions, but also need a surprising level of guidance in respectful engagement so as not to create a hostile work environment for the Native staff. Visitors must be instructed not to arrive in "Indian" costumes or refer to the homes (*wetu*) as "huts."[42] Native interpreters endured "war whoops" from guests until a small sign was recently posted at the entrance to the homesite and drastically reduced this upsetting behavior.[43] Coombs explained to us that the sign intended to communicate "the rights and wrongs on stereotypes before entering the Wampanoag Homesite" and asserted that "this sign means the most for Native people."

Another dimension of the emotional labor performed by WIP interpreters involves the constant emotional demands of engaging with history. "We just don't come in and play Indian. We are Indigenous people twenty-four hours a day," Coombs said. WIP interpreters must interact with some 3,000 guests a day (6,000 during the Thanksgiving season) and repeatedly relay Native peoples' experiences with colonization, genocide, devastating diseases, and slavery. "We're never going to shy away from the hard issues," he said. "It's what we do." Yet Coombs explains that it's difficult for interpreters to "[talk] about our own people dying off and being taken captive as slaves" without feeling anger rise up. "You know ... it just festers inside. And swoosh, it spills right out." But Native interpreters cannot become visibly upset when discussing these subjects, lest the visitor become uncomfortable and shut down the interaction. "We can teach [Native interpreters] how to talk to the guests" without taking their anger out on them, Coombs explained, "but there's a lot of inner pain in Native people." Each workday involves an emotional trade-off between the comfort of the interpreter and the education of the guests: interpreters are asked to regulate their own emotional experience of living with history to more effectively teach visitors about difficult and painful histories. But, according to Coombs, that is the main requirement of the job. "Changing [guests'] way of thought—that's what we have the opportunity to do at the Wampanoag Homesite. A guest might come in one way, but they're going to leave another."[44] The notion that the WIP interpreters have the power to change visitors' perceptions about Native people in the past, as well as in the present, is a tremendous responsibility with high emotional stakes. Interpreters strive to close the historical distance by evoking empathy for Indigenous perspectives from guests.

From the perspective of Wampanaog and other Indigenous staff in the WIP, programming is a deeply personal embodiment of history, representing the continuation of cherished traditions that carry the unequivocal message that "we're still here."[45] From the carving of a sixteen-foot mishoon (dugout canoe) using traditional methods headed up by Darius Coombs to the 2017 project in which Sokoki Abenaki artisan Bob Charlebois in the museum's Craft Center makes a wampum belt "using ancient methods," Native people close the distance in preserving or reviving Native ways (fig. 36).[46] WIP staff voice the deep meaning of their work: "The program preserves our lives as they would have been led in the past" (James Hakenson, Aquinnah Wampanoag); "The Wampanoag Indigenous Program is a platform where Native people, in our own words, can shape guest perceptions and opinions about Indigenous cultures" (Brian Bartibogue, Mikmaq); "At the Wampanoag Homesite, we have the ability to acquaint the public with a truer, more balanced history" (Erin Weeden, Mikmaq); "The Wampanoag Indigenous Program is one of the few hubs that help Native people maintain traditional skills" (Danielle Hill, Mashpee Wampanoag).[47] When asked about the deeper meaning of working in the WIP on historic arts and technologies, Coombs replied, "It's recovering our culture and maintaining our identity. I would say to any Indigenous person, 'Hold on to what you can and revive what you can revive. You'll be more in tune with yourself and what you are as a person.'"[48]

Other recent interpretive changes at Plimoth Plantation reveal additional complexities that closing the distance may entail. Following a 2014 National Endowment for the Humanities conference that brought Native and non-Native scholars to Plymouth to consult about the plantation's interpretive approach, the year of interpretation was changed from 1627 to 1624, and staff instituted new programming as a result.[49] The year 1624 would become the new temporal benchmark for programming because, according to Plimoth Plantation's 2015 annual report, it "was a year in which the Pilgrims faced seemingly insurmountable spiritual, economic, agricultural and political challenges in Plymouth Colony. 1624 reveals the fragility of the colonial experiment and the complexities of relations with Native communities. Visitors could see that

FIGURE 36. Phillip Wynne with a mishoon being carved with the traditional burn method, Plimoth Plantation. *Courtesy of Plimoth Plantation.*

to the Pilgrims the future was not inevitable (as it seems to us now peering through the lens of 400 years)." Or, as Plimouth Plantation deputy director Richard Pickering put it, 1627 was "too safe a year" that had allowed Plimoth Plantation to skirt around "troubles with violence and Native people." This temporal move emphasizes contingency and opens new interpretive possibilities for conveying what it was like for colonists and Native people "on a knife edge of survival and diplomatic challenges."[50]

The programming revisions were intended to explore "1624 and other seventeenth-century subjects in multiple presentational formats: demonstrations, tours, theatrical performances, hands-on experiences and podcasts."[51] One major innovation involved staging performances of certain scenarios and then moving from first- to third-person interpretation to discuss with the audience the meaning of what they had witnessed. The Native and English interpreters engage one another in these historical scenarios to demonstrate for the audience how certain events can be understood from different perspectives. In addition to their educational value for visitors, Darius Coombs explains that such performances enable Indigenous staff to actively participate in the reconstruction of historical narratives by presenting their own interpretations of the past. Coombs illustrated this interpretive power by improvising during a trading scenario. In the performance, when the governor attempted to break up a trade between a Wampanoag man (performed by Coombs) and colonist John Jenny, Coombs simply walked away with his newly acquired brass kettle, seemingly in defiance of the governor's authority. In the debriefing with the audience that followed this performance, he explained, "The reason I walked away is that I don't go by the laws at Plymouth Colony. Maybe John Jenny has to but I don't. . . . He's the governor of Plymouth Colony; he's not my people's. He's not my chief."[52] As for reenacting scenarios more generally, Coombs observes that it allows the staff to "push the envelope all the time. . . . Let's see how people are going to react. . . . That's why we like doing a debriefing afterward. . . . 'What do you think of all that?' It makes it come alive. Scenarios like that need to come alive."[53]

Through his work cocreating and performing in these scenarios, Darius Coombs engages on a deep level with the figure of 8sâmeeqan. Coombs performs the role of 8sâmeeqan in numerous scenes that take place from 1621 through 1627, wearing carefully researched painted buckskin clothing, a black wolfskin, and a wampum belt reproduction crafted by Bob Charlebois (fig. 37).[54] The clothing allows Coombs to answer guests' questions about local materials and speak to the Massasoit's status as a tribal leader (something the mute and minimally clad monument cannot convey, especially to curious stu-

FIGURE 37. Darius Coombs in a performance at Plimoth Plantation.
Courtesy of Plimoth Plantation.

dents on the BYU campus). The clothing also serves as a culturally informed corrective to previous depictions of the Massasoit, when his role was performed by non-Indians wearing tan flannel outfits inspired by the theatrical look of the Wild West shows.[55] But material culture, even when it is carefully researched for historical accuracy, can only convey so much about the past. Performing 8sâmeeqan requires Coombs to develop a deeper understanding of the man's social, cultural, and political context in order to interpret his actions in the scenarios. "I got to really think about Massasoit when I played him. I had mixed feelings about some of the things he did, you know?" Coombs reflected. He may have been a steady friend to the Pilgrims and a shrewd diplomat who tested his allies' loyalty — Coombs interprets 8sâmeeqan in both ways without a sense of contradiction — but the end result of his actions cannot be changed and weighs heavily upon the educator. "I don't know if I really care for a whole lot of what he did in a way, you know? Sure, he was great for his diplomacy, when the colonists got here," Coombs explained. "But then, in reality, [Wampanoag people] face a lot of [the impacts] ourselves." He has encountered people from western Native nations who, upon learning that he is Wampanoag, accuse him of "let[ting] the people in" who unleashed colonialism across the continent. This awareness of present-day readings of the Massasoit's actions has shifted his interpretation to incorporate ambivalence and doubt. Was 8sâmeeqan as powerful as we have assumed? Could he have made different choices? "We hear about Massasoit being the great leader of the Wampanoag, but we can't be sure 100 percent. . . . We could be wrong there," Coombs explained.[56] As a Wampanoag man who has embodied the sachem in dramatic reenactments, Coombs knows what it means to grapple with a complex history that continues to shape the present: "[As] you learn more and more, you do look at him in a lot of different ways, you know?"[57]

Other educational programming at Plimoth Plantation also embraces multiple perspectives to close the distance between unbalanced and stereotypical representations of early seventeenth-century encounters. August 2002 witnessed a major undertaking at the plantation when the exhibit *Thanksgiving: Memory, Myth, & Meaning* opened to the public. Embracing multiple perspectives on the fateful events of 1621, this project drew on the expertise of the Wampanoag nation, its own Native staff, and more than 100 Natives who participated in the production of a video that re-created the 1621 scene.[58] Linda Coombs, associate director of the Wampanoag Indian Program at the time, wrote that "the exhibit peels away layers of the Thanksgiving myth until it arrives at the truest history, and uses not just a single author to present and interpret all aspects of that history, but incorporates the actual voices of historic participants in order to achieve a much more complete history."[59] This project entailed inclusion of Wampanoag peoples and perspectives that sought to address centuries of inaccuracies surrounding this myth-laden history. Challenging the Thanksgiving myth was no small undertaking, considering how the story has long been propounded in print and replicated more recently in everything from museum exhibits to the silver screen in productions such as the film *Squanto: A Warrior's Tale* (1994), which depicted Indigenous history in ways that Linda Coombs and other Indigenous people of New England find unrecognizable. As part of the exhibit, she secured funding to film a reenactment of the Thanksgiving scene that involved 100 Indigenous people in Native dress over a three-day shoot. Darius Coombs helped assemble the cast from the Native community, an experience he described as "awesome!"[60]

Linda Coombs points out that meaningful collaboration is "a gradual and ongoing process that must be consistently maintained and monitored. It is the process and not just the end result that is important—the process of the museum's two cultures working collaboratively when necessary, separately if that is what is needed, and recognizing when either is the appropriate method."[61] The coproduction of *Thanksgiving: Memory, Myth, & Meaning* throughout the entire process and including the entire Wampanoag community "shows much respect for the Wampanoag."[62] In striving for accuracy, Coombs adds, "what we would like to change are the attitudes that keep us in that place of omission; where one part or 'side' of history is perceived as the whole. It is not just a matter of Wampanoag People having the opportunity to tell our 'side of the story'. It is a matter that all of us see the history of the seventeenth century (or of any time period) holistically. There are no sides, but only one whole story."[63]

How do visitors experience these efforts to close the historical distance? Plimoth Plantation remains extremely popular: it ranks number one of sixty-two "things to do in Plymouth" and has received a Certificate of Excellence from TripAdvisor.[64] Reviews available in August 2016 translated into four and a half stars out of five. Most reviewers reported overwhelmingly positive experiences, although some found the Wampanoag Homesite underdeveloped and less friendly than other parts of the plantation, which hints at the costs of the emotional labor expended by Indigenous educators. One observer from Boston clearly grasped the perspective of Indigenous public historians at the homesite when he observed, "The Native American village is staffed by tribal members, they are NOT actors. . . . The pilgrim village was wonderful too, and so real!" Others thought the experience dull, and some thought it expensive. But the favorable ranking is reflected in the comments guests made about how Plimoth made them experience the past. A mother from nearby New Bedford wrote, "I love seeing the Pilgrims in their cottages, working as if we really just stepped back into the 16th century [sic]. . . . The Native Americans are amazing as well, a very educational experience that is fun as well for all ages."[65] A woman from Florida reported it was an "awesome experience. You step back into history—total immersion. The people you meet in the plantation have become the real people who lived there—it feels real."[66] And another, from London, Ontario, wrote, "It's like you are talking to somebody through a time warp."[67] "We're 65 and everything we ever learned about the Pilgrims went down the drain. Now the REAL story of what happened comes out—and we like truth better than fiction!" noted a couple from San Diego.[68]

Plimoth Plantation invites active engagement in a sort of embodied history meant to convey the sense of time travel so clearly revealed in guest reactions. Guests are encouraged to imagine themselves in the place of seventeenth-century historical actors as a leisure, educational, experiential activity. This approach to historical memory making contrasts with the ways *Massasoit* stands mute on Cole's Hill and elsewhere, allowing passersby and those motivated by active engagement with the statue to consider historical complexity only when plaques prompt such contemplation, as in the case of Plymouth. Both of these kinds of experiences involve historical representation, but in very different ways, one dynamic and participatory, and the other passive and contemplative.

A very different way of embodying history to close the distance came in the form of *Colonial House*, a reality TV–style PBS series produced by New York–based Thirteen/WNET and Wall to Wall Television in the U.K., which premiered in May 2004. This was what now appears to be the final installment in what PBS calls "experiential history," which followed other period-based series beginning with *The 1900 House*, followed by *Manor House*, *1940s House*, and *Frontier House*. The eight-part *Colonial House* is billed as being about "indentured servitude. No baths or showers. Public punishments. Welcome to daily life in the year 1628!" The website seeks to entice viewers by declaring, "Think colonial life was all about pious Pilgrims, powdered wigs and freedom for all! Think again! Two dozen modern-day time travelers find out the hard way what early American colonial life was really like when they take up residence in *Colonial House*."[69] The cast brings together men, women, and children from the United States and England, who arrive on shipboard to "their New World," charged with building a profitable colony, "like those of America's first settlers, using only the tools and technology of the era." The website teases that *Colonial House* will challenge viewers' understandings of the new colony, and let them watch the cast members in their daily struggles with each other, the weather, their living conditions, and intense physical labor. Viewers will witness disputes over the class and gender expectations of the times that have been left in the past, strict religious observance regulations, and strictures on cast members' behavior around even profanity.[70]

Though set in 1628 coastal Maine on Passamaquoddy land, *Colonial House* is clearly a project about re-creating the landing of the Pilgrims in Plymouth and their initial struggles to build a colony, complete with staged encounters with Native people meant to replicate that element of the story. The show takes place a year after the baseline of interpretation that Plimoth Plantation moved to in the 1960s. But the parallels intended by this historical reality show are unmistakable, and it is no surprise that Plimoth Plantation played a leading role in shaping the series. *Colonial House* drew on expertise from Plimoth in building the village where it is set, and Plimoth Plantation personnel served as living history experts (along with counterparts from England) in preparing "the colonists for life in 1628."[71] The seventeen chosen for the experience spent two weeks at Plimoth Plantation in intensive training in the technology, material culture, and attire of the time. Staff began building the structures on location in late 2002 and working on the furnishings and provisions, familiar tasks for Plimoth Plantation staff but now imparted to people who would spend four months living the experience in a remote location for the cameras.[72] Plimoth Plantation followed up on its involvement with an exhibit on the series, *Setting the Scene for* Colonial House, which opened in 2004.

Colonial House also relied on Native experts. John Bear Mitchell (Penobscot), a lecturer of Wabanaki studies at the University of Maine and the Wabanaki Center outreach and student development coordinator, writes of his experience as both a historical consultant and participant in several encounters between the cast and the Passamaquoddy and Penobscot, on whose land the village was constructed, for the series website. He points to the historical documentation revealing "a future of uneasiness" between these peoples, who established trade in the early years, but hoped the audience was able to see "the humanness of our interactions and my tribal people as a very hospitable people."[73] Other Native experts from the Native homelands of the village site included Donald Soctomah (Passamaquoddy)—an expert on the tribe's history and culture, whose career with the tribe included work with its forestry service and as the tribe's representative to the Maine legislature—with involvement as well from George and Patrick Sabattis and the Passamaquoddy Joint Tribal Council.

Linda Coombs, now program director of the Aquinnah Cultural Center on Martha's Vineyard, and Ramona Peters, director of historic preservation for the Mashpee, joined Mitchell and Soctomah as Native American consultants for the series. Both are highly visible Native intellectuals, and they appeared in one of the most powerful of the episodes, the seventh, called "The Reckoning." Several Native people affiliated with Plimoth Plantation also appear in this episode, which features a clan of Wampanoag traveling to visit relatives in the area. In one important exchange inside the village, Wampanoag Nancy Eldredge chastises a fellow Native for accepting food from the colonists, which they had all agreed not to do once they decided to enter the village. She sternly corrects him, "We just don't want it to appear like, you know, happy Indians with the first Thanksgiving . . . because it wasn't like that at all. And if we were being treated in a good way even today and our land wasn't still being taken and we weren't still thought of as unintelligent savages, then, you know, I would say fine."[74] Following this tense exchange, which includes nervous acknowledgement from the colonists, the voice-over informs the viewer, "Relations between the colonists and Native Americans are romanticized in the traditional Thanksgiving story. It's commonly thought that in 1621, the Wampanoag joined the colonists in a friendly three-day feast." Ramona Peters points out that "we know that wouldn't have been the case," which the colonists also acknowledge must be "right." The voice-over adds detail Peters herself has cited to underscore her point: "The real story is that ninety Wampanoag men showed up after hearing gunfire. Instead of war, they found the Plymouth colonists preparing for a feast. In the interests of diplomacy, the Wampanoag joined in. But the event was never to be repeated." The voice-over subsequently informs the viewer about the Day of Mourning that has been held on Thanksgiving Day in Plymouth since 1970.

This scene sets up one of the most soul-searching moments in the whole series. At a solemn meal in the evening, the colonists process their day. Paul Hunt, an Englishman who portrayed a servant for the company in the series, laments how one Native woman in the encounter "kept mentioning the English and looking at me in particular, and said, 'You guys, the English, came over here, and you did this, and you did that.' . . . If she said 'your ancestors,' it would be one scenario. . . . I just found that quite offensive." Carolyn Heinz, a vocal character who was at that time in the series portraying the governor's wife, retorted, "Your society was the imperial power that colonized for 300 years half the world, so if you've got a little bit of discomfort about it, probably does you a little bit of good, too. . . . Nobody really likes to have it pointed out that your people and your culture has been responsible for their suffering. . . . We need to have it pointed it out, though." Michelle Voorhees-Rossi, sited in a free household in the village, assents. The scene shows her real-life husband, John Voorhees, who revealed himself in the first episode to be a "half-breed" Paiute who felt uncomfortable with the *first* first contact scene depicted in the series, looks similarly uncomfortable here. Carolyn continues, "It suddenly sunk in in a way it hadn't up till then. That I'm going along with being an imperialist." (Some murmur in assent.) She adds, "It didn't really sink in on me that I'm engaging—I'm reenacting a whole system that I don't believe in and disapprove of. And yet it's the roots of our own nation, who we are." The contemplation of the group continues, and not for the first or last time in the series, Carolyn gets the final say. She reflects that being troubled over the United States in the context of the world (by calculation, post-9/11) prompted her to think of participating in the project: "I thought how good it might be to go back and to relive an earlier, simpler, purer point in our national history. So here I am, and of course, what I'm discovering is there were no pure moments in our national history. This is not a pure moment. We were already moving in. We were already driven by greed and ambition. And we were willing to shove away the Native people. So what was better then than now? [Sniffles are audible.] I don't know." The episode closes with silent contemplation over a fire.

From the first episode, the intent of Native consultants and participants to confront efforts to freeze them in a sanitized past was revealed when Mitchell announced to the cast members, "We have been through the largest genocide, the largest holocaust on the soil of the United States. We are recipients of all that death, and the holocaust that happened on this soil was one of embarrassment for this country." "The Reckoning" brings this Indigenous perspective into bold relief, with the buildup to the confrontation in the village. The narrator foreshadows the action in the episode by announcing, "The Natives are prepared to confront the settlers over the issue of colonization." Over the course of several scenes, the argument unfolds. Aquinnah Wampanoag Jonathan Perry points out, "Being here is a chance to represent our people to show that we are a continuing culture and a continuing people. A modern people. As well as having deep roots with our ancestors. And to have our story heard."[75] In the same scene, Eldredge justifies Indigenous anger as legitimate, "especially when it seems like America in general doesn't like our history to be told." Mashpee Alice Lopez illustrates the ongoing impact of the structure of settler colonialism by insisting that "Indian land is still being taken all over the country, and as long as you don't acknowledge Native people, then you don't have to acknowledge that you're doing anything wrong to anyone."

In contrast to the confrontation so boldly embodied in "The Reckoning," there are ways in which, in spite of the laborious efforts to hew closely to an "authentic" re-creation of this American origin story, *Colonial House* instead engages in the production of generic narratives about encounters between Native and non-Native people. Liz Lodge looked back and remembered thinking, "We had, at the production team's request, not focused on colonization from the perspective of the Indigenous people. First encounters with both Passamaquoddy and Wampanoag would occur in the colony, rather than in a classroom and the manner in which colonists interacted with them would draw as much on twenty-first-century mindsets as on seventeenth-century world view."[76] There is a wrestling with the past in these scenes to try to capture a visceral sense of the time, such as in the first encounter scene when Passamaquoddy John Bear Mitchell observes, "When I first walked into the village it was a little scary. Fear would be felt on both sides." George Sabattis adds that, in this scene, "we just tried to make it as they felt, years ago." These and other scenes grapple with what first encounters must have felt like even while the voice-over points out here and elsewhere details of scholarly, Native-centered interpretations of historical encounters between Natives and non-Natives. The narrator at this point, clearly drawing from historical scholarship, informs the viewers that "in the 1620s, the English settlers and Native Americans depended on each other for trade. . . . Relations between Native Americans and settlers were always unstable." "The Reckoning" elevates the grappling for experiential meaning to a different level, confronting the first Thanksgiving narrative directly and in a way that provokes cast members to seriously engage with conflicting narratives about history. As Carolyn Heinz said to Ramona Peters when the Wampanoag confront the cast in the village, "I have been deeply moved by meeting you, and it's making me think about my own role and my ancestors. And this has been very meaningful to me." "The Reckoning" represents a crescendo in the collision of historical narratives about origins and a powerful rejection of frozen narratives that refuse to explain the origins and still-reverberating consequences of the United States as a settler-colonial state.

How did viewers process the embodiment of this experiment in historical experience? Judging from the ten viewers who posted reviews of *Colonial House* on its Internet Movie Database (IMDb) page, the series escaped widespread acclaim and appreciation. One who took the time to reflect on it noted, "Many viewers seem to fault the program for its lack of rigor in forcing the colonists to stick with seventeenth-century laws. Overall I found the program educational but it really did teach more about twenty-first century views toward the colonial period than it did actual seventeenth-century life." This viewer added particular criticism for Native accounts of what this history would have been like for their ancestors as being "tedious modern day politicized rants," suggesting that they preferred historical distancing to reckoning with a contested past.[77] Others echoed the critique that *Colonial House* failed to properly

adhere to early seventeenth-century laws and codes of conduct around everything from gender roles to class hierarchies. Overwhelmingly, those who took
the time to post their reactions on the IMDb site faulted the series for its failure to close the distance between the present and the past. Overall, the show
ranked 7.6 stars out of 10 from the 140 viewers who ranked the series.[78]

The executive director of Plimoth Plantation, Nancy Brennan, wrote in
2004, "No contemporary individual can occupy the space, time, preoccupa-
tions, and mindset of other individuals living centuries ago," but efforts at historical reenactment such as *Colonial House* open a particular kind of window
on grappling with the past.[79] Paul Hunt, the laborer from Manchester, England
in real life who took such umbrage at the confrontation with the Wampanoag
in the village, reflected on the experience by saying, "I learnt more about religion, history, appreciation and understanding of people and my own life and
personality than I ever thought I would, and consider myself very lucky to experience what I did."

Among the actual people involved in this virtual history project were Indigenous people meant (by implication) to be Wampanoag. Linda Coombs
pointed out that the producers never followed through on creating a Native
council composed of both Passamaquoddy (on whose land the series was
filmed) and Wampanoag people to consult with for "appropriate representation of Native People in the program." They instead took the easier route of
working mostly with Passamaquoddy people on whose land they filmed the
series, thus treating Indians who are not the same as generic. While Coombs
applauded Passamaquoddy efforts to counter imagery of savagery in their
friendly interactions with the cast members, this left out the larger "issues of
colonization the producers were looking for." This is the backdrop of "The
Reckoning," which involved what, she stated, "must have been THE worst day
of everyone's life." Filmed during a twelve-hour day in the pouring rain without
provisions or the means to cook for themselves, the Wampanoag delegation
faced the ordeal with determination. The sun broke the next day for filming
in the village. Having decided sharing food with the cast would send a signal
of cordial relations, the Natives made the decision to decline any such offers,
because "we were attempting to impress upon the audience the full aspects of
colonization" and "the power of visual images."[80]

Those Wampanoag who participated in "The Reckoning" believed they
would have an opportunity to provide input on how the footage was used,
which never happened. Yet Coombs relates that the incident in the village
(and another one about a stolen chicken, which prompted rebukes from the
other Wampanoags) did not garner the negative reactions they feared. In-

stead, the incidents illuminated Wampanoag culture, and "some came to the realization of what colonization means then and now to Native Peoples, and what it means for all Americans." As Coombs powerfully points out, "Colonization is still something that is part of our lives. It is not something that has ended, but whose connections start in the past and maintain a strong hold on the present. It has wrought profound changes in our lives and cultures from the seventeenth century to the present that were not of our choice or of our making." After all, *Colonial House*, inadvertently or not, conveyed the larger meanings the Wampanoag people hoped for: "Such awareness is not just good for some of us, but for all of us."[81] From this perspective as well, "'play-acting' a colony for the purposes of having a certain type of 'experience' is a stunning thought."[82] The Wampanoag puzzled, too, over what would motivate the four people of color who became cast members to participate in a venture that would not have included them.[83]

Linda Coombs reflected on *Colonial House* from her perspective as a long-term associate director of WIP: "Working in a forum such as [WIP] . . . where one is immersed in analyzing and interpreting the seventeenth century, at times places one squarely in the face of dealing with the uncomfortable, difficult, and sometimes very painful issues of history. In WIP we constantly field these issues. We need to keep them subjective in order to relate Native perspective on them (the primary charge of our job), and we also need to stay in a place where we are not overwhelmed by the full depth of the meaning of the manifestations of colonization. It is a balancing act, but Native People have learned to accommodate having 'a foot in two canoes,' living in two worlds, as the sayings go. . . . Being involved in the *Colonial House* project was often an odd mixture of the above."[84] While the producers insisted they wanted "Native involvement and Native perspective," they did not follow through in such a way that would "qualify for what would be respectful treatment of Native staff and community members during the process of getting us on film."[85]

RECKONINGS

One possible take-away from the divergent readings of *Massasoit* in its far-flung locations is the capacity of a statue to offer a safe way to wrestle with the discomfort involved in coming to terms with settler colonialism as an ongoing structure. Except in Plymouth since 1970, the other *Massasoit* installations offer passersby the opportunity to do so on their own time and place and in their own way, with the message of the historical markers virtually erasing the possibility of contesting a simplistic message of pacific colonialism or even an Indigenous history rooted in narrative specificity. Our interviews in places other than Plymouth indicated a strong inclination for passersby of *Massasoit* to internalize the distancing message the Improved Order of Red Men hoped people would take away with them: the affirmation of colonial settlement through the welcoming posture of the statue. In Plymouth since 1970, the new markers and the annual protests (in addition to revisions to the curriculum insisted upon by the UAINE) demand a fuller engagement with a contentious history to be reckoned with in places where Indigenous people are dramatically a part of the narrative in the present and future, and where they had more than a thing or two to say about the past and how it reverberates in the present.

At Plimoth Plantation, guests occasionally voice discomfort over the presence of the Wampanoag Homesite and the approach to depicting Indigenous people, but most regard that element of the site as secondary to the experience they seek, which is to put themselves in the place of the Pilgrims. In *Colonial House*, cast members experience history as hardship, though mostly at a safe distance from Indians, except for the periodic visits of Passamaquoddy and Penobscot people meant to convey the fear of the unknown and uneasy negotiations for coexistence until "The Reckoning," an episode that drips with discomfort. Taken together, these three very different kinds of encounters offer different windows onto the role of discomfort in public history venues that engages with the problem of political, cultural, and historical distance. There is ambivalence about closing the distance manifested in each of these locations, and there is a connection to commercial appeals. Those who profit from historical tourism of various sorts run a risk if they hew too closely to the actual (or revised) narrative they seek to commemorate.

All three of these kinds of public history venues, *Massasoit*, Plimoth Plantation, and *Colonial House*, attest to the durability of national narratives of origin attached to Plymouth and, in particular, the place of the Massasoit (whether depicted as he was or generically) in mediating the history of encounter. In all three of these settings, the generic message of peaceable embrace stands in tension with Indigenous interventions about what really happened, and all of them revolved around this history transpiring in the place (approximated, in the case of *Colonial House*). A mobile *Massasoit* reveals differing receptions of history: once uprooted from his homelands, 8sâmeeqan's likeness is more likely, though not conclusively, to be read as generic, and the likelihood of *Massasoit* inviting complex narratives about Indigenous history and the nation plummets, underscoring rather than closing the distance between the past and the present.

Chapter Four

MARKETING

Like most public memorials, *Massasoit* was sculpted, cast, and installed as a result of fund-raising based on a particular historical narrative. The fund-raising
process adapted Pilgrim-centered stories of 8sâmeeqan to a philanthropic
marketplace that, in the first decades of the twentieth century, responded to a
rhetoric of civic duty. The resulting *Massasoit* installation fixed those stories in
place with stone and metal and contributed to the development of a lucrative
heritage tourist industry on the Plymouth waterfront. But unlike most memorials, *Massasoit* did not remain in Plymouth—or *only* in Plymouth. *Massasoit*
has continued to travel from a specific commemorative geography into bound-
less commercial realms. The monument has been folded into the consumer
landscape of Plymouth, while innumerable replicas have been dispersed into
the commercial spaces of shopping malls, auction houses, souvenir shops, and
eBay. While many scholars have examined memorials in place, little is known
about the commercial appeal of commemorative Indian statuary and the resulting narrative effects over space and time. How did *Massasoit* help to commercially brand Plymouth as a tourist destination, and what happens to the
memorial and consumerist function of *Massasoit* when it is removed from
the Plymouth context and made available on a shelf beside seashell charm
bracelets or alongside a collection of LPs on eBay? When *Massasoit* became
a commodity and memorial at the same time, the original intention of those
who commissioned the statue would be secondary to its commercial potential. No longer a symbol for a singular historical narrative, the replicas could
be usurped for market purposes—whether branding, advertising, or outright
profit. The consumptive modes surrounding *Massasoit* reveal how capitalism is
intertwined with settler-colonial fantasies while standing in tension with place
and memory.

As Marita Sturken has argued in connection to concepts as disparate as AIDS memorialization and memorial culture around 9/11 and the former World Trade Center site, consumerism represents a response to national trauma that resembles a "tourist" relationship to complex histories that helped trigger violent events, and it encourages a sense of innocence and victimhood through tragedy on the part of the consumer. Just as purchasing a teddy bear clad in an NYPD T-shirt or a snow globe resurrecting the Twin Towers brings comfort to the consumer and papers over the fraught global political economy that gave rise to the events of 9/11, tourists who collect miniature *Massasoits* or Pilgrim salt and pepper shakers are consuming a comforting history of peaceful coexistence and welcoming embrace as the origin story of the United States, which they can take with them to the far reaches of the country and beyond.[1] Although Sturken's book takes up contemporary and very different kinds of national events, we wish to extend her arguments in order to think about how comfort culture, which the tourist industry and the commercial art market seek to target, structures the story of national origins in Plymouth. She argues that reenactment through popular culture, including the consumption of souvenirs, represents responses to trauma that are meant to bring comfort in what many experience as terrifying times. In the case of *Massasoit* as a signifier of Thanksgiving and national origins, what is elided in this comfort consumerism is the long and deeply uncomfortable actual history of settler colonialism that sits on the sidelines in Plymouth in favor of a story of national innocence.[2]

FUND-RAISING

In the late nineteenth and early twentieth centuries, public fund-raising for statuary art could be a decades-long endeavor that proceeded in fits and starts, often stymied along the way by economic, cultural, and political factors. Economic conditions in the United States shifted rapidly with cycles of booms and depressions in the late nineteenth century, and conflicts in Europe destabilized the global commodity market in the early twentieth. When workers faced cut wages and unemployment, it was difficult to convince Americans to send money for the construction of a statue, particularly when churches, hospitals, and libraries also relied upon donations.[3] Even at the height of "statue mania" in the United States, numerous memorial projects, both national and local, competed for subscriptions. Potential donors had to be convinced not only that a project could be completed but also that the monument reflected their values, a shared sense of identity, and didactic goals targeted at future generations.

Although the fund-raising campaign for *Massasoit* stretched over eight years and was interrupted by World War I, it ultimately met its goal by attaching a national significance to the historical figure and thus encouraged financial investment. The idea for the publicly funded monument was first proposed in 1913, and by 1915, the Committee on the Massasoit Memorial had begun soliciting donations from its national membership. In a motion in the national meeting, the committee announced the sale of limited-edition souvenir pocket pieces to the 400,000 members for twenty-five cents each. The large coins featured a facsimile of one of Dallin's early clay models on one side and the inscription "To the Memory of Massasoit, by the Improved Order of Red Men. 1620–1920" on the other. The pieces would be of such "historic character," the committee promised, that every buyer would wish to hand down the souvenir to his or her descendants.[4] The committee then used a combination of patriotism and shaming to encourage sales.

A nine-and-a-half-foot bronze statue depicting 8sâmeeqan, the fund-raising committee asserted, was perfectly in line with the mission of the IORM to honor (through imitation) the noble features of Indigenous life as founding principles of the United States.[5] In order to appeal to the wider membership, and to convince the order that the monument would represent the national membership rather than "any particular Reservation" (using the terminology of the local and regional chapters of the IORM that spun off from the Indian play of the organization), the committee made a case for 8sâmeeqan's importance to the creation of the nation. The memorial was to be a tribute to the Massasoit for making it possible "for the Pilgrims to lay the foundations of this great Nation."[6] A truly patriotic soul would be moved by the sentiment of such a memorial; in fact, one's devotion to the ideals of the nation could be measured in *Massasoit* pocket piece orders. "Who, therefore, can refuse to purchase one of these souvenirs at such a small outlay, when such contribution is to be used for such a glorious purpose . . . ?" the committee rhetorically asked.[7]

To the surprise of the Massachusetts Improved Order of Red Men, the Massasoit (and *Massasoit*) did not initially represent a national icon, and the subscriptions for the pocket pieces did not flow in as expected. After a year, the committee admitted to being "almost discouraged" by the lukewarm response to its efforts and chastised the members for failing to honor "the most noted Chief in the history of this country."[8] The problem, perhaps, was that the committee failed to convince the leadership of the local chapters that the Plymouth statue represented the nation, and thus all the membership. A case had to be made to the larger organization for the importance of the memorial. The committee then targeted the Tribes, or local chapters, by suggesting the leaders purchase coins for a quarter of their members and take on the task (and financial risk) of collecting the donations from individuals.[9]

The narrative of the Massasoit's friendship was not the only story to be marketed with the memorial. Although the statue would depict Šsámeeqan, the committee prophesized that the effect on Plymouth tourists would be a greater appreciation for the work of the fraternal order. The future statue would be accompanied by a bronze plate identifying the Improved Order of Red Men as the donors and would therefore "create a feeling of admiration [in the tourist] for our Order as a great American Institution." Clearly, the bronze was meant to say a lot more about the settler nation and the IORM than about the Pokanoket leader and the persistence of Wampanoag people in New England.

The national membership was convinced by the motion and voted unanimously to support what they deemed "a project conceived in patriotism, and born of honor."[10] The next year the newly incorporated body known as the Massasoit Memorial Association announced that 10,000 pocket pieces had been sold, and the effort had collected over $2,000.[11] The fund-raising effort fixed on the sentimental and performative to link consumption of objects to patriotism. As ideal citizens, IORM members were encouraged to experience the founding of the nation through souvenir pocket pieces; these objects would convey a connection to a place and a particular historical narrative.[12] As Marita Sturken has argued, consumer culture has long played an important role in shaping American national identity: "The equation of patriotism with consumerism not only reveals the paucity of national identification in the United States, with its ready-made symbols and disconnection from history, but also demonstrates the central role that innocence plays in American culture."[13] The patriotic purchase of a souvenir pocket piece would make possible the erection of a monument that would, in turn, beget pride in the nation and honor the work of the organization in communicating the nation's greatness. The effort to fund it also tells us a great deal about the connection between patriotism, public memory, and consumerism.

In early 1917, two years into the fund-raising campaign and facing lagging support as the United States entered World War I, the Massasoit Memorial Association decided to encourage donations by expanding and personalizing the souvenir offerings. While members could continue to purchase the pocket pieces for a quarter, the association decided to direct its efforts to the sale of a "beautiful photogravure certificate, with the name of the subscriber engrossed thereon" for a dollar.[14] Perhaps a certificate that could be framed and displayed in one's office offered members greater public recognition as patriots and benevolent donors than a pocket piece. In a last-minute special offer in 1921, the association advertised an eleven-and-a-half-inch "perfect Replica" of the statue for members who made a personal donation of twenty dollars.[15] These fund-raising techniques, in addition to opening the call for subscriptions to the wider public—mainly Plymouth residents invested in boosting their town's reputation and tourist visitation—helped the IORM to finally reach its goal of $22,000 (roughly $275,000 in 2017 dollars). In the final accounting, the Massasoit Memorial Association reported that the eight-year campaign had successfully raised enough money to pay Dallin and to cover the outlay of $7,277 associated with producing and distributing the souvenirs.[16]

Dallin completed the final version of *Massasoit* by 1921 and entered into a contract to provide a bronze cast of the statue to the buyers for the scheduled unveiling in July. The Massasoit Memorial Association agreed to pay Dallin $15,500 (nearly $200,000 in 2017) for *Massasoit* and the foundation for a pedestal.[17] It was up to Dallin to pay for the bronze cast, which could have cost him a sizable portion of his commission; he sent his plaster model to the Gorham Manufacturing Company foundry and was likely directly involved in the casting and finishing process.[18] The long fund-raising campaign for the monument illustrates the challenge of a publicly funded project. In many ways, the *Massasoit* campaign was typical; the fund-raising efforts for the Statue of Liberty in the 1870s and 1880s also involved the sale of small replicas and an informative book, and depended on donations from individuals and organizations across the country.[19] So, too, did schoolchildren in Knoxville, Tennessee, mount a penny campaign to erect a monument to Tsali in the service of mythic Cherokee Trail of Tears memorialization.[20] Hundreds of individuals gave money for the *Massasoit* project, and about a third of the total cost was devoted to producing and disseminating souvenirs with its image. The fund-raising process prompted promoters to articulate the relevance of the monument to the nation, and the public response affirms that the narrative struck a chord.

In the proposed placement of the statue in Plymouth (rather than in 8sâmeeqan's home) and with a plaque inscription honoring the fraternal organization, the purported intent to commemorate the Massasoit became a prize that patriotic Americans could award themselves. As Andrew Denson noted of the erection of a memorial to Tsali in the tourist town of Gatlinburg, the donors' "effort to honor the Native American past became an act of possession."[21] The IORM considered *Massasoit* an opportunity to promote the organization while contributing to the formation of national identity associated with (Native) sacrifice and peace. And even before the statue had been officially unveiled, hundreds of smaller consumer exchanges had taken place around its image and the meaning of the memorial nominally devoted to 8sâmeeqan.

The Massasoit Memorial Association invoked tourism to encourage subscriptions for the statue in two related ways. First, IORM members could visit Plymouth for the tercentenary and see the outcome of their generosity as part of a larger commemorative event.[22] Second, the association reasoned that the placement of *Massasoit* a few paces away from the famous rock would be the best way to reach tourists and give the memorial the greatest impact. On this account, the Massasoit Memorial Association was on point. After the collapse of the whaling industry and decline of milling, the village sought to profit off the heightened interest in colonial history by remaking Plymouth Harbor into a tourist destination. By 1921, the statue of the Wampanoag leader contributed to a consumerist monumental landscape that promised visitors a view back in time and into the English colonial origins of the nation.

A memorial landscape around Plymouth was not a modern American invention. Wampanoag people had long crafted physical memorials to their ancestors and communicated historical information through features in their homeland. Christine DeLucia notes that "the Northeast was already a memorial terrain and had been for millennia" by the time Europeans arrived on the scene, even though this fact has remained "undervisible to outsiders."[23] Edward Winslow noted that Wampanoag people around Plymouth dug small holes in the ground to memorialize an event. Other colonists noted the appearance of heaps of stones at significant sites or graves. When a knowledgeable traveler passed the hole or stone heap, the feature would bring to mind the story of the event or person, and the traveler would make their own small contribution. These ritualized ceremonies of remembrance connected the living to their ancestors and to specific places. The English colonists who landed at Patuxet noted some burial grounds, but largely failed to recognize and acknowledge the cultural features that formed memorial webs across the landscape and over thousands of years.[24]

In addition to these constructed rock memorials, Wampanoag people also regularly visited places significant to their cultural, physical, and spiritual lives to put their ancestors' wisdom into action and ritually root their memories and cosmology in place. Linda Coombs described seventeenth-century Wampanoag society: "They knew not only what to get for food, clothing, shelter, warmth, utility, medicine, ceremony or any other need that would arise, but where to get it, when to get it and how to get it. This was accumulated knowledge that was thousands and thousands of years old, handed down from countless generations."[25] The ritualized visits to certain places—to gather the first berries of the season, or to pull in the first herring — were an enactment of historical knowledge and memorialization. Waterways and springs, in particular, were known meeting places and spiritually important sites. When settlers from the Plymouth Colony sought to control access to freshwater springs in the seventeenth century, tempers flared and contributed to the end of 8sâmee-qan's long peace. As Christine DeLucia argues about the wake of King Philip's War, "Both Natives and colonists transformed such springs into sites of memory, which attempted to convey their respective — and frequently divergent — understandings of historical violence." While English settlers frequently wrote books and occasionally erected carved stone monuments, Wampanoag people told stories, wept, placed stones, and conducted other acts of caretaking on ritualized visits to important sites of memory.[26] The placemaking traditions of southern New England Native people were inflected with ceremonies of remembrance, and were inseparable from the natural contours of land and water of their homelands. It was not until the late nineteenth century that the settlers in Plymouth, motivated by cultural as well as commercial concerns, began a collective effort to remake their village and waterfront into a monumental pilgrimage site in its own right.

As in many western societies, the memorial impulse in Plymouth emerged as a way to mark change over linear time. From the late eighteenth century, the town held an annual Forefathers' Day sermon in December that regularly drew connections between the Pilgrims' landing site and the providential success of the nation. This commemorative practice (and rhetorical strategy) secured Plymouth's self-fashioned identity as "the most ancient town in New England." The sleepy town of farmers, millers, and cod fishermen had little else to distinguish it. In 1851, when Henry David Thoreau traveled the fifty miles by rail from Boston to Plymouth, the remote town struck him as the "end of [the] world." Noting the section of Plymouth Rock on display at Pilgrim Hall (the other half remained at the shore after a disastrous attempt to move the stone split it in two), and relaying how pieces had been chiseled off for tourists, Thoreau ungenerously concluded in his journal, "Nothing saves Plymouth but the Rock." Although Plymouth developed mills and factories that attracted many European immigrants in the late nineteenth century, it was ultimately the rock (and the traffic in its fragments) that saved the town.[27] The heightened interest in historic attractions in Plymouth coincided with the decline of mill industries and shipping in New England coastal villages. Tourism became a popular phenomenon after the Civil War, which dovetailed with heightened concern for commemoration to produce fertile conditions for the heritage tourist industry.[28]

The commemorative impulse that began with the Forefathers' Day sermon shifted into more participatory spectacles and reenactments that incorporated Plymouth's physical surroundings, which encouraged demolition and restoration efforts to capture (and freeze) a sense of authenticity in place. The direction of the tourist trade in Plymouth did not emphasize preservation of the town's historic structures (wharves and warehouses from the industrial boom had already replaced colonial-era buildings) as much as the construction of memorials. In 1859, celebrants gathered to lay the cornerstones of two structures designed by Hammatt Billings—a canopy for the rock and the National Monument to the Forefathers—that would serve as the foundations for the tourist industry. The local newspapers, recognizing the importance of promoting Plymouth as a destination, cooperated on their coverage of the event. The Victorian canopy over the rock was formally dedicated in 1867, just in time for the next Pilgrim-centered anniversary.[29] In 1870, the Pilgrim Society of Plymouth organized a celebration to commemorate the 250th anniversary of the landing at Patuxet. In addition to historical speeches, some guests were treated to a walking tour featuring the "solitary vestiges of the first-comers" (meaning the English colonists) and a portion of the rock under the canopied structure.[30] By 1895—the year of the 275th anniversary celebration—visitors could add the National Monument to the Forefathers to their walking tour, though the statue is installed far away from the main circuit of monumental Plymouth. The enormous monument (the tallest freestanding monument in the world) was completed in 1889 after decades of planning, and the unveiling festivities reportedly attracted a crowd of 15,000 people—double the population of Plymouth at the time.[31] Along with monuments and anniversary celebrations, the town took other steps to establish a tourist economy by staging annual historical pageants and printing guidebooks to lead visitors to memorial sites and local businesses alike. In the process, Plymouth joined other southern New England communities on "the cutting edge of capitalism" by marketing historical attractions with sophisticated modern techniques.[32]

The tercentenary celebration of the Pilgrims' landing and the first year of settlement to be observed in 1920–21 offered the perfect opportunity to completely remake Plymouth into a tourist mecca. In 1915 the Massachusetts legislature passed a resolution to create the Pilgrim Tercentenary Commission, which proposed two projects in 1916: the preservation and construction of a monumental landscape in Plymouth; and a historical pageant that would tell the story of the Pilgrims alongside the settlement's role in "the progress of the nation." The citizens of Plymouth, meanwhile, formed a town committee to make recommendations to the commission, advocating for the first project

FIGURE 38. *Reconstruction of the First House on Leyden Street, Plymouth.*
Photograph by Edward P. McLaughlin, courtesy of the
Plymouth Public Library, Tercentenary Photo Collection.

in the form of permanent renovations and structures that would enhance the tourist industry. Residents voted to purchase land for the construction of a "public memorial building" that could host the proposed tercentenary events, "bringing thousands of visitors to the town" and thus taking advantage of the injection of federal and state appropriations around the anniversary to ensure a modern tourism infrastructure for generations to come. Indeed, *Massasoit* was destined to contribute to this venture, but the memorial would not be the centerpiece that the Improved Order of Red Men had hoped.

Plymouth residents invested in building the local tourist economy must have been delighted by the Tercentenary Commission's plan to remove Plymouth's "unsightly wharves, coal shed and other buildings," which presumably communicated unpleasant and anachronistic notions of commerce (figs. 38 and 39).[33] The shoreline around Plymouth Rock needed to be transformed from an aging commercial seaport into a commemorative space that resembled how it looked to Pilgrims 300 years earlier (that is, a supposedly

FIGURE 39. *Plymouth Waterfront, 1920. Photograph by Edward P. McLaughlin, courtesy of the Plymouth Public Library, Tercentenary Photo Collection.*

empty wilderness). A seawall was constructed in 1920, and the canopy over the revered rock was replaced with a neoclassical portico at the shoreline (a gift of the National Society of the Colonial Dames of America), a setting more fitting of a sacred relic that could withstand the pilgrimage of generations of tourists.[34] In fact, the attempts to display the rock as an icon for the nation may have done the greatest damage to it; the rock suffered a second cracking in the course of restoring it to the "original" base on the waterline.[35] Once imprisoned in a granite structure at the bottom of a fifteen-foot drop, it practically invited adventure-seeking vandals, whose messages were sure to receive public attention. For nearly a century, the rock has been the target of purposeful anger directed at state power and public order: it was painted red on May Day in 1937, buried in the sand in 1970, attacked with a stick of dynamite in 1976, and defaced with a black swastika in 1991. "This kind of thing happens two to five times a year," the state park supervisor responded after a teenager spray painted "LIES" across the rock in 2014. "It's just the nature of where it is."[36] The sizable structure erected in 1921 also had the unintended effect of empha-

Marketing

sizing the rock's diminutive size and the town's anxious efforts to profit from it. As John Seelye wryly put it, the rock's sanctity was "negated by the pompous granite canopy surrounding it, which is in turn surrounded by the tawdry commerce in souvenirs and like tourist businesses that characterize the waterfront street."[37] From this vantage point, the *Massasoit* statue is a picture of artistic elegance that would be joined by a handful of other monuments and reconstructions around Cole's Hill and a full-scale replica of the original *Mayflower*.[38] The physical transformation of the Plymouth waterfront into a tourist destination that presented visitors with modern conveniences and opportunities to consume experiences, narratives, and souvenir items came along with subscriptions and government capital investments of nearly $1 million.[39] The turn to heritage tourism on Plymouth's waterfront, as in other New England towns in the early twentieth century, meant that visitors could experience an idealized yet largely imaginary colonial place that signified simpler times and deeper moral convictions.[40]

Once the Plymouth shoreline was set on the path of becoming a memorial complex, state and local committees planned events to introduce visitors to the narrative that placed Pilgrims and Plymouth at the center of America's exceptional origin story. With congressional aid, the Pilgrim Tercentenary Commission planned a number of commemorative performances to take place from 21 December 1920 to 21 December 1921 in what would be deemed the Year of the Pilgrim.[41] The Massasoit Memorial Association had long hoped to hold an unveiling ceremony for the statue to coincide with the tercentenary celebration of the 1621 peace treaty and Thanksgiving feast, but *Massasoit* did not fit into the tercentenary commissioners' plans for a truly exciting tourist draw.

The commission proposed a tercentenary celebration in 1921 that would contribute in material ways to the tourist infrastructure. But how to draw sizable crowds for the tercentenary? Although the idea of a world's fair was discussed, ultimately the planners thought an overly commercial atmosphere and gaudy spectacle was not fitting for the solemnity of the occasion. The commission settled on a series of events that were ephemeral and temporary, but which had drawn large crowds to Plymouth in the past. And to the delight of Plymouth residents who capitalized on the new industry, the tercentenary events brought in unprecedented numbers of tourists. Severe storms hit Plymouth in July and forced delays for many of the tercentenary's outdoor spectacles, which also pushed back the date for the *Massasoit* unveiling ceremony, but the unpredictable weather hardly dampened tourists' enthusiasm. The grand procession commemorating the Pilgrims' departure and the Shriners parade— both held in August 1921— reportedly attracted 100,000 spectators and snarled

FIGURE 40. *Pilgrim Progress Procession, Plymouth. Photograph by Edward P. McLaughlin, courtesy of the Plymouth Public Library, Tercentenary Photo Collection.*

traffic into the town (fig. 40). One guidebook from 1921 includes a tantalizing reference to a free tourist attraction of a "real native Indian camp" just over a mile from the town center and accessible by frequent bus service (figs. 41, 42, and 43). Forty Passamaquoddy individuals contracted with the town's tercentenary committee to establish the camp, which according to the guidebook and the local newspaper, offered visitors a "complete presentation of real Indian life under real native conditions," along with special events such as "water sports on the pond" and "war dances in full native costumes."[42] In addition to the Indian camp display, which was reportedly one of the most popular attractions of the tercentenary, commission records reveal contract bids from Pawnee Bill (who advertised "lots of experience in putting on big pageants, spectacles, and in handling Indians") and a "Chief Manabozho" (who offered the services of "[his] band of Indians for the pageantry").[43] The commemorative summer of 1921 looked a lot like the kind of commercial world's fairs the commissioners claimed would be unfit for the occasion, particularly with the added element of "real Indians" that reliably drew tourists in this period.

FIGURE 41. *Indian Camp at Tercentenary, Man with Bow and Arrow.*
Courtesy of the Boston Public Library, Leslie Jones Collection.

The main tourist attraction of the year (made possible with a generous appropriation of $50,000 from the state of Massachusetts) was a grand out-door drama, *The Pilgrim Spirit*, performed along the Plymouth waterfront for the summer of 1921.[44] The pageant featured 1,300 locals cast as Pilgrims, and a 300-member chorus and orchestra told the dominant and celebratory Pilgrim story to enormous crowds (the town built a 10,000-seat amphitheater) during its month-long summer performance run.[45] The elaborate production focused on the colonists' journey and hardships, and included a couple of scenes with 8sâmeeqan and his warriors. As with other such pageants of the era, *The Pilgrim Spirit* reenacted a story that could be used to incorporate and acculturate recent immigrants into the nation. In Plymouth, the sizable Italian and Portuguese immigrant communities participated in the crowd scenes, but the pageant's major roles were given to "old-stock Plymoutheans." The majority of Indian roles went to non-Indians; Plymouth resident Harry Nickerson played the Massasoit, costumed in a flannel pant and fringed tunic inspired by Plains Indian Wild West shows.[46] Absent from *The Pilgrim Spirit* was any representa-

FIGURE 42. *John Dana and Another Performer at the Maine Indian Camp in Plymouth, Massachusetts. Courtesy of the Boston Public Library, Leslie Jones Collection.*

tion of the first Thanksgiving. The pageant author had considered including it in his script, but he bucked the trend of the Pilgrim Thanksgiving movement just as it was beginning to explode in American celebratory culture.[47] It was an odd omission, given that so much of the memorial landscape along the waterfront capitalized on the first Thanksgiving myth to attract tourists (fig. 44).

If anything, the tercentenary was just as focused on showcasing the latest technology to tourists as it was on re-creating the past. Although hints of the seaport's nineteenth-century industrial character punctuated the spacious memorial façade — a telegraph line here, empty clapboard buildings there — promoters emphasized the modern comforts that made historical tourism more appealing and accessible than ever before. Directly atop Cole's Hill, within a few feet of the proposed site of the *Massasoit* memorial, the commission erected a 40-foot-high tower to illuminate the 400-foot-wide stage below.[48] The light was touted as an attraction in its own right; the tercentenary chronicler devoted a full page of the program to "electrical facts" and

Marketing

FIGURE 43. The organizers could have drawn from the nearby community, such as these Mashpee Indians depicted on Cape Cod in 1929. *Courtesy of the Boston Public Library, Leslie Jones Collection.*

proclaimed that "the electric lighting plant for the pageant field was reputed to be the largest and most complete of anything of that kind ever erected in this country."[49] Building a tourist industry around history meant that modern technology and tourist conveniences might occasionally take priority over the monuments and historical sites themselves. Nearly all of the buildings below Cole's Hill and along the southern waterfront were removed by 1921, including the last original house on Water Street and the neighborhood known as Little Italy, to open the waterfront for the tercentenary performances.[50] The well-lit pageant, which included a scene featuring the historical Massasoit, would ironically (though temporarily) displace the *Massasoit* memorial. When the storms caused delays for the pageant through August, the Massasoit Memorial Association conceded that it had been physically pushed out by a lighting fixture. "We shall be obliged to wait until the Pageant is over and the Tower removed," the association announced, before "we can hold our celebration."[51] And so, only after the tercentenary pageant was cleared off the grounds would

FIGURE 44. *The Pilgrim Spirit*, scene of treaty signing. *Tercentenary photograph by Edward P. McLaughlin, courtesy of the Plymouth Public Library.*

the statue be unveiled atop Cole's Hill on 5 September 1921.[52] It was a year after that that the Improved Order of Red Men held a dedication ceremony, with what the organization hoped was a fitting level of fanfare, that would not be overshadowed by tercentenary events.[53]

MONUMENT ON THE HILL: WALKING
TOURS AND TOURIST SHOPS

Once *Massasoit* was unveiled on Cole's Hill in 1921, the statue was incorporated into several commercial contexts based in the local tourist industry. City boosters and entrepreneurs successfully branded Plymouth as the nation's birthplace thanks to the strategic marketing of memorials (including *Massasoit*) and historical narratives. The sale of *Massasoit* to Plymouth tourists perhaps exceeded the Improved Order of Red Men's expectations, but it also meant the memorial would be repackaged and reframed in ways the group did not intend. Shortly after its installation, the statue was visually associated with the town of Plymouth in tourist-directed media. The statue was featured

Marketing

on the cover of the 1920s guidebook *Springtime Motoring in Beautiful New England*.[54] As city boosters and entrepreneurs no doubt realized following the popularity of the Passamaquoddy camp and tercentenary pageant, when Indians and commemorations of Indian history are included in the town's promotional material, tourist ventures can become commercially viable.[55] In addition to drawing tourists off the main highways to Plymouth, one of the most active ways in which the statue buoys the local economy today is through entrepreneurial walking tours. The *Massasoit* installation is a regular stop on historic tours because the top of Cole's Hill offers a high vantage point for other features of the waterfront and memorial landscape, particularly Plymouth Rock. The statue serves tour guides as a helpful conduit for place stories that delight, inform, and most important, entertain tourists.

One place to begin a tour is the Pilgrim Hall Museum, "the oldest continuously operating public museum in the country and America's museum of Pilgrim possessions." Opened in 1824 by the Pilgrim Society (established in 1820), this venerable building houses an array of seventeenth-century artifacts, including some directly from the *Mayflower* itself. Pilgrim Hall is dedicated to "the hazardous voyage, the 1620 landing, the fearful first winter, the first Thanksgiving at Plymouth" as "the founding story of America," and houses permanent, temporary, and online exhibits and resources.[56] The museum was renovated in 2008 and reorganized; the entrance-level gallery is devoted to the Pilgrim story in art and myth (and includes one of Dallin's early *Massasoit* models), while the lower hall, according to one guidebook, "presents the true history of the Plymouth colonists."[57] It is in the lower level that visitors also encounter the story of the Wampanoags, "the Native People who inhabited this area for 10,000 years before the arrival of the new settlers and who are still here today." The interpretation does not completely ignore conflict, depicting a world of interdependence that came unraveled in the 1670s and exploded with King Philip's War.[58] Although Wampanoag history gets a nod in these and other ways, the lower-level welcome video, *One Small Candle*, makes it clear that it is the Pilgrims who get top billing. The video opens by announcing the story of two cultures coming together and sets the drama of the passage on the *Mayflower*, but it is only toward the very end that the story of Samoset, Tisquantum, 8sâmeeqan, and the treaty ushering in fifty years of peace takes the stage. The story of peaceable ways and Indian assistance is highlighted as necessary for survival: "Despite their differences there was common ground. The personal bonds that were built up were very important." The video closes with a snapshot of the first Thanksgiving (with a credit to Edward Winslow), with 8sâmeeqan and his men joining in during the celebration. This story of Pilgrim survival represented "the beginning of what will ultimately lead to what we call the country of America." Even though Plymouth Colony was absorbed by Massachusetts after seventy-two years, the Pilgrims left a deep impression; as the video closes, it notes, "If you're going to have symbolic ancestors, let's have these guys."[59] Tourists prepared to engage with the memorial landscape outside the museum will be primed to witness a satisfying and emotional narrative of peaceful national origins in Plymouth.

But paying tourists may also encounter narratives of an Indigenous place that challenge their expectations for a celebratory settler origin story. Pilgrim Hall housed the traveling exhibit *Captured! 1614* during the spring of 2016. Created under the guidance of Mashpee Wampanoag Paula Peters with a team of Wampanoag designers, researchers, and historical interpreters who had complete content and editorial control over the process, the exhibit panels and series of short films first opened to the public in 2014 at the Plymouth Public Library. *Captured! 1614* presents the Patuxet Wampanoag perspective on the slaving expedition of Thomas Hunt, who seized twenty men and boys from Patuxet, including Tisquantum (and seven more Wampanoag men from Nauset on Cape Cod), for sale in Spain.[60] Peters explained in a press release, "This is a critical piece of the history of Plymouth that can't be told accurately without a Wampanoag voice and I'm excited for this opportunity to tell our story on an international platform."[61] According to Peters, the reception of the exhibit has been overwhelmingly positive among Wampanoag communities and non-Indian viewers.[62]

The target audience of *Captured! 1614* was non-Indians, and so Peters focused on careful documentation (using English written sources) so it would be "very truthful" and beyond reproach.[63] Despite her careful attention to citations, it was the creative and emotional aspects of the exhibit that seemed to most impact non-Indian viewers. Indeed, the deeply disturbing imaginative recounting of the abduction of the twenty male family members from Patuxet by English slavers — as told by Wampanoag women as first-person interpreters in the films — packed an emotional punch that made the narrative memorable. When the exhibit first opened at the Plymouth Public Library, the staff reported that some visitors pulled chairs up to the screen and watched the videos repeatedly. Peters interacted with one such visitor at the library who became visually moved by what he had seen; when the man learned that Peters had helped to produce the exhibit, he expressed his gratitude and insisted that she continue to tell this story.[64] Several other visitors to the Pilgrim Hall Museum left online reviews praising *Captured! 1614* for offering fascinating information about Wampanoag experiences with colonists. One reviewer articulated a sense of surprise at "how they were able to live side-by-side with the pilgrims . . . despite having less than positive experiences when . . . explorers had kidnapped Wampanoag men to sell as slaves."[65] The commercial memorial landscape around Plymouth increasingly incorporates Indigenous perspectives in a way that problematizes the origin story of peaceful colonization, and visitors seeking out new voices responded positively. As Peters reflected on the exhibit and its potential to shake up non-Indians' comforting narratives, she asserted that the truth "had to be told to them in a way that did make them think."[66] These complex narratives are both historically grounded and emotional, yet they do not promote the celebratory patriotism that the Improved Order of Red Men and the tercentenary planners initiated. However, they are also not fully incorporated into the dominant historical narrative most easily consumed along the Plymouth waterfront.

Plymouth's tourist industry encourages visitors to seek out ever more guidance, and many turn to tour companies and other private institutions to fill this demand. Most tourists to Plymouth are directed toward the Visitors Information Center on Water Street, which is staffed by volunteers (the city voted to deny public funds to the center in 1939, indicating residents' ambivalence toward the tourist industry) who are eager to present visitors with a tourist map of the waterfront and their own opinions of the town's highlights.[67] On our visits in 2014 and 2017, the volunteers recommended the most popular tourist destinations: Plimoth Plantation, the Jenney Grist Mill, and the *Mayflower II* (when it was not removed for restoration work). On the latter visit, the volunteer offered her own narrative of Plymouth history, including the startling observation that the original inhabitants of Patuxet had "all died off."[68] The interior walls of the center are lined with maps and pamphlets so visitors can choose their own experience, from marine activities to hotel packages and guided tours. One of the most common tourist guidebooks for the 2014–15 season, produced by Destination Plymouth (with funding from the Massachusetts Office of Travel and Tourism, the Plymouth County Convention and Visitors Bureau, and the Town of Plymouth's promotional fund), features a foldout map of the memorial landscape. While visitors could use the map for a self-guided tour, many of the attractions are indicated on the map with the phone number for a local tour company. The statues and memorials, including *Massasoit*, are drawn on the map, but one must book a walking tour and hire an interpreter to learn more.[69]

The most prominent activities are ghost tours and heritage tours of the major sites. If tourists time their visit deliberately at the close of the season, they may conduct a circuit in which they disembark from the *Mayflower II*, walk through the Wampanoag Homesite, and sit down to an elaborate Thanksgiving dinner at the Plimoth Plantation Visitors Center.[70] The commemorative landscape adds value to the dinner, and the tickets are highly coveted. In 2016, Plimoth Plantation planned seven events for Thanksgiving Day: three full-scale seatings of "America's Thanksgiving Dinner" (ninety-eight dollars for adult nonmembers, fifty-eight dollars for children) and four seatings of the "Thanksgiving Day Buffet" (seventy-three dollars for adult nonmembers, thirty-six dollars for children).[71] The tourist industry, although composed of institutions with educational missions, nevertheless relies on the celebratory narrative of national origins to draw crowds. At Plimoth Plantation, interpreters from the English Village circulate through the crowd, creating a festive atmosphere. Wampanoag Homesite interpreters also work during the dinners but refuse to act jovial for the occasion. "I'll go around and talk to people, educate people about the history, but you will not see Native people singing as a celebration. You might hear and witness an honoring song for our ancestors who paved the way for us so we can be here today," Darius Coombs said. "I wear black face paint on purpose in order to trigger questions," he explained, which opens the opportunity to inform visitors that Thanksgiving represents a day of mourning for his people.[72] This technique of public history is intended to invite engagement with a complex narrative rather than provoke confrontation about opposing perspectives on the national origin story. And because Plimoth Plantation relies upon the Thanksgiving dinner as an important and reliable revenue stream, the myth around the holiday actually enables the organization to support cutting-edge interpretation in the Wampanoag Homesite that visitors may not seek out otherwise (especially after a visit to the Plymouth Visitors Information Center).

After perusing the array of offerings marketed in the Visitors Information Center, tourists are confronted with two connected features of Plymouth's tourist industry. First, the local economy of Plymouth is based on stories about Pilgrims and Indians, which are conveyed through tour guides' interpretations of a landscape of reconstructed and commemorative sites. *Massasoit* appears on promotional materials, indicating the success of the figure to city branding. Second, the heritage walking tour business (which includes *Massasoit*) is booming and highly entrepreneurial. According to the volunteer at the information desk in 2014, the town does not require licenses for guides nor promote a standard manual or historical narrative; the very suggestion of such oversight is offensive.[73] Plymouth is not necessarily an outlier in this regard, although some American cities including New York, Charleston, South Carolina, and Washington, D.C., have introduced licensing and registration requirements in an effort to prevent overcrowding in historic districts and to protect consumers. Such regulatory efforts have met with resistance, including by a group of Savannah, Georgia, guides who filed a federal lawsuit against the city arguing that the requisite history test placed an "unconstitutional burden on free expression."[74] In Plymouth, the unregulated nature of guiding allows us to see how private tour offerings targeting specific consumer groups can flourish and evolve alongside American commemorative culture.

Some free public programming is available to tourists: Massachusetts Department of Conservation and Recreation (DCR) employees offer thirty-minute tours regularly throughout the summer tourist season. On one pleasant July day in 2014, DCR guides lead their groups from Plymouth Rock to *Massasoit* to orient the visitors and briefly introduce the memorial landscape. The first guide, a seasoned DCR employee, gives a five-minute introduction to the Massasoit, the treaty, and the elements of his story visible from where they stand on Cole's Hill: the *Mayflower*, the William Bradford statue, the site of the first Thanksgiving, and the plaque explaining the Day of Mourning. The group moves on and is replaced a short time later with another—this one led by a young male DCR guide. This guide's wording is precise and emphasizes 8sâ-meeqan's political strategy within a complex Indigenous world. The two park guides offer the same general story with different details; the older guide focuses on 8sâmeeqan's role in helping settlers who later steal Native Americans' land, while the younger guide places the alliance in a larger Indigenous context. These guides are informative and seem determined to offer a balanced, complex historical story, but they are also self-taught and poorly paid. What they know they gather in their own free time from available published sources in the local public library. After the thirty-minute tour, Plymouth visitors are then encouraged to explore more on their own, and they often turn to more in-depth private tours.

Among the most popular Plymouth heritage tours are those led by a God-fearing retiree clad in Pilgrim attire named Leo Martin. Along with his wife, Martin owns the Jenney Museum, a private business with a curious interpretive angle that combines a celebration of the Christian nuclear family with a glorification of presumed Pilgrim values of private property ownership and political liberty. Located next to the Jenney Grist Mill (a reproduction built in 1970 on the original mill site as a tourist attraction and now run by Plimoth Plantation as a stop on the popular tourist circuit), the Jenney Museum capitalizes on sidewalk traffic by drawing in visitors with a bookstore and gallery space. The three exhibits on display in 2017 respectively celebrated the Christian family as the cornerstone of society, explained different dimensions of liberty (a photograph of *Massasoit* appears in the "Constitutional Liberty" section), and suggestively asked whether the Pilgrims were the first abolitionists. From this site, the Jenney Museum launches a variety of tour products, such as a free "Pilgrim Progress Reenactment" (re creating the march of the surviving colonists of the first winter of 1620–21 from Plymouth Rock to the First Parish Church) and themed walking tours including ones called Christian Heritage, Pilgrim Economics, and Discover Plymouth's History.[75]

On a spring 2017 Discover Plymouth's History tour, which cost fifteen dollars per person, the costumed guide weaved a Christian story of national origins firmly rooted in Plymouth, torturously reading American free enterprise and democratic patriotism back into the early seventeenth century. Leo Martin began the tour at the grist mill to explain why the area appealed to the Pilgrims and pointed to details of the structure that demonstrated the colonists' industrious nature. He then presented a number of admiring claims about the Pilgrims: their high level of education ("the governor could speak five languages"); their devotion to self-rule and equal protection under the law ("they were people of character and integrity who stood by their word"); and female colonists' patriotic decision to starve to death that first winter ("sacrificing themselves for the next generation knowing if [the children] did not survive, *we* would not survive"). The guide's insistence on presenting a celebratory portrait of the Pilgrims and the nation's founding characteristics led him to a peculiar reading of Indian history. When addressed at all, Wampanoag history was either misinformed or put to the task of justifying a glorified version of colonial history. "There was one other tribe in Plymouth [besides the Wampanoag led by the Massasoit], and that was the Patuxet," the guide explained, confusing the relationship between the villages of Patuxet and Pokanoket within the Wampanoag confederacy. When the guide mentioned Tisquantum's ability to speak English, it was not intended to illustrate Wampanoag intelligence and dedication to learning (as such multilingualism signified for Bradford). Rather, the guide quickly relayed Tisquantum's enslavement in Europe mainly as a setup for a joke; with a dramatic pause, he revealed that Tisquantum had been invited on board a ship by "a hunter by the name of Hunt. You can't make this stuff up, can you?" Thus, the tourists' attention could be diverted from an understanding of what Tisquantum's language abilities revealed about the colonial world — or even the simple terrible fact that English slaving ships abducted Wampanoag men along the coast — and onto a more comforting thought of a quaint coincidence of English naming.

Martin routinely glossed over complexities of English-Wampanoag relations in favor of a creative reframing that casts colonists as well-meaning innocents and Native people as their understanding helpmates. From the beginning of the tour, Leo Martin addressed the uncomfortable truth of Native land dispossession and attempted to put his audience at ease. "The reason I bring [Tisquantum] up," he explained, as though any mention of Native people on a Plymouth tour demanded an explanation, is because "most people believe that the Pilgrims stole the land from the Indians. They did not. The Indians did not want the land . . . because of the plague. The Pilgrims took land nobody wanted. After that, they paid for it to the chief, Massasoit." It is quite a leap in logic to assume that because a village was struck by a devastating epidemic at the time of the Pilgrims' arrival that Wampanoag people no longer wanted the land (with its freshwater springs, resources, and footpaths). The issue was further muddled with the guide's dubious claim that Pilgrims paid 8sâmeeqan for the land, thus suggesting that Wampanoag interest in the land persisted and Pilgrims understood that paying for their right to occupy it was the ethical thing to do.[76] The tour guide continued to grasp for a narrative that cast the Pilgrims as moral paragons while accounting for the undeniable fact of Wampanoag land dispossession. He took the opportunity to distinguish the Pilgrims from the Puritans at Massachusetts Bay, arguing that he could not "make excuses for the Puritans that came ten years later; they even took land from us." Since the guide insisted that private property is the bedrock of power, it was important to him to point out that the Pilgrims did not gain their power through theft, and they "did not touch" land occupied by Indians.

Yet the guide also offered a contradictory argument based on the Pilgrims' inherent goodness: when they did take from the Indigenous people, it was justifiable. The guide pointed out that when the Pilgrims first landed on the tip of Cape Cod, they had run out of food. They looked around and found "corn buried in the ground by the Indians and they took it. They didn't steal the corn, they borrowed it. They did pay it back later. If they had not taken it, they would not have survived." The logic is as tortured as it is common in New England narratives: stealing is not stealing when perpetrated by the Pilgrims. The mythic founders of the nation could literally do no wrong if their survival on the continent was at stake. On the other hand, the outbreak of King Philip's War, customers learn on the tour, was largely due to Pometacomet's hubris and personal failings. In sum, the guide suggested that the Pilgrims had been the true victims of history, their reputations besmirched by assumptions of land theft.

Pausing at the *Massasoit* statue, the guide repeated the narrative championed by the Improved Order of Red Men 100 years earlier: 8sâmeeqan was "a very important man" and "our friend. Without him the Pilgrims would not have survived." But rather than explain what made 8sâmeeqan an important historical figure beyond agreeing to a peace treaty, the guide used him as a foil to illustrate the colonists' honorable intentions. Most of the tour time in front of the statue involved a story that emphasized the hardship Edward Winslow endured in order to offer 8sâmeeqan medical attention when the sachem fell ill. The guide brought the tourists' attention briefly to the Day of Mourning plaque ("If you'd like to come back on Thanksgiving Day you can join my Native American friends in their National Day of Mourning, which takes place right at that rock"), but he did not explain the origins or intent of the event, nor stop to allow the tourists a moment to read the plaque before moving on to the next Pilgrim monument.

For audiences listening to this Plymouth history tour, many aspects of seventeenth-century New England no longer make sense because Native perspectives and actors have been removed. While the guide pointed out the duration of the peace established through the treaty at least three times, he displayed little patience for the possibility of Native interpretations for the events he related. The guide completely glossed over the complex events of King Philip's War at the site of the UAINE plaque addressing the war. However, he paused to relate the gruesome details of Pometacomet's dismemberment, accounted for because the colonists believed "he didn't deserve to be buried, so they didn't bury him" and justified because it was "quite the deterrent." At one point, Martin assured the tour group that his one-sided narrative passed scholarly muster because "our historian, Governor Bradford, wrote a book called [Of] Plymouth Plantation. Everything I tell you comes right out of the book, a primary document, everything is true."[77] Although Bradford did chronicle the early years of Plymouth up to his death in 1656, that fact alone does not mean Martin's interpretations of those events could be called true. His choice to uncritically and unapologetically adopt a seventeenth-century colonist's perspective on Native people suggests that the guide neither expected, nor receives, much pushback from paying customers.

Indeed, tourists' reviews of the 2015 season on TripAdvisor give the Jenney Museum the highest ratings, one even suggesting readers "put aside your history books. Instead, take this tour." It should be noted that reviews on TripAdvisor capture only a small fraction of customers' experiences, and because anyone can post reviews on TripAdvisor (there is no screening mechanism for actual customers), the company has been charged with both hosting fake reviews and removing negative content.[78] Whether written by paying customers or not, online ratings help to advertise the Jenney Museum's various tours and draw consumers to the business with promises of an interpretation of "heritage" from an English perspective. The Jenney Museum tours offer an inspiring story to visitors hungry for this particular version of national origins, prompting one visitor from Schenectady to compare it favorably to Plimoth Plantation, which "has become so watered down and revisionist in telling about the pilgrims that I find it hard to love it like I used to." Most reviews conclude that the Jenney Museum tours offer "an accurate portrayal" of Plymouth life and describe the guide as a "true patriot and American hero." Several reviewers also appreciated the Jenney Museum's Christian Heritage Tour, which was described as "fact- and God-based" and helpfully teaching "the Christian roots of freedom in America."[79] This tour (and its online reviews/advertisements) encourages visitors to see Plymouth as an exclusively Pilgrim site — a hallowed ground infused with comforting English memories that left Patuxet, Indigenous history, and Native views on the sidelines.

There are alternatives to this Pilgrim-focused heritage tour for visitors with the energy and inclination to seek out Indigenous history and Wampanoag sites. By private arrangement and fifteen dollars, one can also book a ninety-minute walk with Native Plymouth Tours for more complex and less comfortable interpretations of Plymouth's place in the nation's origins. Tim Turner began the business in 2010 with his brother in order to fill a glaring hole in heritage tours: Plymouth history from a Native perspective.[80] Turner, a citizen of the Cherokee Nation, grew up in Plymouth and is now employed as the guest experience manager for the Wampanoag Indigenous Program at Plimoth Plantation. Like other leading figures in the program, Turner conducts extensive research into Wampanoag history and culture, and his work has the support of Wampanoag scholars. At Native Plymouth Tours, he applies educational techniques from Plimoth Plantation to the specific landscape of Plymouth. On a summer evening in 2014, Turner began a tour with the two of us at Plymouth Rock to first acquaint us with the shoreline and how it would have looked as Patuxet shortly before the Pilgrims' arrival.[81] Turner then leads tourists through unmarked clearings, waterways, and hillsides to point out where Wampanoag people built their homes, buried their dead, and traveled on well-worn paths to build relationships and conduct diplomacy. In the storied site of the first Thanksgiving, Turner pauses to point out a modest spring feeding a creek that meanders through a manicured memorial park and empties into the bay. To the untutored visitor, the creek and surrounding greenery form an attractive park with a convenient path connecting commemorative sites. To residents of Patuxet, Turner reminds tourists, freshwater springs were highly valued and often visited. This kind of tour not only interprets the landscape from a Native perspective, but also transports the tourist into a seventeenth-century Wampanoag worldview in which landscapes are memory, and each generation gives voice to the stories of, in, and on the land.[82] He even includes a 200-year-old tree with gnarled roots heaving below a downtown Plymouth side yard to affirm the persistence of Wampanoag people's historical experiences amid a memorial landscape largely devoted to Pilgrim fathers. In Turner's conception of Plymouth, the landscape is storied, but not frozen in time. Wampanoags have always been there, and they continue to present tourists with an unsettling narrative of national origins that challenges the innocent story that gave rise to Plymouth as a tourist mecca.

In addition to the environmental features and Pilgrim monuments, Turner gives ample attention to the plaques and statues dedicated to, or written by, Indigenous people. Turner leads the group first to the *Massasoit* statue to discuss the historic leader as well as the memorial's creation. The guide points out the features of the statue that his research confirms to be authentic, as well as the details he suspects to be fabrications or culturally inconsistent elements (originating either from seventeenth-century English writers or Cyrus Dallin). He also recasts the bond between 8sâmeeqan and the English in the Wampanoag context of war with the Narragansett; the treaty was a "mutual defense" agreement, not a peace treaty. Turner challenges the narrative intent of the memorial by asserting that 8sâmeeqan was primarily interested in protecting his people, not the colonists, and speculates that if 8sâmeeqan had known how things would turn out, he would not have allied with the English.[83] This tour uniquely treated the memorial as sculpture art and a window into seventeenth-century Wampanoag perspectives rather than a conduit for a story of 8sâmeeqan's contribution to Pilgrim survival and America's founding character.

In addition to a wide-ranging analysis of the statue, Turner provides a richly detailed history of the Day of Mourning plaque installed near *Massasoit*'s pedestal. Rather than allowing the content of the plaque to stand alone or quickly leading visitors away, as other observed guides had done, Turner explains how the plaque resulted from a 1970 event in which Native people's perspectives had been censored and their voices silenced. The physical fact of the United American Indians of New England plaque can achieve a kind of revered glow in Turner's narrative; it is a solid representation of Native voices fixed in place — unavoidable, undeniable, and potentially uncomfortable for those who pause to reflect on the import of its message. Customers on the Native Plymouth tour are invited to wrestle with the complexity of *Massasoit* and other Pilgrim-centered installations. Turner's goal is to provide context for the memorial landscape by discussing the controversies and very human dramas behind the bronze plaques and statues, always emphasizing Native persistence.[84] Turner's tour is not limited by and to Plymouth's constructed memorial landscape; the springs, trees, pathways, and contours of the land all provide windows into Wampanoag history, perspectives, and perseverance.

Ratings for Native Plymouth Tours on TripAdvisor, which come largely from Massachusetts and New England residents (perhaps because the tour is not overtly promoted at the Visitors Information Center although they do stock pamphlets of the tour), laud the tour for offering "a history lesson you won't find in text books." Most reviews appreciate the "other," "different," and "authentic" perspective of Plymouth history offered on the tour, reaffirming both the multiplicity of perspectives on the past and the perception that Indigenous history is an alternative, nonmainstream narrative that supplements the generally accepted version. Several Massachusetts residents expressed gratitude for the tour for debunking myths, providing a more complete picture of America's origins, and helping them to identify inaccurate or excluded aspects of dominant Pilgrim and Thanksgiving stories.

Turner's narrative complicates celebratory narratives by discussing Wampanoag people's experiences and acknowledging the historical fact of settler colonialism. An Israeli tourist in 2013 confirmed that Turner's narrative resonated with general histories of colonialism while bringing the local manifestations into stark relief: "We all know the Pilgrims [came] to occupy [the land] but this tour shows you location, stories and history of the first colonization." Stripping back the layers of American innocence and exceptionalism to discuss the reality of English settler colonialism hit tourists at different registers, with local customers expressing greater satisfaction than out-of-state tourists, and revealing an ongoing tension in the historical memory of Plymouth. One local visitor suggested the tour prompted a kind of healing for citizens of Plymouth that collapsed the seventeenth century into the present; Native people and European settlers "finally can share the truth about their shared history good and bad." But another visitor from Florida in 2011 acknowledged that "there is much to be said about the treatment of the natives by the English," but nevertheless critiqued the tour for giving "a bit too much emphasis and guilt trip for the whites and English," making the tour "a little uncomfortable for the non indian tourists."

Tourists affirmed that the Native Plymouth tour was "non-biased" and "well-balanced," revealing suspicions or expectations that such a tour might be otherwise. While most of the local tourists deeply appreciated learning about familiar places from a Native perspective, and one New Bedford resident credited the tour for her realization that the mainstream interpretation offered at other local sites was only superficial without Indigenous stories, glimpses of

Indian stereotypes nevertheless bubble to the surface. One tourist from the U.K. who took the tour in 2013 titled his glowing review of the tour "Honest Injun," and one New York tourist in 2012 appreciated how the history of what "the Native American Ancestors endured at the hands of the white man" was "told to us without bitterness from a forgiving and evolved perspective."[85] This New Yorker, at least, suggested that ensuring the tourists' comfort with the historical narrative was a service that the tour guide was expected to deliver.

By comparing private Plymouth tours, we can see how narratives can be packaged for different consumer interests and variously received according to visitors' expectations. On a single day in 2014, all of the guides—from public institutions and private companies alike—mentioned Thanksgiving on their tours, as well as the gathering for the Native American Day of Mourning held at the statue. But the private Plymouth tours appeal to different clients, as online reviews reveal. While the most common words associated with the Jenney Museum in online reviews were "Christian heritage," for Native Plymouth Tours the terms "Native American" and "myths" occur most often. The commercial context in which *Massasoit* is enveloped can at least partially account for the development of these divergent histories and conceptions of heritage in Plymouth. The fact that the Town of Plymouth has not opted to license or otherwise regulate individual guides has resulted in tours that present perspectives that can fall outside of the mainstream. While both private tours offer nominally educational tours, clients might choose a Jenney Museum tour to find affirmation in a triumphalist origin story of Pilgrim survival and spiritual strength, while others seek out Native Plymouth Tours to be challenged to see a familiar story and place from a different and potentially more unsettling perspective. The open and entrepreneurial approach to heritage tourism in Plymouth makes both the Jenney Museum and Native Plymouth tours possible. The question of where to spend fifteen dollars and maximize tourist time is at its heart an economic calculation for the tourist, and *Massasoit* is a primary site at which the market in heritage tours finds definition and the possible narratives multiply and fracture in different directions.

To a large extent, the marketability of historical narratives determines their dissemination, and *Massasoit* is at the center of this consumer exchange. The commemorative impulse reaffirms the centrality of English colonialism to the nation's origin story while stamping narratives in place. To attract tourists, Plymouth must be sold as a site where history comes alive and collective memory is palpable. As the only statue to an Indigenous person in the town, *Massasoit* not only sets memories in place—it sells them. The tourist industry that associates the Massasoit with Plymouth has effectively branded the town with the Pokanoket leader's image. But the presence of *Massasoit* on Cole's Hill also enables Indigenous people such as Paula Peters, Tim Turner, and activists who come together on the National Day of Mourning to unsettle settler narratives that assert mythic peaceful national origins in Plymouth.

MASSASOIT SOUVENIRS

Once the tourism industry associated the Massasoit with Plymouth, the *Massasoit* memorial could be packaged for ease of travel and sold as a mobile commodity. Tourists consume the commemorative landscape surrounding the statue on Cole's Hill and are constantly invited to purchase memorabilia connected to this act. As Marita Sturken points out, "Tourism is defined by the activity of taking things away from the places we have visited."[86] If walking tours promise an experience for the consumer, the souvenir shops present opportunities to express one's connections to a place story through a consumer activity in which one may carry away a physical reminder of that experience.

The items found in current-day Plymouth shops are largely the same as those offered since the 1890s: Pilgrim spoons, Pilgrim figurines, booklets, paperweights, charms, guidebooks, and postcards.[87] The tercentenary and unveiling ceremonies in 1921 precipitated the addition of commemorative plates and even a puzzling Christmas greeting card featuring the statue's stern face.[88] As the storied site of the first Thanksgiving, Plymouth shops burst with replicas and representations of the shared feast. Notably, the nostalgic first Thanksgiving table has expanded over time to include the Native guests in this commercial setting, with mixed results. At the turn of the twentieth century, the most sought-after souvenir items were sets of replica Pilgrim place settings.[89] In 2013, the latest variant on the dining décor has taken on a more cartoonish edge: Puritan and Indian salt and pepper shakers, gourd-printed tablecloths, plush turkeys, and porcelain cornucopia centerpieces. In our visits to Plymouth tourist shops in 2014 and 2017, we found many souvenir items representing the "Indian" side of the equation: plastic warbonnets, tomahawks, and arrowhead replicas mix with postcards and coffee mugs decorated with depictions of the *Massasoit* statue (figs. 45, 46, and 47). Kitschy references to Thanksgiving and stereotypical depictions of Indigenous people accompany *Massasoit* in other Plymouth consumer spaces outside of souvenir shops as well. A restaurant across the street from a row of shops on Water Street presented a similar mash-up of Pilgrim and Indian stereotypes: *Massasoit* pictured on a wallpaper collage with photographs of a buckskin bikini–clad Native American doll; Geronimo; a pinup blonde woman in a Pilgrim

FIGURE 45. Headdress souvenirs, Plymouth waterfront shop.
Photograph by Jean O'Brien.

hat and fishnet tights; and a drawing of the Plymouth peace treaty council. The revered values of the Thanksgiving holiday—gratitude, peace, and mutual understanding—have been confused, if not completely undone, by this assortment of images and souvenir items. In these commercial contexts, *Massasoit* is a place-specific reference that functions to call to mind and confirm Indian

FIGURE 46. Thanksgiving figurine souvenirs, Plymouth waterfront shop.
Photograph by Jean O'Brien.

stereotypes for the tourist. In shops just a few paces from the *Massasoit* memorial, visitors are treated to their expectations of Natives mirrored back to them rather than provided with confirmation that they walk on historic Wampanoag land. If the memorial to 8sâmeeqan was meant to honor the Pokanoket leader for brokering a peace agreement that secured the English colony, much of the kitschy souvenir items referenced Plains Indian warfare — another place, time, and set of relationships altogether. These ethnic memorabilia (or racialized icons) tell us about "the inner desires of those who create and consume them," notes Larry Levine, as well as "some of the forces that shape reality" for Na-

FIGURE 47. Small *Massasoit* for sale, Plymouth waterfront shop.
Photograph by Jean O'Brien.

tive people.[90] The jarring disjuncture presented to visitors in Plymouth tourist shops—coffee mugs with depictions of *Massasoit* on a shelf beside a framed collection of "Indian arrowheads" and a stand of plastic feathered warbonnets—attests to the complex layers of imperialist nostalgia and consumerist appropriation at the heart of settler colonialism. When consumers of souve-

Marketing

nirs such as headdresses and tomahawks transport these items to places with no other representations of Native people, such stereotyped icons become the singular understanding of Indianness.

The consumer desire for Indian kitsch works against the intent of the *Massasoit* memorial while also shaping how *Massasoit* is "read" outside of Plymouth. In a commercial marketplace saturated with ethnic memorabilia, *Massasoit* may be more readily seen as a generic representation rather than one of a historical actor. And one need not search far to find a small souvenir replica *Massasoit* that can be carried home in a suitcase. In the Pilgrim Hall Museum gift shop, we found among the children's books and "highbrow" Thanksgiving souvenirs a two-inch figurine and a charm-bracelet *Massasoit*. We learned that these were the last of the shipment; the souvenirs were popular enough to sell out. What is the function and meaning of *Massasoit* souvenirs? According to Sturken, souvenirs are "objects [that] convey . . . a connection or attachment to a place."[91] The nature of that connection depends on a tourist's interests and willingness to engage with available place memories, but the dominant narratives in the memorial landscape encourage messages of peaceful colonization and English national origins. The seventeenth-century sachem (or, rather, his likeness) grasping the peace pipe is forever frozen in a moment of welcoming. This moment is condensed and distilled — intended to stand for a larger and complex historical context (much like the tourist-friendly town of Plymouth). It is a whole seventeenth-century New England world represented through one of its parts. "This mode of conveying meaning," writes Celeste Olalquiaga, "invests souvenirs with a large fetishistic potential: souvenirs begin to stand in for events or situations they were contingently associated with or were supposed to represent, gaining a life of their own."[92] Souvenirs are remembrances crystalized into an object, yet the process of commodification empties the souvenir of its singularity of experience. Each souvenir can be invested with meaning according to a consumer's universe of experiences and values. The souvenir can be educational, inspirational, decorative, mnemonic. *Massasoit* souvenirs, these small replicas of the body of an Indigenous man, may be owned by anyone, invested with any meaning, and transported anywhere.

The memorial, once converted into memorabilia, can be commodified as an art object and traced in the marketplace. For example, we can follow the fate of one eleven-inch bronze acquired in Plymouth as a souvenir in the 1950s. This particular piece sold at auction for $6,500 in 2009.[93] Three years later the same piece was resold at auction for a mere $850, demonstrating the high stakes involved in market transactions. This time, the mouthpiece of the pipe had been broken off and lost, and the auction house identified the piece as a posthumous cast.[94] Despite its damaged state and the fact it was an unauthorized cast, the eleven-inch statuette may have retained market value from the history it accumulated as a souvenir. A typed note affixed to the bottom of the damaged figurine offered vague historical information but precise provenance: "Chief Massasoit who saved the settlers from massacre in 1620–30. Given me at Plymouth, U. S. A. by the Town on my visit there with Sir Julian Gascoigne & Jack Hill in 1955."[95] Maj. Gen. Sir Julian Gascoigne, a British World War II officer, went on to serve as governor of Bermuda, where he hosted a summit with John F. Kennedy to discuss the construction of the Berlin Wall in 1961.[96] The souvenir could be sold and resold as a condensed reference to Plymouth or the Cold War—whichever might have greater bearing on the exchange value of the piece—or simply as an art object that fulfills a consumer's desire to own a stylized Indian figure for display.

MASSASOIT STATUETTES

However widespread the reach of *Massasoit* souvenirs acquired in Plymouth, these reproductions may pale in comparison to the number of the statue's replicas circulating in the art market with no connection or reference to Plymouth at all. One of the causes (and results) of the memorial's commodification is that it could be easily unmoored from a specific place or memory and made ever more mobile. In this sense, *Massasoit* fits into the generic Indianness we see in Indian statuary. Even the National Congress of American Indians, the preeminent organization of tribally elected officials in the United States, confused *Massasoit* for a representation of Tisquantum, as featured in a 2014 advertisement produced to protest the Washington National Football League team's mascot, an ironic error in a video that celebrates historical precision and Indigenous diversity.[97] The story of the mobility of *Massasoit*—or more appropriately, the dispersal of *Massasoits* from southern New England—cannot be separated from the capitalist marketplace in which the statue was sculpted, cast, and exchanged. To trace the commercial reproductions of the statue (rather than the place-based souvenirs), we must return to the 1910s. At the turn of the twentieth century, sculpture works displayed at world's fairs popularized the art form, and changes in plaster and metal casting made it possible to reproduce smaller sculptures faster and cheaper. Sculptors could make a great profit by selling small versions of their larger public monuments while increasing their exposure.[98] Because the market for sculpture multiples was vast and eager, Dallin knew he could earn an income on these works while also building a national reputation that would encourage commissions of heroic-sized hand-hewn pieces. Like many artists struggling to make a living from their creative labors, Dallin readily engaged with the art marketplace by pursuing catalog sales and large-scale reproductions of his work.

Cyrus Dallin, like other sculptors, sent his plaster model of the first version of the statue to a manufacturer so the small reproductions could be made to pay for his decade-long work on the commissioned memorial. Dallin registered a copyright for the statuette *Massasoit #1* in 1915 and contracted with P. P. Caproni and Brother, a Boston terra-cotta company, to produce and sell plaster reproductions of the forty-inch piece. According to the contract, Dallin would receive a royalty and an additional plaster reproduction for each statue sold. The contract also included the plan for the proposed six-foot statue with the same terms and conditions; the sculptor was to receive $150 for the life-sized model of the statue, "and thereafter the sum of $20 as a royalty for each plaster reproduction sold."[99] The terra-cotta company wasted no time in selling reproductions: the catalog from 1915 offered a forty-inch reproduction for thirty dollars and the six-foot cast for $100 ($700 and $2,400 in 2015 dollars, respectively).[100] Given the terms of the agreement, the company stood to make high profits on each reproduction sold after the first two. If the number of forty-inch reproductions available today is any indication, the *Massasoit #1* casts sold well, but Caproni failed to sell a single lifetime cast of the six-foot statue by catalog.[101]

The unveiling of the Plymouth *Massasoit* in September 1921 no doubt drove increased consumer interest in the statuette, and the company consequently began to offer the replica of the Plymouth version that had previously been limited to Improved Order of Red Men members. The final 1928 Caproni catalog offered for sale forty-inch casts of both versions of *Massasoit*, with *Massasoit #1* priced at forty dollars and the Plymouth replica at thirty-five dollars.[102] It is not known how many forty-inch statuettes were sold in the period in which Caproni held reproduction rights, but the subsequent value of each piece in the art market depended upon the seller's claim about its rarity. According to the Christie's auction house, Caproni contracted with the Gorham Manufacturing Company foundry to cast only three forty-inch statuettes in a limited lifetime edition. As of 2008, two of these pieces are on public display, one in the Woolaroc Museum in Bentonville, Oklahoma, and another in the Algonquin Club in Boston, and the third was sold to a private collector at auction in 2008 for $266,500.[103] The original clay model of *Massasoit #1* now stands on permanent display at the Pilgrim Hall Museum in Plymouth.

Dallin apparently also approved a limited series of 100 eleven-inch bronze replicas of his revised *Massasoit* sculpture to cover the Massasoit Memorial

FIGURE 48. Small *Massasoit* reproduction on a storage shelf at the Springville Museum of Art. *Courtesy of Springville Museum of Art.*

Association's final $1,500 debt a month before the statue's unveiling (fig. 48). It is not clear how many of these eleven-inch figures were ultimately distributed (in exchange for a twenty-dollar donation to the Massasoit Memorial Association fund), but only one member had contributed twenty dollars by the time the statue was installed on Cole's Hill.[104] However, at some point after Dallin's death in 1944, the art and souvenir markets were flooded with eleven-inch *Massasoit* statuettes. We can assume that at least some of these pieces were cast and distributed as part of the original IORM fund-raising effort. The Red Men Museum and Library in Waco, Texas, currently owns a few of the figurines, and the Cyrus E. Dallin Museum in Arlington, Massachusetts, prominently displays a *Massasoit #1* statuette.[105] But a great number of unauthorized eleven-inch statues can be traced to the Springville Museum of Art, which received Dallin's nine-and-a-half-foot plaster original from BYU in the early 1980s. Soon after acquiring the plaster on loan, the museum commissioned and distributed replica statuettes of *Massasoit* to advertise its newly expanded collection of Dallin's work. For many years the museum offered what were called "museum reproductions" for about $150 each.[106]

The Springville museum also used the statuettes to advertise itself as a world-class art institution by spreading them around the globe as souvenirs.

Marketing

Around the same time that the original plaster model arrived, the annual Springville World Folkfest began, which grew into one of the largest festivals of folk dance and music in the country. Today many international visitors descend upon the small town in late summer, and the city puts forth great effort to host the performers and spectators.[107] For years, the museum extended its welcome by gifting performance groups with a statuette of *Massasoit* to commemorate their time in Springville. According to museum director Rita Wright, who has only heard about the practice, which was from before her time at the museum, the gifts to international groups ceased because the cost of reproduction was too high for the museum to sustain. As a result of the museum's choice to sell and gift *Massasoit* statuettes, the small replicas decontextualized and deterritorialized the subject of the statue itself. "There may be *Massasoit*s in Russia," Wright joked.[108]

The licensed casts and posthumous replicas made as recently as the 1990s mix and circulate through the market and among private art dealers and collectors with little differentiation. In 2014 the Mayflower Society deaccessioned one of the lifetime eleven-inch casts, which fetched about $1,000 at a Plymouth auction.[109] Statuettes of similar size in good condition but produced later sold for $450 and about $2,500; other auction houses listed estimated sale prices from $1,000 to $3,000 but did not find buyers.[110] At the moment of writing, an eleven-inch "original" statuette was for sale on eBay for $1,000.[111] The ephemeral and private nature of these auctioned items—not to mention the rapidly shifting availability of online records of such sales—gives the impression that the statuettes are both always available and rare collectibles. For example, David Lintz, archivist at the Red Men Museum and Library, recalled that one of the statuettes sold on eBay for over $4,000 in late 2014, yet records of this sale cannot be confirmed.[112] The precision of information about the statuettes ranges wildly as well, sometimes misidentifying the posthumous cast as an IORM fund-raiser original and 8sâmeeqan as a leader of the "Wampanogas" or "Wampananos."[113] The subject of the memorial ceases to matter as the object swiftly changes hands in the art marketplace. Within placeless online auction spaces, value is determined based upon ephemeral and self-referential stories of a statuette's provenance and the artist's fame, rather than stories of the Massasoit's diplomacy and Plymouth's memorial landscape. This placelessness stands in stark contrast to the meticulous way Wampanoag history and memory is dependent on intimate grounding in particular places.[114] As commodities, the statuettes do not embody the solid realities of 8sâmeeqan's historical existence or Dallin's craftsmanship cast in bronze on Cole's Hill. Novelist and art collector Gertrude Stein's famous quote "There is no there there," about the ruptures of memory and place that contribute to a self that exists only in the immediate present, might be aptly applied to the *Massasoit* statuette at the point of sale.[115]

MARKETING *MASSASOIT*

Thanks in large part to the tercentenary of 1920–21 and city boosters' marketing strategies, the figure of the Massasoit has become deeply intertwined with Plymouth origin stories and the heritage tourism industry. Within Plymouth tourist shops, *Massasoit* souvenirs were incorporated into a commercial realm in which generic Indian figures and stereotypes continue to captivate consumer interest. These kitsch items, by virtue of their placement beside other racial icons, appealed to the popular notion of the noble savage. Kitsch, Sturken argues, "responds to particular kinds of historical events and indicates particular kinds of political acquiescence."[116] Souvenir items such as cherubic Indian figurines and magnets depicting Native people and Pilgrims feasting together invokes comforting stories and comfortable responses. This kitsch, according to Sturken, "is meant to produce predetermined and conscribed emotional responses, to encourage pathos and sympathy, not anger and outrage." In a place that seeks to fashion itself as the origin of the nation and its founding values, tourists can come to believe that because they feel sympathetic and innocent, so too is their nation.[117] The event marketed in Plymouth, whether the first Thanksgiving or the unlikely survival of the Puritan settlement, helps to reinforce the notion of American innocence, and the consumerist engagement through the purchase of *Massasoit* souvenirs suggests a universal agreement on the value of this origin story; after all, consumerism and patriotism are closely linked. Yet once *Massasoit* souvenirs left Plymouth, these commodities lost their link to a specific place. What does it mean for Plymouth history to be scattered around the country and the world?

Massasoit's marketing, replication, and dispersal from Plymouth have allowed consumers to acquire the stories, likeness, and labors of others. For decades following his death in 1944, Dallin's works continued to be replicated and scattered across the country. His sculptures became increasingly recognizable, yet seldom attributed to and associated with Dallin specifically. Dallin's Massachusetts descendants manage his estate in Arlington, but Dallin's commissioned works around Arlington (and elsewhere) deteriorated over time without proper conservation. Out of concern for Dallin's legacy (and his ties to the Boston suburb), the Cyrus E. Dallin Art Museum was established in 1995 as a nonprofit institution dedicated to preserving his works and educating the community about the artist.[118] Yet the museum is small and its reach is limited; it is a massive challenge for a modest institution to ensure that Dallin's name is just as recognizable as his famous Indian statuary displayed in dozens of cities across the country.[119]

The dispersal of the commodified memorial has certainly posed a challenge for those most deeply concerned with the statue's meaning. Yet the scale of mobility and the nature of sale have also made the figure more accessible and open to interpretation than if it had remained fixed in Plymouth. *Massasoit* souvenirs can be purchased by anyone for a few dollars, and given the esteem in which Wampanoags hold their ancestors, it is possible that Wampanoag and other Native people collect the figurines for proud display.[120] As our research at the Utah capitol grounds indicated, Native viewers appreciated that the memorial honored a Native individual, regardless of the fact that the Massasoit had no ties to Utah. Even if the statue is seen as a generic Indian figure, it may be claimed as a symbol for the dignity of all Indigenous peoples. The ubiquity of *Massasoit* casts, statuettes, charms, mugs, and postcards holds the possibility of spreading 8sâmeeqan's fame, even while the deeper implications of settler colonialism for Indigenous peoples are easily elided in these representations. For Wampanoag people, places are sites for keeping historical memory alive, and when they intervene as Indigenous public historians in comforting American narratives, in the case of *Massasoit*, his actual story becomes unmoored and disconnected from narratives, and those unmoored narratives in turn spread his fame as a generic signifier for the innocence of the American nation. The monumental mobility of *Massasoit* reveals the instability of memory surrounding this deeply contested foundational story of the nation. In this larger sense, *Massasoit* cannot so easily be owned and controlled.

For Wampanoag and other Indigenous people in southern New England, the long history of marketing *Massasoit*, particularly as a Plymouth brand, opens the door to reclaiming Indigenous space and renewing place memories. With a tourist infrastructure already well established and a consumer interest in authentic experiences and unique perspectives, Plymouth and its memorial landscape may be reinterpreted and effectively repackaged, which will (at least to some degree) impact the meaning of the *Massasoit* reproductions. The first step in this process was the creation of the United American Indians of New England "Day of Mourning" plaque, which introduced a counternarrative to the first Thanksgiving story in a place many tourists were sure to see it: at *Massasoit*'s feet. The UAINE plaque suggests to tourists that they walk on hallowed ground not because Pilgrims were once buried beneath them in Cole's Hill, but because they stand on the site where settler colonialism unleashed generations of suffering and loss. Some passersby we interacted with took up the challenge of thinking about conflicting interpretations of this history because of this new plaque. The more complex historical narratives presented at the Plymouth installation do not accompany the statuettes, however, and have thus far not traveled with the *Massasoit* reproductions.

Will consumers shy away from challenging stories that may cause discomfort? Or will more tourists gladly pay for diverse perspectives and unexpected insights? Native Plymouth Tours offers a valuable complication to the narratives set in stone and metal on the town's historic waterfront, yet the longevity of the tour is not assured: it is a tour one must seek out, and it does not command the clientele of the Jenney Museum tours. These facts render this historical alternative precarious from a financial perspective. The marketplace for historic narratives evolves alongside political and social ideology, and private tour companies that do not fulfill consumers' expectations will not succeed. Political winds shift over time and tourists who experience the nation in crisis may wish to return to more comforting and comfortable origin stories. All kinds of factors, from the price of gas to online consumer ratings, might impact the financial futures of private tour companies and, subsequently, the kinds of historical narratives offered at the base of *Massasoit*'s pedestal.[121]

Furthermore, the economics of Plymouth heritage are more complex than consumer choice, as evident in comparisons of the public history offerings. Paula Peters expected to be challenged and therefore sought out numerous primary documents and recent scholarship when developing the *Captured! 1614* exhibit. She diligently documented all the claims and posted detailed "white papers" with sources on the Plymouth 400 website for viewers who wish to learn more.[122] The level of scrutiny over Indigenous tellings of their history demands heroic and meticulous work in order to pass muster with a general public when it is prompted to reconsider conventional narratives that have long buried and ignored Indigenous perspectives, bringing to mind an additional dimension to the emotional labor of their public history efforts.[123] The Jenney Museum tour guide, by contrast, did not provide the same level of research and factual precision. Indeed, Indigenous public historians and educators devote great energy to historical research and making new perspectives available in a memory marketplace in which simplistic and celebratory Pilgrim-centered colonial histories are both plentiful and demonstrably lucrative. In Plymouth, Wampanoag public history must be subsidized (or undertaken as a labor of love that comes with a tax — the burden of gauging the degree to which tourists are willing to accept challenges to their understandings of history without turning those audiences away). Given the time and emotional energy that goes into challenging dominant narratives that tourists consistently seek out, how can the work of Indigenous public historians be sustained in the heritage tourist industry?

The questions of marketing and historical memory are pressing ones for planners of the quadricentennial scheduled for 2020. As of this writing, Plymouth 400, the trademarked name of the planning organization, has begun to establish programming, exhibits, and marketing strategies. Consumers can already purchase clothing, posters, and commemorative license plates in anticipation of the event. Construction is currently underway on the interactive Plymouth 1620–2020 exhibition, *An American Story—A National Legacy*. Meanwhile, the exhibit titled *"Our" Story: 400 Years of Wampanoag History*, of which *Captured! 1614* was the first thematic installment, continues to grow as it is sent on tour around Wampanoag homelands in the months leading up to the quadricentennial. When on display at Massasoit Community College in 2017, the exhibit presented two new themes and panels: one of communication traditions and territory, and the other, titled "The Great Dying," depicting the "catastrophic effects of a plague that devastated the Wampanoag Nation between 1616 and 1619."[124] Contrasting perspectives and complex legacies appear to be of central concern in the framing of the 2020 commemoration, opening the possibility for new understandings of *Massasoit*. Not surprisingly, marketing is a chief consideration. The trademarked brand for Plymouth 400 features the outline of a male Indian figure within an outline of the *Mayflower*. Depending on one's perspective, the figure could be seen as standing in the shadow of the ship—or the other way around.

EPILOGUE

Anniversaries of Rupture / Disruptions of Memory

To get at the politics of time you need to go to memory.

KEVIN BRUYNEEL, "The Trouble with Amnesia"

Time is carefully marked, and demarcated, in Plymouth. Every year since 1769, Plymouth residents have celebrated Forefathers' Day on 21 December to commemorate the landing of the English colonists. The historical narratives of Plymouth begin in 1620, even though the first colonists set foot in the well-established village of Patuxet. The creation of a "year zero" in settler time makes anniversaries possible, which then foster potent forms of collective memory. The 250-year anniversary convinced tourists to make a pilgrimage to a rock on the shore to behold the symbolic origins of the nation. The tercentenary served as the occasion for the Improved Order of Red Men to commission a statue of the Massasoit. Each year in late November, American families reenact a Thanksgiving ritual in which people come together to share a bounty. Time is a structuring force, in Plymouth and across the nation, that shapes collective memory. It nurtures narratives of peaceful colonization and Indigenous acquiescence, of European settlement as a force of modernity and Indian disappearance as a yardstick for progress. Such calendrical commemorations reproduce the political temporality of settler colonialism.[1] The viewer who glances up at the heroic-sized bronze *Massasoit* and reads the plaque honoring "the protector and preserver of the Pilgrims" has been invited to recognize the existence and justify the power of settler colonialism in the present moment.

But there are other possibilities. As President Barack Obama said in a speech at the dedication of the Smithsonian National Museum of African American History and Culture in 2016, memorials offer the opportunity to reconsider how history is told and make choices about what to retain and what to cast aside. Monuments and plaques tell us only a sliver of the past, "a singular event that we once chose to commemorate as history," but "that same object reframed, put in context, tells us so much more."[2] Indigenous people have taken on the task of reframing *Massasoit* and placing the story of the sachem's mutual defense agreement within a larger context of Indigenous suffering, survival, and resilience. The monument thus serves as a site of intervention, an opportunity to disrupt settler memory and install an alternative temporal consciousness. The annual National Day of Mourning protests that take place at the statue embody counternarratives to Thanksgiving Day celebrations that violate Indigenous understandings of settler colonialism rooted so particularly in Plymouth. The revisionist marker installed next to *Massasoit* addresses the violence unleashed upon Indigenous people after the English arrived, effectively closing the cognitive distance between 8sâmeeqan's time and our own. With these interventions, a space can open up for a reconsideration of our history and identity, and viewers have the opportunity to grapple with discomfort and new forms of memory.

The National Day of Mourning was born in response to a significant anniversary in settler memory, yet it set in motion an alternative timeline that emphasizes Indigenous resilience throughout a shared past. In 1970, when James was disinvited from speaking at the 350-year anniversary of the Pilgrims' landing because his interpretation of the event was unacceptable to the planners, he initiated a new timeline of Wampanoag protest and visibility. His "unauthorized" speech at the *Massasoit* statue declared Thanksgiving a day of mourning, one that would be observed from that point forward in calendrical time. The next year, under the leadership of Tall Oak and Brian Miles, Plimoth Plantation established the Wampanoag program, to be staffed by Native people. Linda Coombs recalled that establishing the program, which allowed visitors for the first time to "hear our story from our perspective," was a "knock-down, drag-out" fight, but it was initiated in 1971 "as a direct result of the first National Day of Mourning."[3] The program created the opportunity for generations of Wampanoag and other Native employees to conduct intensive research into the seventeenth-century world and learn skills and techniques their ancestors had mastered. In addition to re-creating artifacts, the Indigenous staff also learned how to interpret their history and gauge their presentations to different audiences. Coombs noted that when visitors were directed to the Wampanoag Homesite before entering the English Village (an interpretive change in the late 1990s), "that just flipped the whole script." Visitors released their reverence for the colonists and demanded to know why the English stole Indian land. "The effect was noticeable," Coombs recalled.[4]

The long-term impacts of the Day of Mourning can be seen in other ways as well. The annual Day of Mourning protests picked up urgency and attracted more militant activists in the 1990s. The marches through the city and more extreme acts of protest provoked fear of disorder that the town of Plymouth was anxious to quell. One significant result of negotiations between Plymouth and the United American Indians of New England was the installation of a plaque with an explanation of the Day of Mourning beside *Massasoit*. If our interviews with passersby in Plymouth are any indication, local residents and tourists alike have taken note of the plaque, and many have reflected on the alternative narrative of Thanksgiving and settler colonialism it explains. Ever since its installation, visitors who have been moved by the plaque's words have taken this more complicated narrative home with them. The annual Day of Mourning protest and the plaque beside the statue change interpretations of *Massasoit* and disrupt the ritualized Thanksgiving mythology in Plymouth.

The decades of work of Indigenous people that has gone into "flipping the script" in Plymouth reverberate, illustrating how memorial interventions can foster dialog about the legacies of settler colonialism far from the New England coast. In spring 2017, a protest erupted in Minneapolis over a controversial interactive sculpture called *Scaffold* installed in the Walker Art Center's sculpture garden. The white multimedia artist of the piece, Sam Durant, who had grown up near Plymouth, intended his work to represent the gallows used in executions of political dissidents, freedom fighters, and Native Americans (specifically the thirty-eight Dakota men hanged in Mankato, Minnesota, in 1862) to explore issues of inequality, race, and state violence in U.S. history. But Dakota protesters argued the artwork trivialized a traumatic event in their history; viewers could walk on and off the scaffold without having to grapple with the deep pain the executions inflicted in the region. "This is a murder machine that killed our people because we were hungry," said Sam Wounded Knee, Crow Creek Dakota.[5] Durant listened to Dakota elders and agreed to remove the piece and sign over the intellectual rights to the Dakota Nation. As he recalled from the conversations, "The Dakota people basically saw something that looked like a monument to their massacre."[6] Durant admitted that he had not understood the local context, which included the fact that state history textbooks had only acknowledged the forced removal of the Dakota people in 2015; the legislature had decided over the protests of Native citizens not to relocate most of the artworks in the state capitol's Senate chambers glorifying cultural and racial superiority over the Dakota Nation; and a controversy has arisen over how to commemorate the bicentennial of a military fort built on a site of Dakota spiritual significance that served as an internment camp for Dakota women, children, and elders after the Mankato execution.[7] Although the details are specific to the region and the Dakota Nation, such controversies over the persistence of settler memory in public spaces, halls of government, commemorations, and historical narratives can be found across the country. As he reflected on his evolving awareness of the presence of the colonial past, Durant recalled witnessing a protest at Plymouth Rock in the early 1970s when he was quite young. "It was the United American Indians of New England. They were saying, 'Hey America, this is a catastrophe for us, not a celebration. It's a day of mourning.' I remember thinking, 'Oh, there's another side to this.'"[8] As he saw in Plymouth and belatedly learned in Minneapolis, acknowledging that the nation has been built on dispossession and violence involves an uncomfortable dialog about the structure of power that continues to shape collective memory *in place* and *in time*. Durant's failure to anticipate the heart-wrenching responses of Dakota people begs the question of the power of settler colonialism to isolate moments of rupture in settler memory rather than to generalize them as a larger unsettling of antiseptic national narratives. For Durant in this particular moment, colonialism was effectively an event rather than a structure, underscoring the power of settler colonialism to erase its ubiquitous pulverizing of Indigenous peoples, places, and rights.

And yet as such episodes enter the larger stage of public debate, they suggest that a reckoning with a violent and conflicted past still reverberating in the present is an ever-larger element of public consciousness. As the mythologized origin of the nation (and English settler-colonial memory), Plymouth is a crucial site for disrupting the dominant narrative of Indian acquiescence and disappearance at the root of so many other memorial controversies across the country. In anticipation of the 400-year anniversary of the Pilgrims' landing, Wampanoag citizens see an opportunity to teach people about the complexities of colonial history and foster an alternative temporal consciousness. Similar to the creation of the Wampanoag program at Plimoth Plantation, the Plymouth 400 Board, tasked with planning commemorative events for 2020, was formed in response to Indigenous protest. Linda Coombs recalled how the board invited Wampanoag perspectives "because they really do not want to do what they did a hundred years ago [when white residents performed as Wampanoags in the pageant and *Massasoit* was installed on Cole's Hill] or have another whole Frank James thing like in 1970."[9]

Wampanoag elders' and educators' involvement in Plymouth 400 has resulted in the temporal reconfiguration of settler memory in two ways. The first is to insist upon James's 1970 speech act as a "year zero" of Wampanoag perspectives on history that will no longer be ignored or silenced. In this alternative timeline, 2020 represents the fifty-year anniversary of the creation of the Day of Mourning rather than the 400-year anniversary of a different event. If anniversaries help us to recall and ritualize memories in calendrical time, Wampanoags insist upon an acknowledgment of additional events in a shared history between Indigenous people and non-Native residents.

The second way in which Wampanoag elders and teachers have crafted a new historical consciousness around the Plymouth 400 anniversary is through their work on the regional traveling exhibit *"Our" Story: A Wampanoag History Exhibit*. The Wampanoag team launched the project in 2014 with the first installation titled *Captured! 1614*. To more fully contextualize English-Wampanoag relations when the *Mayflower* Pilgrims founded their colony on the bay, Wampanoag educators insisted on moving the timeline back six years to include the 1614 kidnapping of twenty-seven Wampanoag men and boys (including the iconic Tisquantum) from coastal villages for sale as slaves in Spain. The exhibit explains that this traumatic abduction and Tisquantum's subsequent escape and return to Patuxet form "a critical backstory to colonization and the roots of the American holiday, Thanksgiving." A panel titled "The Great Dying" opened in 2016 to mark the anniversary of "the catastrophic plague that killed tens of thousands of native people between 1616 and 1619 from Cape Cod to Maine." The exhibit includes emotionally moving video of Wampanoag descendants trying to imagine how these episodes of trauma and violence must have been experienced by their ancestors. From the Wampanoag perspective, the agreement of mutual defense that 8sâmeeqan famously negotiated with the English can only make sense when taking into account the ways in which the epidemic devastated their ancestors, threatened their understanding of their entire cosmos, and weakened the Wampanoag nation politically and militarily in the years immediately prior to the Pilgrims' arrival.[10] By centering crucial events in Wampanoag history, the exhibit designers are both enlarging the historical consciousness of America's shared past and disrupting the settler memory that insists history begins when the *Mayflower* Pilgrims set foot on the beach.

Wampanoag educators have responded to the settler-colonial narrative, particularly the myth of peaceful first contact and Thanksgiving, rather than exclusively crafting their own separate history in public protests, plaques, performances, and exhibits. They thus illustrate the creative potential of directly confronting a deeply painful history of settler colonialism. As Ira Berlin noted of African American organizations of all kinds created within and after slavery, these organizations became the sites of new languages, aesthetics, and philosophies. "They produced leaders and ideas that continue to inform American life, so much so that it is impossible to imagine American culture without slavery's creative legacy."[11] While the disruptions to settler memory may focus on undoing myths, challenging narratives of disappearance, and especially addressing the anniversaries of the peaceful founding of the nation, Wampanoag historical interventions have been likewise generative and creative rather than simply passive or reactionary.

Interventions are not easy and require sustained courage on the part of Indigenous public historians, who undertake exhaustive research in creating their interventions and costly emotional labor in engaging with the non-Indian public. Such undertakings demand that viewers unflinchingly look at embarrassing and uncomfortable truths about the past and acknowledge the pain that historical narratives continue to inflict today. Because Americans use public monuments to articulate stories about the past and set their perspectives in place, they have become the sites for deeply emotional battles over memory. The fervor with which Americans hold on to their long-cherished narratives is laid bare in recent efforts to question and dismantle memorial sites and installations. Scrutiny of Confederate memorials increased after a white supremacist murdered nine black members in a Charleston, South Carolina, church in 2015, and municipal governments across the South removed or renamed sixty (of roughly 1,500) publicly funded symbols of the Confederacy in response.[12] These actions sparked an immediate reaction; the Southern Poverty Law Center reported 350 pro-Confederate flag rallies in the year after the Charleston attack. The controversy over the removal of Confederate statues hit fever pitch in the summer of 2017, when several cities voted to move Confederate monuments installed during the height of Jim Crow (1890s–1930). The first in a series of confrontations took place in New Orleans in May; after receiving death threats, city contractors donned protective gear to remove four statues in the dead of night to evade the threatened violent encounters. The city of Charlottesville, Virginia, which had voted in April to move two of its Confederate statues and rename a city park, then became a lightning rod for reactionary violence. In August, the governor of Virginia called a state of emergency when white nationalists under the guise of "Unite the Right," who had gathered in Charlottesville to oppose the removal of a statue of Robert E. Lee with semiautomatic weapons and chants of "you/Jews will not replace us," clashed with counterprotesters. The event reached a terrible crescendo when a white nationalist drove his car into a crowd of antiracist protesters, killing

Heather Heyer and injuring nineteen others.[13] In the days that followed, a crowd pulled down a Confederate monument in Durham, North Carolina, the city of Baltimore quietly removed four statues overnight, and the governor of North Carolina announced his desire to remove all Confederate monuments on public property in the state.[14]

The violent scenes of hatred and bigotry on display in Charlottesville appeared to be a game changer; after watching neo-Nazis and other white supremacist organizations from around the country rally together in defense of the Robert E. Lee statue, it became clear that Confederate memorials were potent political symbols to those who wish to maintain white supremacy. In addition to direct action in sympathy with the counterprotesters, many Americans began to debate difficult historical issues in the days after the events in Charlottesville. Historians, for their part, entered the public dialog to supply context for the erection of Confederate monuments during Jim Crow and to clarify the distinction between history and memory. An event in the past can never change, for the past is irretrievable and incontrovertible. But depending on whether that event holds significance in the present, it may be represented (in language or in symbol) or ignored. Memory is meaning; it is an interpretation of the past that can help us to know who we are and what we value. As one historian described the tenor of public discourse in late summer of 2017, "Central to the discussion has been the place of memory in the identity of the nation. . . . [Citizens] are prompted to think about the ethics of remembrance."[15] What stories do our monuments tell about history, and do those stories reflect our values today and who we want to be tomorrow? Although public polls taken after the events in Charlottesville in 2017 indicate that a majority of American adults would oppose the removal of a statue to a Confederate leader "as a historical symbol" (the poll question itself blurring the distinction between history and memory), the debates over the removal of monuments have involved, to some extent, an acknowledgment that statues glorifying racist ideologies and regimes have an impact on race relations today. The New York Times described the political climate after the shocking events in Charlottesville as a potential moment for a "long overdue national reckoning with Southern and American history."[16]

As monumental as this moment seems, with crowds tearing down statues and citizens flocking to city council meetings to passionately express their views on public memorials, this is not a full reckoning with American history. Confederate monuments force an acknowledgement of the persistence of the ideology of white supremacy, drawing a direct line between the defense of slavery, the terrorism of Jim Crow, and racial inequalities today. Yet uncomfortable silences remain; missing from the passionate conversations about the nation's history is the system and logic upon which slavery was built. As well, if Americans acknowledged the history and ongoing violence of settler colonialism, we might have seen the sympathy expressed for antiracist protesters in Charlottesville who confronted white supremacists also extended to Standing Rock Sioux protesters of the Dakota Access Pipeline gathered in 2016 to defend their homes, vital resources, and sacred sites from the destructive incursions of a private company (with backing from the federal government). If Americans understood the destructive force of settler colonialism, the shock and horror that swept the nation when a man drove his car into a crowd of protesters in Charlottesville would have also gripped the country upon reports that Morton County police officers pelted Native protesters with rubber bullets, tear gas, concussive grenades, and water hoses mounted on armored vehicles in subfreezing temperatures, sending at least seventeen protesters to the hospital. A reporter of the events at Standing Rock commented that "the systematic violation of Indigenous land rights is an old story" and one that is not often linked to Indigenous people's lived realities in mainstream public consciousness.[17] The cognitive distance reinforced in settler narratives and calendrical time therefore obscures the connection between historic violence and present-day injustice. Even if Americans voice regret for past violence and land dispossession, the failure to recognize that Indigenous people are still fighting for the same things they were centuries ago suggests that non-Indians cling tenaciously to their stories of Indian disappearance. If Americans are finding the "lost cause" narrative a tough one to dismantle and disentangle from history, the narrative of peaceful colonization poses an even greater challenge. A full reckoning with American history would mean taking a long, hard look at the monuments, memorials, and other public sites dedicated to the commemoration of colonialism writ large.

The skewing of political discourse to ignore settler colonialism even in the midst of debates over historical memory and monuments has been achieved through the role of settler memory, which Kevin Bruyneel defines as "the practices of memory that allow those in the United States to both see and to not see Indigenous people and settler colonialism, to remember and forget at the same time."[18] We see performances of Indians in Thanksgiving observances, representations of 8sâmeeqan installed and reproduced, and consumerist practices around replicas and souvenirs of *Massasoit*. We see this and other memorials that declare "good" Native peoples to be both supportive of American progress and relegated to the past, and that mark space in a way that naturalizes the American state's authority and ownership over Indigenous land. But the violent dispossession of land from Indigenous people—in the past or as an ongoing legacy shaping the present—rarely or only fleetingly enters public debates. Settler memory thus operates to "disavow on-going settler-ness as an active practice," enabling and reproducing the "violence and dispossession of settler-colonialism itself." The lack of talk about Indigenous people and their resistance against settler-colonial expansion is settler memory "doing its work."[19]

Wampanoag elders and educators have taken on the demanding task of both teaching about their history and disrupting narratives of settler colonialism. Every year on the Day of Mourning, in every guest interaction in every workday in the Wampanoag Homesite at Plimoth Plantation, at each Plymouth 400 meeting and in each curatorial decision, in each scheduled tour to the *Massasoit* statue, in each interview with researchers like us, and in countless other ways, Native people share their histories of violence, dispossession, survival, and resilience. In each of these moments Native educators demand that Americans confront their discomfort and grapple with a shared history of settler colonialism. Discomfort stands in counterposition to mythic national origin stories of innocence and purity in Plymouth and in other sites of memorialization of Indian history such as the Sand Creek Massacre National Historic Site, the Battle of Little Bighorn Battlefield National Monument, and the various Cherokee efforts to intervene in Trail of Tears memorialization and Potawatomi commemorative practices around the Trail of Death, which begins in Plymouth, Indiana.[20] Struggles over history and memory in these sites and others dramatize the importance of the past and its meaning in "what can and can't be said" about Indigeneity, race, and nation in the United States. But these struggles also beg the question of why discomfort as an affect is so frequently momentary rather than internalized and struggled over: it erupts to the surface then recedes, prompting us to ask, "What comes *after* discomfort?"

On a spring afternoon in 2017, we navigated through the narrow streets of the small industrial town of Warren, Rhode Island, in search of the only physical memorial to the Massasoit in the vicinity of his seventeenth-century home. We located the 1907 monument on a short street that ran to the edge of the Warren River, where an assortment of storm drains seeped onto rubble piled on the shore (fig. 49). A fisherman on a nearby dock saw us walking around with cameras and asked if we were there to inspect what the locals suspected to be a toxic chemical waste dump site. Ancient tree roots had pushed the sidewalk bricks up into a disorderly jumble, and a fence for a neighboring property pressed up against the cracking concrete base of the monument (fig. 50). A

FIGURE 49. Drain pipes at the river shore in Warren, Rhode Island.
Photograph by Lisa Blee.

portable toilet stood on the sidewalk nearby. The setting in Warren presented a jarring juxtaposition to the scene evoked on the monument's bronze plaque:

THIS TABLET
PLACED BESIDE THE GUSHING WATER
KNOWN FOR MANY GENERATIONS AS

FIGURE 50. Massasoit Spring Monument, Warren, Rhode Island.
Photograph by Jean O'Brien.

MASSASOIT'S SPRING
COMMEMORATES THE GREAT
INDIAN SACHEM MASSASOIT
"FRIEND OF THE WHITE MAN"
RULER OF THIS REGION WHEN THE

Epilogue

PILGRIMS OF THE MAYFLOWER
LANDED AT PLYMOUTH
IN THE YEAR OF OUR LORD 1620

At some point, the water that sustained 8sâmeeqan and his people stopped gushing and the monument itself seemed to be neglected and forgotten. "Massasoit Spring is blocked up," Linda Coombs had told us the previous day. "They tarred it in or something. I wish they would unblock it and dig out that tar and just let that water flow . . . out to the bay. Symbolically, I think that if it was unblocked that would be a good thing."[21] What would it mean to restore the spring, to make the deep history of Wampanoag experiences visible at this site and show an alternative to the environmental degradation that symbolizes "progress" here? What does it take to unleash that which has been simultaneously invoked and covered over by settler colonialism? Monuments can give us a place to start revising and reenvisioning. Engaging with monuments allows us the opportunity to examine national stories, to grapple with the pain of suppressed and silenced truths, to determine which narratives fully reflect our shared past. They may be formed of stone and metal and appear set in place, but monuments are not fixed. While the United States is a nation formed by settler colonialism (and in immeasurable ways, the decisions of 8sâmeeqan), the mobility of *Massasoit* shows that such sites of memory contain monumental potential.

Acknowledgments

This book has been a long time in the making, and at the risk of neglecting to extend our appreciation to all those who helped shape it along the way, we'd like to give it a try. We benefited from the assistance of many archivists, collections managers, librarians, and fellow researchers in our quest to understand the larger context surrounding each copy of *Massasoit* in Utah, Kansas City, Dayton, and Plymouth.

In Salt Lake City, Stephanie Angelides from the Utah State Capitol and Gregory Waltz from the Utah State Historical Society gamely went through their records to find traces of Cyrus Dallin and *Massasoit*. Rita Wright at the Springville Museum of Art opened up the museum archives and shared institutional memories that helpfully contextualized Cyrus Dallin in his hometown and in Utah art history. In Provo, the Brigham Young University Museum of Art's senior registrar, Emily Poulsen, provided access to museum collection files, and Virgie Day generously shared her research findings on sculpture reproductions. Officer Arnold Lemmon at BYU was instrumental in helping us piece together the story of *Massasoit* reproductions; he was kind enough to share his art fraud investigation files, patiently explain how all of the pieces fit together, and check our work for accuracy. Finally, Dallin's descendant Denice Wheeler graciously invited Lisa into her Wyoming home to share her collected materials on the Dallin family, and through her own research and a guided tour, Wheeler provided a wonderful introduction to the region's history. David Boutros and Nancy Piepenbring at the State Historical Society of Missouri in Kansas City helpfully guided us through the Miller Nichols papers and provided invaluable documents for our research. George Peso helped us to fill in holes in our timeline by sharing his memories of the *Massasoit* in the Evergreen Plaza shopping center before the mall closed.

In Plymouth, Massachusetts, we benefited from the knowledge of many public intellectuals. Tim Turner's fantastic Native Plymouth tour helped us to see Plymouth in new ways and set us on a fruitful path through Wampanoag landscapes. Darius Coombs met with us several times—in D.C., Honolulu (in conjunction with a Native American and Indigenous Studies Association meeting), and Plymouth—to teach us about the accomplishments and daily physical, creative, intellectual, and emotional work that Native interpreters pour into the Wampanoag Homesite at Plimoth Plantation. Richard Pickering enthusiastically welcomed us to Plimoth Plantation and provided important background information on the institution's past programming and future plans. Linda Coombs and Paula Peters generously made time to talk with us about our project, and their insights helped transform this book into one that is much better for their wisdom. Ramona Peters contributed important information and saved us from committing a couple of embarrassing gaffes. We could not have written this book without the crucial work and insights of these patient teachers and public intellectuals.

David Lintz from the Red Men Library in Waco, Texas, generously shared invaluable materials about the commission of the original statue and provided us with background information on the organization. Other archivists, collections managers, and individuals who provided materials include Denise Mahoney (Art Institute of Chicago); Stuart Hines (LaBudde Special Collections, Miller Nichols Library, University of Missouri at Kansas City); Sally Kurtz (Dayton Art Institute); Ann McFerrin (Kansas City, Missouri, Parks and Recreation); Valerie Wahl (Northwest Museum of Arts and Culture); Karen Shafts (Boston Public Library); Bob Cullum (Leslie Jones Collection, Boston Public Library); Chad Emmett (BYU); Cindy Brightenburg (L. Tom Perry Special Collections, BYU); Heather Leavell (Cyrus E. Dallin Art Museum); Jeannine Levesque (Leominster Public Library); Elizabeth Dube (Plymouth Public Library); and Julie Ahlers.

We also wish to thank all of the passersby in Salt Lake City, Provo, Kansas City, Dayton, and Plymouth who agreed to pause and answer our questions about *Massasoit* as they went to class, work, and on tours. Jessica Leslie Arnett amazed us time and again with her transcription of our many interviews and on-the-ground research at the Dayton Art Institute, where she gathered the final insights from passersby. We are so grateful for her assistance.

We have benefited greatly from audiences where we presented elements of this book in progress, including numerous appearances at Native American and Indigenous Studies Association meetings, the Western History Association Conference, and the American Society for Ethnohistory meeting, which resulted in the publication of the first iteration of this book in the journal *Ethnohistory* and the realization that we were not quite done with this project. We thank fellow panelists and audience members at these conferences for their wonderful feedback and encouragement. Pamela Klassen, Carol Duncan, and other participants in the Sites of Memory Workshop at the University of Toronto lent us generous support. Jeani would also like to thank Heidi Kiiwetinepinesiik Stark, Ann Stahl, and others at the University of Victoria for supportive feedback on chapter 3, and Julie Reed for the kind invitation to deliver the Milton M. Klein lecture at the University of Tennessee, which yielded helpful insights. Lisa thanks members of the Carolina Seminar in American Indian and Indigenous Studies at the University of North Carolina at Chapel Hill for their thoughtful questions and insistence that this research needed to become a book. Lisa would also like to thank colleagues at Wake Forest, especially writing group members Nate Plageman, Ben Coates, Monique O'Connell, and Jake Ruddiman, for reading early drafts of this work and helping to puzzle through several chapters. Participants in the University of Minnesota's American Indian and Indigenous Studies Workshop read multiple versions of manuscript elements and, as always, offered fabulous and good-humored advice. They are literally too many to mention by name.

Generous funding from our respective institutions supported research on this book, dating back to research assistance for Lisa at the University of Minnesota. The Wake Forest University Department of History supported Lisa's research and conference travels, and the Humanities Institute Summer Writing grant made it possible to focus on writing and revision at a crucial stage. Jeani also drew on an Imagine Fund grant from Minnesota for research travel as well as research funds for conferences.

Mark Simpson-Vos, Jessica Newman, Mary Carley Caviness, and countless others at the University of North Carolina Press have been unstintingly helpful and supportive along the way. Mark, editor extraordinaire, extended enthusiasm for the project when we first pitched it to him and has been fabulous in every respect in hearing us out, reading our work, and going along with our demands for rich illustration of our book.

Finally, we have the great fortune of not just a long-standing personal relationship that deepened with our many wonderfully stimulating research trips but also terrific support systems at home. Lisa thanks Eranda Jayawickreme for the bottomless cups of tea and thoughtful insights that made the morning writing routine a joyful one, and cats Pancho and Sadie for their reliable lap warming and keyboard stomping. Jeani thanks Tim Kehoe, always there with an encouraging word and an abundance of fun, and wants to note the helpful pestering of her cats, Pancho and Lupe.

Notes

ABBREVIATIONS

AAA   Cyrus E. Dallin Papers, Archives of American Art,
        Smithsonian Institution, Washington, D.C.
BYUPIS Brigham Young University Police Investigation Summary, University
        Fine Arts Collection, Arnold Lemmon Files, Provo, Utah
CCC   Capitol Commission Correspondence, Utah State
        Historical Society, Salt Lake City, Utah
CLDSCHL Church of Latter-Day Saints Church History
        Library, Salt Lake City, Utah
MEFMCF Massasoit Excerpts from Master Case File,
        Arnold Lemmon Files, Provo, Utah
MF   Massasoit File, Brigham Young University
        Museum of Art Archives, Provo, Utah
MIF   Massasoit Investigation File, Brigham Young University
        Museum of Art Archives, Provo, Utah
MNC   Miller Nichols Collection, Collection No. K1081, Western Historical
        Manuscript Collection, State Historical Society of Kansas City /
        University of Missouri, Kansas City Archives, Kansas City, Missouri
PPLVF   Plymouth Public Library, Vertical Files, Plymouth, Massachusetts
RMML   Red Men Museum and Library, Waco, Texas
TPCP   Tercentenary Planning Committee Papers, Pilgrim Hall
        Museum Archives, Plymouth, Massachusetts
USHS   Utah State Historical Society, Salt Lake City, Utah

PROLOGUE

1. Jennifer McDermott, "Wampanoag Leader's Reburial Will Honor 'Cultural Obligation,'" *Portland Press Herald*, 14 April 2017, http://www.pressherald.com/2017 /04/14/reburial-of-a-wampanoag-leaders-remains-to-the-original-grave-in-rhode -island-will-honor-a-tribal-spiritual-and-cultural-obligation. The Massasoit's name is

spelled variously in the primary and secondary record. In this book, we follow the spelling and orthography of the Wôpanâak Language Reclamation Program, and we thank Judi Urquhart and Jessie Little Doe for their assistance in these matters. His name is pronounced "Oo-sah-mee'-kwun."

2. Peters, "Consulting with the Bone Keepers," 32–43. The seven institutions are the National Museum of the American Indian, Museum of the City of New York, Haffenreffer Museum, Rhode Island Historical Society, Roger Williams Park Museum and Planetarium, Robert Peabody Museum, and the George Hail Free Library / Charles Whipple Museum. "Wampanoag Massasoit Returns to Original Burial Site," capecodtoday: cape cod community news, 13 April 2017, http://capecodtoday.com /article/2017/04/12/231617-Wampanoag-Massasoit-Returns-Original-Burial-Site.

3. "Wampanoag Tribes Rebury Remains of Ancestral Leader Massasoit," Indianz, 16 May 2017, https://www.indianz.com/News/2017/05/16/wampanoag-tribes-rebury -remains-of-ances.asp.

4. The first iteration of this project came out as O'Brien and Blee, "What Is a Monument," 635–53.

5. Homage to Ari Kelman's masterful book, *Misplaced Massacre*.

6. Catherine Cloutier, "How Many US Communities Are Named 'Plymouth?': 30 US Cities, Towns, and Townships Share the Name of the First Thanksgiving Locale," *Boston Globe*, 25 November 2014, https://www.bostonglobe.com/metro/2014/11/25/how-many -communities-are-called-plymouth/XLQlwkRAi3K6IghDbWSsnI/story.html.

7. Linda Coombs interview. On New England Indians in the whaling industry, see Shoemaker, *Native American Whalemen*; and on the centrality of the sea to colonial encounters, see Lipman, *Saltwater Frontier*.

8. Brooks, *Our Beloved Kin*; DeLucia, *Memory Lands*; Warren, *New England Bound*, esp. 91–113.

9. "The Messenger Runner," Plymouth 400, accessed 12 September 2017, http://www .plymouth400inc.org/messenger-runner.

10. "Celebrating 40 Years," 16. Mishoon, the Wampanoag word for boat, is singular; mishoonash is plural. DeLucia discusses the commemorative journeys, including via *mishoonash*, as a process of "regrounding in meaningful memorial geographies," in contrast to the disorientation of the many removes of Mary Rowlandson during her captivity in King Philip's War. In this sense, Indigenous memorial mobility is inherently connected to the intimacy of place. DeLucia, *Memory Lands*, 106–12.

11. *Affiliate*, 1.

12. *Annual Report.*

13. "Celebrating 40 Years," 16.

14. *Affiliate*, 1.

15. See, for example, Morgan Lee and Felicia Fonesa, "US Monuments of Spanish Conquest Facing Mounting Criticism," *Seattle Times*, 8 September 2017, https://www .seattletimes.com/nation-world/us-monuments-to-spanish-conquest-facing-mounting -criticism/; Alan Freeman, "As America Debates Confederate Monuments, Canada Faces Its Own Historical Controversy," *Washington Post*, 28 August 2017, https:// www.washingtonpost.com/news/worldviews/wp/2017/08/28/as-america-debates -confederate-monuments-canada-faces-its-own-historical-controversy/?utm_term =.29831aa8e975; Ian Austen, "Canada, Too, Faces a Reckoning With History and Racism," *New York Times*, 27 August 2017, https://www.nytimes.com/2017/08/28/world

/americas/canada-john-a-macdonald-kingston.html?_r=0; Daniella Silva, "Christopher Columbus Statue in New York City Could Be Considered for Removal," NBC News, 23 August 2017, https://www.nbcnews.com/news/us-news/christopher-columbus-statue -new-york-city-could-be-considered-removal-n795316; Stephani Zillman, "Northern Territory Commits to Changing Racist Place Names," ABC News, 31 August 2017, http:// www.abc.net.au/news/2017-08-31/northern-territory-to-change-racist-places-names /8859814; and Faiza Mahamud, "Minneapolis Park Board Votes to Change Lake Calhoun Name to Bde Maka Ska," *Minneapolis Star Tribune*, 5 May 2017, http://www.startribune .com/minneapolis-park-board-to-vote-tonight-on-lake-calhoun-name-change/421157163.

16. The commission was tasked with reviewing public art and historical monuments on property owned by the city and developing guidelines for city action. "Mayor de Blasio Names Mayoral Advisory Commission on City Art, Monuments and Markers," NYC, accessed 19 September 2017, http://www1.nyc.gov/office-of-the-mayor/news/582-17 /mayor-de-blasio-names-mayoral-advisory-commission-city-art-monuments-markers.

17. Steve Cuozzo, "De Blasio's 'Monuments' Squad is an Absolutely Terrifying Idea," *New York Post*, 8 September 2017, http://nypost.com/2017/09/08/de-blasios-monuments-squad-is-an-absolutely-terrifying-idea/. Just days before, a resident of Yonkers, New York discovered that a Columbus statue there had been beheaded, with the head later discovered in Columbus Memorial Park. This followed a similar act of vandalism of a Columbus statue in Baltimore. Mandy Mayfield, "Beheaded Statue of Christopher Columbus Found in New York Town," *Washington Examiner*, 30 August 2017, http://www .washingtonexaminer.com/beheaded-statue-of-christopher-columbus-found-in-new -york-town/article/2632978.

18. Ku Klux Klan founder Nathan Bedford Forrest scored highest, with 87 percent of readers voting to take down his monument, followed by Confederate leaders Jefferson Davis (77 percent) and Robert E. Lee (72 percent), while George Washington came in at the bottom with 4 percent supporting removal. Christopher Columbus fell toward the lower end of the spectrum at 30 percent, nestled between Andrew Jackson (39 percent) and William McKinley (23 percent), and followed by Theodore Roosevelt (17 percent) and Ulysses S. Grant (9 percent). Emily Badger, Kathleen A. Flynn, and Samuel Jacoby, "Which Statues Need to Come Down? You Decide," *New York Times*, 29 August 2017, https://www.nytimes.com/interactive/2017/08/29/upshot/statues-quiz.html?_r=0. After Forrest, Davis, and Lee, came Joe Paterno (80 percent), Roger B. Taney (79 percent), Strom Thurmond (66 percent), Frank Rizzo (54 percent), J. Marion Sims (50 percent), "Silent Sam" (48 percent), and Stephen Foster (45 percent).

INTRODUCTION

1. Sociologist Iwona Irwin-Zarecka, who argues that collective frames of reference shape individuals' interpretations of past events, uses the term "memory work" to describe how individuals engage in concerted efforts to make a usable past. We seek to extend the knowledge of this process beyond collective memory formation by tracing its cultural development over time and in conversation with cultural-political questions at the heart of Indigenous studies. See Irwin-Zarecka, *Frames of Remembrance*.

2. Savage, *Monument Wars*, 4, 7–8.

3. Temkin, "Freeze-Frame."

4. Savage, *Monument Wars*, 6.

5. Moorehead, *Finding Balance*, 34–35.

6. Quote from Linda Coombs interview; Darius Coombs and Pickering interview.

7. Linda Coombs interview.

8. Edward Lodi reviews the battle and suggests that both sides were correct. He posits that because settlers understood that Pokanoket villages were often located near springs, and springs abound across the region, it is likely that the Massasoit frequented springs in both Warren and Barrington. Virginia Baker, *Massasoit's Town*, 67–70. On the contest over Sowams, see Virginia Baker, *Sowams*, esp. 4–8, who claims the evidence lines up in favor of Warren, Rhode Island; Fessenden, *History of Warren*, 13–31; and Bicknell, *Historical Address and Poem*, 21.

9. On replacement narratives, see O'Brien, *Firsting and Lasting*, chap. 2.

10. Kelman, *Misplaced Massacre*, 5.

11. Denson, *Monuments to Absence*, 3–9.

12. Wolfe, "Settler Colonialism."

13. Blight, *Race and Reunion*, 381.

14. For examples of First Nations artists' interventions in settler memory in Canada, see Phillips, "Settler Monuments, Indigenous Memory," 281–303.

15. Young, "Holocaust Memorials in America"; Brundage, *Where These Memories Grow*, 6–7.

16. Savage, *Standing Soldiers, Kneeling Slaves*, esp. 155–59. He includes the never-realized vision of the United Daughters of the Confederacy to erect a Mammy monument on the national mall. For more on that project and the ubiquity of Mammy stereotyping in American popular culture, see McElya, *Clinging to Mammy*; and on the embrace of Mammy in another context, see Duncan, "Aunt(y) Jemima."

17. Bergstrom, "Tough Telling." On the discomfort with histories of slavery, see also Horton and Horton, *Slavery and Public History*; and on the controversy over revising portrayals of slavery in dialog with the new social history at Colonial Williamsburg, see Handler and Gable, *New History*. See also DeLucia, *Memory Lands*.

18. See, for example, Sturken, *Tourists of History*; Frei, "Towards Memory, Against Oblivion"; and Jacey Fortin, "Toppling Monuments, a Visual History," *New York Times*, 17 August 2017, https://www.nytimes.com/2017/08/17/world/controversial-statues-monuments-destroyed.html?mcubz=0&_r=1.

19. Cosson, "Transcript of New Orleans Mayor Landrieu's Address on Confederate Monuments," Pulse, 19 May 2017, http://pulsegulfcoast.com/2017/05/transcript-of-new-orleans-mayor-landrieus-address-on-confederate-monuments.

20. Mike Signer, "Mike's Statement on Charlottesville's Confederate Statues," website of Mike Signer, 18 April 2017, http://www.mikesigner.com/news-events/2017/4/18/mikes-statement-on-charlottesvilles-confederate-statues.

21. W. Fitzhugh Brundage, "I've Studied the History of Confederate Memorials: Here's What to Do About Them," Vox, 18 August 2017, https://www.vox.com/the-big-idea/2017/8/18/16165160/confederate-monuments-history-charlottesville-white-supremacy; Joe Sterling and Ralph Ellis, "Charlottesville Mayor: I Changed My Mind about Confederate Monuments," CNN, 20 August 2017, http://www.cnn.com/2017/08/18/us/charlottesville-mayor/index.html.

22. The National Trust for Historic Preservation's Preservation Leadership Forum has assembled tool kits and offered examples for ways to address Confederate monuments

through community-based discussion and education. See Stephanie Meeks, "After Charlottesville: How to Approach Confederate Memorials in Your Community," Preservation Leadership Forum, 21 August 2017, http://forum.savingplaces.org/blogs /stephanie-k-meeks/2017/08/21/after-charlottesville-how-to-approach-confederate -memorials-in-your-community. See also *Whose Heritage?*

23. Ari Kelman examined the contentious process of memorializing the 1864 massacre of Cheyennes and Arapahos perpetrated by the U.S. Army (who are typically depicted as heroes in a war to destroy slavery); non-Indians, historians, National Park Service (NPS) employees, and Cheyenne and Arapaho descendant communities struggled to find agreement on the meaning and location of the Sand Creek Massacre National Historic Site. The process revealed the depth of mutual distrust between academic and traditional Native American ways of knowing the past. The site opened to the public in 2007, but the NPS has yet to determine an interpretive plan. Kelman, *Misplaced Massacre*, 2–3, 274–79.

24. Doss, *Memorial Mania*, 59, 116.

25. Upton, *What Can and Can't*, vii.

26. Batten, "Myall Creek Memorial," 93.

27. Denson, *Monuments to Absence*, esp. 190–220.

28. Kelman, *Misplaced Massacre*, 279.

29. Borowsky, "Telling a Story."

30. Bitgood and Shettel, "Overview of Visitors Studies," 6–10; Chang, "Interactive Experiences," 170–86; Batten, "Myall Creek Memorial," 82–96.

31. Savage, *Monument Wars*, 310; Savage, "Self-Made Monument."

32. Deloria, *Indians in Unexpected Places*.

33. The principal sources regarding these momentous times are Bradford and Winslow, *Mourt's Relation*; Wisecup, *Good News*; Bradford, *Of Plymouth Plantation*; and tribal histories. Besides tribal stories, only *Mourt's Relation* and *Of Plymouth Plantation* contain descriptions of what came to be called the first Thanksgiving, and only *Mourt's Relation* mentions Indians, indicating the arrival and presence of "King Massasoit, with some ninety men." This leaves a lot to the imagination, and though there is fairly broad agreement on details, various interpretations of these events are asserted.

34. Wisecup, *Good News*, 36–43; Salisbury, *Manitou and Providence*, 114–15; Humins, "Squanto and Massasoit," 56.

35. Wisecup, *Good News*, 146; Salisbury, *Manitou and Providence*, 115.

36. Wisecup, *Good News*, 38–48; Humins, "Squanto and Massasoit," 56–57.

37. Humins, "Squanto and Massasoit," 58.

38. Wisecup, *Good News*, 36–44; Humins, "Squanto and Massasoit," 58–70.

39. Bragdon, *Columbia Guide*, 49, 154; Wisecup, *Good News*, 19–32.

40. Pilgrim Hall Museum.

41. James Baker, *Thanksgiving*, 12–13, 64.

42. Baker, 64.

43. Baker, esp. introduction and chaps. 1 and 4.

44. Baker, 3–4, quote p. 13, and on the infantilizing of the holiday, see esp. chap. 7.

45. Baker, 4, 70–73, 152–53. Sarah Josepha Hale, who edited *Godey's Lady's Book*, campaigned for this national holiday fervently since 1837 and may have influenced Lincoln. Baker, 70–73.

46. Baker, 98–114, esp. 111–14.

47. Tahmahkera, *Tribal Television*, 49. Indians also made Thanksgiving appearances in, for example, *The Brady Bunch* (Tahmahkera, 18, 80–81), *Happy Days* (18, 87), *Everybody Loves Raymond* (18), and *Roseanne* (30).

48. Wisecup, *Good News*, 29–36.

49. Here is the full description of the "first Thanksgiving" from Bradford and Winslow, *Mourt's Relation*: "Our harvest being gotten in, our governor sent four men on fowling, that so we might after have a special manner rejoice together after we had gathered the fruit of our labors; they four in one day killed as much fowl, as with a little help beside, served the company almost a week, at which time amongst other recreations, we exercised our arms, many of the Indians coming amongst us, and among the rest their greatest King Massasoit, with some ninety men, whom for three days we entertained and feasted, and they went out and killed five deer, which they brought to the plantation and bestowed on our governor, and upon the captain, and others. And although it be not always so plentiful as it was at this time with us, yet by the goodness of God, we are so far from want that we often wish you partakers of our plenty." The Plymouth Colony Archive Project, accessed 29 July 2016, http://www.histarch.illinois.edu/plymouth/mourt6.html. And from Bradford, *Of Plymouth Plantation*: "They begane now to gather in the small harvest they had, and to fitte up their houses and dwellings against winter, being all well recovered in health & strengt, and had all things in good plenty; for as some were thus imployed in affairs abroad, others were excersised in fishing, aboute codd, & bass, & other fish, of which they tooke good store, of which every family had their portion. All the sommer ther was no wante. And now began to come in store of foule, as winter aproached, of which this place did abound when they came first (but afterward decreased by degrees). And besides water foule, ther was great store of wild Turkies, of which they tooke many, besids venison, &c. Besids they had aboute a peck a meale a weeke to a person, or now since harvest, Indean corne to that proportion. Which made many afterwards write so largly of their plenty hear to the freinds in England, which were not fained, but true reports."

50. Grace and Bruchac, *1621*, 32.

51. Gale Courey Toensing, "What Really Happened at the First Thanksgiving? The Wampanoag Side of the Tale," Indian Country Today, 23 November 2017, http://indiancountrytodaymedianetwork.com/2012/11/23/what-really-happened-first-thanksgiving-wampanoag-side-tale-and-whats-done-today-145807; Dunbar-Ortiz and Gilio-Whitaker, *"All the Real Indians,"* 36.

52. James Baker, *Thanksgiving*, xx, 108–11.

53. Baker, 75.

54. Converse, "Indian's Capacity to Advance," 16.

55. John Baker, introduction, xviii; "Improved Order of Red Men," Wikipedia, accessed 29 July 2016, https://en.wikipedia.org/wiki/Improved_Order_of_Red_Men; Deloria, *Playing Indian*, 62–68.

56. Weeks, *Massasoit of the Wampanoags*, ix.

57. *Record of the Great Council of the United States* 2 (1915): 24, RMML.

58. O'Brien, *Firsting and Lasting*, 62.

59. *News from Headquarters*, March 1915, 3, RMML.

60. Weeks, *Massasoit of the Wampanoags*, vii–xi.

61. *Record of the Great Council of the United States* 2 (1915): 24–25, RMML.

62. O'Brien, *Firsting and Lasting*, 72–84.

63. Seelye, *Memory's Nation*, 590. *Mayflower II* postcards are available at tourist shops

in Plymouth by Scenic Art, Inc., printing. The *Mayflower II* is currently undergoing restoration at Mystic Seaport in advance of the Plymouth 2020 commemorative activities. "Mayflower II Restoration," Mystic Seaport, accessed 29 January 2018, https://www .mysticseaport.org/category/mayflower-ii-restoration/.

64. Senie and Webster, *Critical Issues in Public Art*, xii–xiii.

65. Savage, *Monument Wars*, 2; Doss, *Memorial Mania*, 48; Bogart, *Public Sculpture*, 6.

66. Bogart, *Public Sculpture*, 4–5.

67. Bogart, 2.

68. *Whose Heritage?*

69. See Benjamin, "Work of Art." Beginning in 1919, critics, artists, and art societies took issue with the nation's expanding commercial art industry and discussed ways to halt the "plague of war memorials." Rather than the figurative statues like doughboys, critics recommended original artistic pieces that not only memorialized, but also encouraged the development of aesthetic appreciation in viewers. Wingate, "Over the Top," 27.

70. Wingate, *Sculpting Doughboys*, 4, 9; Wingate, "Over the Top," 27–28; Doss, *Memorial Mania*, 27.

71. Doss, *Memorial Mania*, 20.

72. Clark, "Indians on the Mantel," 26.

73. Oliver Knapp, *Chief Kisco*, 15–16.

74. The connection between Native Americans and classical art was well established by this time, evidenced by Benjamin West's purported 1760 comparison between a Mohawk warrior and the *Apollo Belvedere*. Clark, "Indians on the Mantel," 26.

75. Clark, 25–26.

76. Oliver Knapp, *Chief Kisco*, 7.

77. Bogart, *Public Sculpture*, 6–7.

78. Francis, *Cyrus E. Dallin*, 7, 27, 147, 150.

79. There is some discrepancy concerning the fourth statue in the cycle because, over time, *The Scout* came to replace *The Protest* in the minds of art critics. Buss, "Appealing to the Great Spirit," 147.

80. See Hutchinson, *Indian Craze*; and Doss, *Memorial Mania*.

81. Oliver Knapp, *Chief Kisco*, 19.

82. Most memorials to specific people would be commissioned and less likely to be commercially reproduced. Non-Indian men and women were primarily the subjects of named memorials, although Dallin produced a few exceptions. Gorham Manufacturing Company to Cyrus Dallin, 28 January 1920, AAA, roll 178; Francis, *Cyrus E. Dallin*, 51.

83. Oliver Knapp, *Chief Kisco*, 20–23, 26, 29; Kearin, "Many Lives of Chief Kisco"; Buss, "Appealing to the Great Spirit," 149. Kearin points out that the generic, mass-produced statue, also an example of "Indian play" by the IORM, was actually intended as temperance propaganda.

84. Buss, "Appealing to the Great Spirit," 163.

85. Savage, *Monument Wars*, 10–11; Kelman, *Misplaced Massacre*, 279.

86. Savage, *Monument Wars*, 11–12.

87. In Muncie, the embrace of *Appeal* does not show an attempt to ignore local history of Indian-settler conflict, but rather the braiding together of fact and fantasy in the context of national narratives of Native disappearance and settler righteousness. Buss, "Appealing to the Great Spirit," 143–67.

CHAPTER 1

1. The reason why the Paul Revere statue was denied final approval, despite its selection by a blind jury and Dallin's multiple redesigns, may be explained by professional jealousy just as much as by cultural elites' rejection of an outsider. Dallin's mentor, Truman H. Bartlett, was unhappy with Dallin's independence and the fact that his young charge chose to pursue a more lucrative opportunity. The city of Boston finally unveiled the Paul Revere statue in 1940; Dallin's struggle for approval of the statue spanned (and arguably defined) his entire professional career in Boston. See Francis, "Cyrus E. Dallin."

2. Shackel, *Myth, Memory*, 11.

3. Mae Huntington, "Dallin with the Indians," *Springville Herald*, 31 March 1938.

4. Speech transcript, "Madam Chairman and Ladies of the Plymouth Women's Club," AAA, Roll 179.

5. Hutchinson, *Indian Craze*, 31.

6. Speech transcript, "Madam Chairman and Ladies of the Plymouth Women's Club," AAA, Roll 179.

7. Sienkewicz, "Beyond the Mohawk Warrior," 5.

8. Cyrus Dallin, "'American Sculpture': A Sketch," undated manuscript, 3, AAA, Roll 179.

9. Dallin, 4, 6.

10. Dallin, 2.

11. Bederman, *Manliness and Civilization*, xi–xii, 7, 14.

12. Leek, "Circumspection of Ten Formulators," 79.

13. Johnson and Francis, *Frontier to Fame*, 28; Francis, *Cyrus E. Dallin*, 6–7.

14. Cyrus Dallin, "The Spirit of Life," Hoopes Scrapbook, CLDSCHL.

15. Johnson and Francis, *Frontier to Fame*, 61–62.

16. Mae Huntington, "Dallin with the Indians," *Springville Herald*, 31 March 1938; Ahrens, *Cyrus E. Dallin*, 42.

17. "Cyrus Dallin, Sculptor," *Arlington Advocate*, series c. 2, 11 June 1970, AAA, Roll 179.

18. F. N. Hollingsworth, "Cyrus E. Dallin—American Sculptor," *Goodwins Weekly*, ca. 1920, 14–15.

19. Undated, unsigned document, appears to be analysis of *Appeal to the Great Spirit*, AAA, Roll 179.

20. For example, at the unveiling of *The Medicine Man* in Philadelphia in 1901, Francis LeFlesch gave a lecture explaining the role of the medicine man in preserving tribal ceremonies and praised the "dignified bearing" of the figure in Dallin's sculptural rendition. Ahrens, *Cyrus E. Dallin*, 42; Mrs. Kirby Davidson, "Cyrus Dallin, Sculptor: The Medicine Man," *Arlington Advocate*, AAA, Roll 179.

21. Heather A. Shannon, "Prominent Americans: Photographs of Treaty Delegates at the Smithsonian," with Sky Campbell, *American Indian Magazine*, Summer/Fall 2014.

22. Hoxie, *Parading through History*, 118.

23. Houston, *Two Colorado Odysseys*, 66.

24. "Antimodernism," which emerged alongside Progressive reforms, is a term coined by T. Jackson Lears. Hutchinson, *Indian Craze*, 16, 31.

25. Hutchinson, 134.

26. Speech transcript, "Madam Chairman and Ladies of the Plymouth Women's Club," AAA, Roll 179.

27. See Perez, "Rough Trade"; and Perez, *Taste for Brown Bodies*.

28. Agnes Edwards, "A Daylight Sketch," source unknown [probably *Boston Herald*], August 1915, AAA, Roll 182. Agnes Edwards Rothery Platt was the author of several historical and literary books, including *The Old Coast Road: From Boston to Plymouth* (Cambridge, Mass.: Riverside Press, 1920).

29. Sargent, "Encounter on Cole's Hill," 401–3.

30. Sargent, 401; Bradford and Winslow, *Mourt's Relation*, 37–38.

31. Ahrens, *Cyrus E. Dallin*, 62n99. The first version of *Massasoit* (1914) was cast by Reed and Barton. "I wish to thank Nanepashemet, Director, Wampanoag Indian Program, Plimouth Plantation, who in his letter of January 14, 1993, pointed out the inaccuracies in the accessories of both versions of *Massasoit*. I also wish to thank Russell H. Gardner, Wampanoag Tribal Historian, for his information concerning the oral tradition that Dallin relied on descendants for models in order to assure the accurate physiognomy of Massasoit." See Weeks, *Massasoit of the Wampanoags*, x–xi; and Bittinger, *Story of the Pilgrim Tercentenary*, 116–20. "Plan Statue to Massasoit," AAA, Roll 182, indicates that "a diligent search was made for the most accurate description of Massasoit." Also see *Arlington Daily News*, 13 October 1931, AAA, Roll 184.

32. Francis, *Cyrus E. Dallin*, 55–56; Blount, "Black Male Nude."

33. Hatt, "'Making a Man of Him,'" 25, 28; Blount, "Black Male Nude," 45; Fairbrother, *John Singer Sargent*, 175.

34. Bederman, *Manliness and Civilization*, 15; Blount, "Black Male Nude," 3.

35. Johnson and Francis, *Frontier to Fame*, 61–62.

36. Sargent, "Encounter on Cole's Hill," 401–3.

37. Virginia Baker to J. W. Converse, *News from Headquarters*, July 1915, 2, RMML; Albert D. Barker, "Newly-Found Relics Held in N.Y. Museum as Massasoit's," *Boston Herald*, 9 December 1923; "An Empty Face at Burr's Hill," *Warren Times-Gazette*, 26 April 2017, http://eastbayri.com/stories/an-empty-face-at-burrs-hill,33w874?; Kopelson, *Faithful Bodies*, 67; Gibson, *Burr's Hill*. These items were included among those repatriated to the Wampanoag in spring 2017.

38. O'Brien, *Firsting and Lasting*, 9.

39. Sargent, "Encounter on Cole's Hill," 403.

40. Bruyneel, "Trouble with Amnesia," 251.

41. Alexander Gilmore, "Massasoit Memorial Association," *Record of the Great Council of the United States*, March 1917, 7, RMML.

42. *News from Headquarter*, June 1915, 2, RMML.

43. Alexander Gilmore, "A Momentous Question," *News from Headquarters*, October 1916, 7, RMML.

44. *News from Headquarters*, July 1915, 2, RMML; "Natives in Grave Controversy," NDN News, 19 September 2008.

45. *News from Headquarters*, February 1921, 4, and no. 6 (June 1921): 2, RMML.

46. The only expense borne by the state of Utah was the cost of transportation of the model from Boston to Salt Lake City. *Salt Lake Tribune*, 2 August 1922, AAA, Roll 179.

47. For discussions on unauthorized casting, see Sylvia Hochfield, "Flagrant Abuses, Pernicious Practices, and Counterfeit Sculpture Are Widespread," *ARTnews*, November 1974; and Day, "Sculpture Reproduction," 1. Day, an art researcher and expert in the administration, policies, and procedures of the BYU art collection and manager of the Fine Arts Collection for a time, was commissioned to write a report contextualizing

illegal sculpture reproduction to support the police investigation into BYU art dealings. For more on American public sculpture, bronze casting, and bronze statuettes of the American West, see the articles on the Metropolitan Museum of Art's website, compiled by Tolles. For example, "From Model to Monument: American Public Sculpture, 1865–1915," The Met, accessed 29 January 2018, https://www.metmuseum.org/toah/hd/modl/hd_modl.htm; and "American Bronze Casting," The Met, accessed 29 January 2018, https://www.metmuseum.org/toah/hd/abrc/hd_abrc.htm.

48. Day, "Sculpture Reproduction," 2.

49. Conner and Tolles, "Double Take," 156–61; Shapiro, *Bronze Casting*; Tolles, *American Sculpture*; Day, "Sculpture Reproduction," 9.

50. Hughes and Rannft, *Sculpture and Its Reproductions*, 3.

51. Day, "Sculpture Reproduction," 2.

52. Cyrus E. Dallin to Heber M. Wells, 12 May 1897, in Hunter, "Monument to Brigham Young," 337.

53. Francis, *Cyrus E. Dallin*, 160. The Capitol Commission had fielded artist bids for sculptures in the capitol for many years, and the plaster of *Signal of Peace* must have appeared as an opportunity for free art for the cash-strapped officials. William Spry to Mary Harriman, 20 August 1913; and Attorney General A. R. Barnes to Mary Harriman, 15 December 1916, CCC, Series 1132, Roll 1. Meanwhile, Dallin sent the governor photographs of the model for a proposed statue of Washakie that he fervently hoped the state would commission for the capitol. State officials responded that the funds were not available for such a commission. Cyrus E. Dallin to Governor William Spry, 16 February 1914; and J. M. Sjodahl to William Spry, 18 March 1914, CCC, Series 1132, Roll 1.

54. Francis, *Cyrus E. Dallin*, 160; *Deseret News*, 3 July 1937, reprinted in Alma Knapp, "History of Cyrus Edwin Dallin," 52.

55. Dallin reportedly recalled this story during a visit back to Utah in 1937. *Deseret News*, 3 July 1937, reprinted in Alma Knapp, "History of Cyrus Edwin Dallin," 52; "Famed Sculptor, Native of Utah, to Attend Unveiling," newspaper clipping in Hoopes Scrapbook, CLDSCHL. The Utah State Archives reported this event: "Friday May 17, 1918: Mr. C. E. Dallin willfully with malice did break the leg from off the Signal of Peace. Repairs made by J. H. Cook, Custodian of Capitol." CCC, Series 11272.

56. A number of years later, the replica was sent to a tourist destination called Pioneer Village in Salt Lake City, where it no longer stands. Francis, *Cyrus E. Dallin*, 161; *Salt Lake Tribune*, 1 August 1922.

57. Francis, *Cyrus E. Dallin*, 161–62. See sales contract dated 23 December 1912, AAA, Roll 178.

58. Brown-Robertson Co., Inc., to Cyrus Dallin, 22 January 1929; Morris and Bendien, Inc., to Cyrus Dallin, 23 January 1929; Release Agreement, 23 November 1927; and District Court of the United States Southern District of New York, In Equity 30–204, *Cyrus Dallin v. John Drescher Company*, notarized 14 October 1924, all in AAA, Roll 179.

59. The statue was displayed in the Gems of the BYU Art Collection section in the B. F. Larsen Gallery of the Harris Fine Arts Center. "Massasoit Goes On Display at 'Y,'" *Salt Lake Tribune*, 31 October 1968. There is no clear trail of ownership or record of transfer of the statue to BYU. Utah state researcher Terry Ellis informed an investigator that the date of transfer was October 1968. Terry Ellis to Wes Sherwood, 27 July 1988, MF.

60. Day, "Misfeasance, Malfeasance and Theft," 4.

61. Day, "Sculpture Reproduction," 35–36.

62. Lemmon interview by Ron Deane, 12 November 1986, MEFMCF.

63. Day, "Sculpture Reproduction," 35–36.

64. Day, 35.

65. Day, 25–26.

66. Day, 41–42.

67. Day, 31–32. See "Losses at Brigham Young University," and especially the featured report by Day, "Misfeasance, Malfeasance and Theft."

68. Day, "Sculpture Reproduction," appendix E, 86. The fraudulent claim of authenticity refers to the claim that the bronze was cast from an original plaster model in the university's collections, when in fact the university never owned or possessed the original. Day, 47–48. Duplicate numbers appeared on casts of the *Chief Washakie* reproduction, indicating the dealer or foundry placed the same edition number on more than one bronze (fraudulently reducing the number in the series inflates the value of each copy). Day, 47; and Lemmon interview.

69. The main actors were Forrest Fenn, Richard Young, Roy Anderson, and Wesley Burnside. Lemmon interview.

70. Forrest Fenn has published several books about his vast collections in Santa Fe. He has made a career of both dealing in Native American items and capturing public interest with his "treasure hunting" antics. See "Treasure-Hunting in the American West," *Economist*, 24 November 2016, http://www.economist.com/news/united-states/21710818 -valuable-hidden-treasure-draws-hopeful-hunters-out-west-treasure-hunting-american ?frsc=dg%7Cc; campus memorandum from Hal Visick to Wes Burnside, 28 July 1976, Art Acquisition Committee Meeting Minutes, 17 September 1976, MF; BYUPIS; and MIF. Arnold Lemmon described Roy Anderson as "a major crook." Lemmon interview.

71. Lemmon interview.

72. In the 16 September 1976 committee meeting, members discussed how the value of each bronze would decrease if the posthumous series increased to more than six. Because of the existing bronzes in Plymouth and Salt Lake City, the committee members may have reasoned that four additional casts would be the limit. In the 21 October 1976 meeting, "questions were raised concerning the legality of the situation such as can we cast a bronze without permission from the estate and could we sell the bronze without permission. There is also the problem of exactly where and from whom we got the Massasoit and what is our claim on the piece." Since there is no title of ownership attached to the plaster statue in BYU's possession, the committee discussed possibility of claims through the Dallin estate. "As far as legal problems with the family, there is only one dissenter who feels he has rights but legally hasn't any claim on the estate." Art Acquisition Committee Meeting Minutes, 18 November 1976, MF.

73. Steven Flint Lowe to Peter Myer, 18 January 1977, Art Acquisition Committee Meeting Minutes, 24 February 1977, MF.

74. Arnold Lemmon surmised that Richard Young was part of the scheme, based on Young's involvement in reproducing other fraudulent "original" statues. Lemmon interview.

75. Clint Barber, "A Monumental Task," *Deseret News*, 2 March 1977. "Lost wax" is a traditional casting method. First, a rubber mold is made from the plaster model. The mold is covered with heatproof ceramic and filled with layers of wax to achieve the desired thickness. The wax is then flushed out and molten bronze is poured in. The bronze is retouched to recapture the detail of the original and oxidized to achieve the desired patina.

76. Arnold Lemmon and Wes Sherwood interview by Neil Hadlock, 8 April 1987, and interview by Richard Young, 24 June 1987, MEFMCF.

77. The newspaper described *Massasoit* in the Evergreen Plaza as one in an edition of five. *Southend Reporter,* 7 April 1977, 36.

78. Campus memorandum from Robert Marshall to Gene Bramhall, 30 December 1980, MF.

79. Seelye, *Memory's Nation,* 78; Horwitz, *Voyage Long and Strange,* 378.

80. Invoice from Young Fine Art Casting to Roy Anderson, 13 January 1981, for a "restoration Massasoit Bust" ($235). The invoice also included reproductions of Dallin's *Chief Washakie* and *The Medicine Man.* Delivery confirmation of "Chief Massasoit Head" to Forrest Fenn, 6 March 1981, MF; Lee Snarr interview by Arnold Lemmon, 15 August 1987, and Mark Maynes interview by Arnold Lemmon, 12 October 1987, MEFMCF.

81. Art Acquisition Committee Meeting Minutes, 19 March 1981, MF.

82. Invoice from Young Fine Art Casting to Roy Anderson, 5 November 1977, for one bronze cast of *Massasoit* ($17,500) with handwritten note, "new order of 3"; invoice from Young Fine Art Casting to Roy Anderson, 26 November 1976 [*sic*: 1977], for three bronze casts of *Massasoit* ($15,000 each); Richard Young to J. Clyff Allen, 17 May 1985; and campus memorandum from J. Clyff Allen to Hal Visick, 25 July 1985, all in MF. See also Art Acquisition Committee Meeting Minutes, 19 March 1981, MF.

83. Dynette Ivie, "Dilemma Besets Indian Sculpture," *Daily Universe,* 26 January 1978; and Steven Lowe to Hal Visick, 27 January 1978, MF. According to Arnold Lemmon, Ken Garff, the original buyer, loaned the statue to BYU but likely received the tax deduction. He then sold it to another buyer, who donated the statue when an investigation revealed that BYU did not have title to the statue. Lemmon interview. The owner donated the statue in the mid-1990s. Day, "Sculpture Reproduction," 53.

84. Art Acquisition Committee Meeting Minutes, 16 September 1976, 17 November 1977, MF.

85. Louis R. Colombo to Peter Myer, 29 December 1976, MF.

86. Art Acquisition Committee Meeting Minutes, 11 December 1980, MF.

87. Art Acquisition Committee Meeting Minutes, 16 September 1976, MF.

88. Miller Nichols recalled that he "found the statue from its owner in Santa Fe. . . . At that time the statue was in storage in Provo." Miller Nichols to Jeane Brashears, 29 November 1993; and Nichols to Forrest Fenn, 23 August 1977, MNC, Correspondence File, Box 28, Folder 23, Art Objects — Massasoit. Forrest Fenn makes a veiled reference to the tax-deduction scheme when negotiating the sale with Nichols: "There are other parties interested in the bronze, but I would much prefer you have it on public display." Fenn to Nichols, 9 September 1977; Nichols to Fenn, 11 October 1977; and Nichols to Frank Vaydick, 17 October 1977, MNC, Correspondence File, Box 28, Folder 23, Art Objects — Massasoit.

89. Walter Janes to Miller Nichols, 29 November 1977, MNC, Correspondence File, Box 28, Folder 23, Art Objects — Massasoit.

90. Invoice from Fenn Galleries, 27 March 1978; Nichols to Fenn, 30 November 1977; and Nichols to Roy Anderson, 9 October 1979, MNC, Correspondence File, Box 28, Folder 23, Art Objects — Massasoit. The appraisal from another Los Angeles dealer, Goldfield Galleries, was $135,000 in 1978. Miller Nichols to Edward Goldfield, October 9, 1979, MNC, Correspondence File, Box 28, Folder 23, Art Objects — Massasoit.

91. The city of Kansas City granted approval for the statue placement in spring 1979.

Patti Brown to Miller Nichols, 27 February 1979. MNC, Box 28, Folder 23, Art Objects–Massasoit. The 1979 appraisal from Forrest Fenn is replacement value (for insurance purposes), and the 1979 appraisal from Brand Galleries is fair market value (for IRS purposes). Roy Anderson to Miller Nichols, 16 November 1979; Miller Nichols to Edward Goldfield, 9 October 1979; and Forrest Fenn to Miller Nichols, 12 November 1979, MNC, Box 28, Folder 23, Art Objects—Massasoit.

92. In materials sent to Nichols from Forrest Fenn, handwritten notes on the catalog page for Dallin's *The Passing of the Buffalo* indicate that the original bronze was sold at auction by Sotheby's for $150,000. MNC, Correspondence File, Box 28, Folder 23, Art Objects—Massasoit.

93. Nichols added at the end of his letter to the Kansas City parks director: "As I have mentioned to you in the past, I do not want publicity concerning the dollar value of the contribution." Miller Nichols to Frank Vaydick, 16 January 1980, MNC, Correspondence File, Box 28, Folder 23, Art Objects—Massasoit.

94. Board of Parks and Recreation Commissioners, *Historic and Dedicatory Monuments*, 36.

95. The Kansas City Municipal Art Commission granted approval for the placement of the statue. Patti Brown to Miller Nichols, 27 February 1979; *Kansas City Times*, 9 May 1979, B2; and Nichols to Edward Goldfield, 9 October 1979, MNC, Correspondence File, Box 28, Folder 23, Art Objects—Massasoit.

96. Miller Nichols to Terry Dopson, 25 October 1994; and Terry Dopson to Miller Nichols, 25 January 1995, MNC, Box 28, Folder 23, Art Objects—Massasoit.

97. Terry Dopson to Miller Nichols, 25 January 1995, MNC, Box 28, Folder 23, Art Objects—Massasoit. For more on the installation, see O'Brien and Blee, "What Is a Monument."

98. Jeane Brashears to Miller Nichols, 23 November 1993; Vernon Cox to Miller Nichols, 14 June 1979; and Miller Nichols to Vernon Cox, 21 May 1979 [probably actually written 21 June 1979], MNC, Correspondence File, Box 28, Folder 23, Art Objects—Massasoit; interviews by Blee and O'Brien, Kansas City. The interviews we conducted were informal—we approached people viewing the statues and asked them questions—and thus we did not record the names of the interviewees.

99. Rubloff also acquired a number of Lincoln statues at the New York auction that drew on regional historical associations with which shoppers would have been familiar; Abraham Lincoln's name is prominent throughout Chicago, including in at least two memorial statues and the naming of Lincoln Park (where Dallin's original *Signal of Peace* now stands). Rubloff, who transformed the city of Chicago and its suburbs, saw little to be gained from preserving the built environment for the sake of commemoration. According to his 1986 obituary, "Rubloff once said that the only landmark in the entire State of Illinois worth saving was Abraham Lincoln's home in Springfield." Jack Houston and Stanley Ziemba, "Arthur Rubloff, 83, Colossus of Real Estate Development," *Chicago Tribune*, 25 May 1986, http://articles.chicagotribune.com/1986-05-25/news/8602070381_1 _magnificent-mile-redevelopment-north-lake-shore-drive/2; *Southend Reporter*, 7 April 1977, 6, https://www.newspapers.com/newspage/8538842/.

100. Rubloff reportedly expected to pay $10,000 for *The Passing of the Buffalo*, but the bidding reached $155,000. The city of Muncie acquired the statue in 1976 and installed it in front of the Balls Department Store—about a mile from an original lifetime cast of Dallin's *Appeal to the Great Spirit*. "Public Art and Sculpture," Muncie Visitors Bureau, 10

February 2016, http://www.visitmuncie.org/what-to-do/arts-and-culture/public-art -sculpture/.

101. Eleanor Page, "One Bronze Got Away, and So Did Bidding," *Chicago Tribune*, 22 November 1975, sec. 1, p. 19, http://archives.chicagotribune.com/1975/11/22/page/111 /article/one-bronze-got-away-and-so-did-bidding.

102. The four other Dallin bronzes added in 1977 were *Chief Washakie, Appeal to the Great Spirit, The Medicine Man*, and *Paul Revere. Southend Reporter*, 7 April 1977, 6, https:// www.newspapers.com/newspage/8538842/; *Southend Reporter*, 2 June 1977, 28, https:// www.newspapers.com/newspage/8554956/. *Chief Washakie* was listed in the police investigation as a piece that had been laundered through BYU.

103. *Chief Washakie* (Young Casting), *Appeal to the Great Spirit* (Wasatch Bronze and Young Casting), *Paul Revere* (Young Casting), and *The Medicine Man* (Wasatch Bronze) are all documented in university records as counterfeit bronzes used in the tax shelter program. Day, "Sculpture Reproduction," appendix E, 32, 86.

104. Day, "Sculpture Reproduction," 10–11.

105. Arthur Rubloff donated a 140-piece collection of bronze sculptures (which he said had been appraised at $4 million) to the Art Institute of Chicago in 1984 as part of the largest single gift in the institution's history. Rubloff, a museum trustee, reasoned that rather than keeping the collection to himself, "thousands and thousands will benefit" from his donation. Bonita Brodt, "Rubloff Reflects on Life of Giving," *Chicago Tribune*, 15 November 1984, secs. 2, 1, 4, http://archives.chicagotribune.com/1984/11/15/page/47 /article/rubloff-reflects-on-life-of-giving (article no longer available); "Real Estate Magnate Arthur Rubloff Has Donated $6 Million," UPI, 14 November 1984, http://www .upi.com/Archives/1984/11/14/Real-estate-magnate-Arthur-Rubloff-has-donated-6 -million/8206469256400/.

106. Ryckbosch telephone communication; Mahoney telephone conversation and emails.

107. Ahlers email; Kurtz emails.

108. Clipping attached to newspaper photo, *Spokane Chronicle*, 7 February 1978.

109. Dealers often did not include sales tax on pieces destined for display in another state (indeed, Fenn did not include sales tax on the sale to Miller Nichols); it was then up to the buyer to pay "use tax" when the piece was shipped to his or her state of residence. But if the artwork were to be loaned to a museum for a very short period, or to a museum in a low-tax state for a longer period, the use tax could be avoided altogether. The state of Washington did not begin to enforce the use tax provisions in earnest until 2004 and subpoenaed records only dating back to 1999. Regina Hacket, "State's Tax Collectors on Trail of Art Collectors," *Seattle Post-Intelligencer*, 14 December 2004, http://www.seattlepi .com/local/article/State-s-tax-collector-on-trail-of-art-collectors-1161974.php.

110. Graham Bowley and Patricia Cohen, "Buyers Find Tax Break on Art: Let It Hang Awhile in Oregon," *New York Times*, 12 April 2014, https://www.nytimes.com/2014/04/13 /business/buyers-find-tax-break-on-art-let-it-hang-awhile-in-portland.html?_r=0.

111. Davey email; Wahl email, 23 March 2017; Forrest Fenn to Miller Nichols, 29 April 1978, MNC, Box 28, Folder 23: Art Objects — Massasoit.

112. *Southend Reporter*, 7 April 1977, 36.

113. Campus memorandum from Robert Marshall to Gene Bramhall, 30 December 1980, MF.

114. Agreement between Robert Marshall and Vern Swanson, 11 September 1980,

BYUPIS; Art Acquisition Committee Meeting Minutes, 16 September 1976; 15 September 1977, MF.

115. Wright interview.

CHAPTER 2

1. DeLucia, *Memory Lands*, 3.

2. *News from Headquarters*, March 1915, 3, RMML.

3. Since 1921, additional monuments to the Pilgrim past include the *Mayflower* replica and increased interpretive signage concerning original homes of individual Pilgrims.

4. Frank R. Arnold, "An American Sculptor of Indians and Soldiers," *Young Woman's Journal* 30 (June 1919): 292–93, AAA, Roll 179.

5. William L. Stidger, "After Fifty-Three Years: Cyrus Dallin's 'Paul Revere' At Last Sees the Light of Day," *Herald the Independent Methodist Weekly* 115 (5 May 1937): 552–53, AAA, Roll 179.

6. See Temkin, "Freeze-Frame," quote p. 132.

7. Kammen quoted in Temkin, 133. (See Kammen, *Mystic Chords of Memory*, 220–21.)

8. The elements of the place 1) are clearly bounded from the surrounding environment and marked with specificity as to what happened there; 2) are carefully maintained for long periods of time; 3) involve a change of ownership, typically from private to public stewardship; 4) attract continued ceremonies, services, or pilgrimages; and 5) attract additional monuments and memorials. All elements can be identified in Pilgrim Memorial State Park on the Plymouth Harbor. Foote, *Shadowed Ground*, 9.

9. Temkin, "Freeze-Frame," 133.

10. We have been unable to determine the reason for the delay between the installation and the "official" dedication.

11. "Massasoit Unveiling," *Old Colony Memorial*, 9 September 1921, PPLVF, Massasoit.

12. *News from Headquarters*, April 1915, 4, RMML; "Converse," *Somerville City Directory* (Boston, Mass.: W. A. Greenough, 1889), 141.

13. *News from Headquarters*, April 1915, 4, RMML.

14. DeLucia, "Locating Kickemuit," 479–80; Cohen, *Networked Wilderness*, 65, 68. Virginia Baker was a published historian of Sowams and engaged in a debate with other scholars over the precise location of Sowams; others believed the Pokanoket village to be near present-day Warren of Mount Hope in Rhode Island. Hodge, "Handbook of American Indians," 275. See also Virginia Baker, *Sowams*.

15. *News from Headquarters*, April 1915, 4, RMML. According to the genealogy published by Zerviah Gould Mitchell in 1878, Mitchell lived in North Abington, Massachusetts, and could trace her lineage to Massasoit. Ebenezer W. Pierce, *Indian History*.

16. Simmons, "From Manifest Destiny," 133; "An Heir to King Philip, October, 1895," *Recollecting Nemasket* (blog), 12 September 2009, http://nemasket.blogspot.com/2009/09/heir-to-king-philip.html.

17. Weeks, *Massasoit of the Wampanoags*, 139–41.

18. O'Brien, *Firsting and Lasting*, 167.

19. Simmons, "From Manifest Destiny," 132; Page, "Descendant of Massasoit," 642, 644; image of original postcard (ca. 1906) in Biron, "Teweelema." See also "Teweelema," *Recollecting Nemasket* (blog), 13 September 2009, http://nemasket.blogspot.com/2009/09/teweeleema.html.

20. Charlotte reportedly admired her great-uncle, and she took his wife's name, Wootonekanuske, as her own. Biron, "Teweelema."

21. Albert Barker, "Newly-Found Relics Held in N.Y. Museum as Massasoit's," *Boston Sunday Herald*, 9 December 1923.

22. Simmons, "From Manifest Destiny," 134; Biron, "Teweelema."

23. Simmons, "From Manifest Destiny," 133.

24. "Massasoit Unveiling," *Old Colony Memorial*, 9 September 1921, PPLVF, Massasoit; George Emerson, "Unveiling of the Massasoit Memorial," *News from Headquarters*, October 1921, 3, RMML.

25. Albert Barker, "Newly-Found Relics Held in N.Y. Museum as Massasoit's," *Boston Sunday Herald*, 9 December 1923. Her memories, as reported to a journalist in 1923, stand in direct contradiction to an account by a local historian who claimed the opportunity to unveil the *Massasoit* memorial in 1921 was the highlight of Charlotte's life. Quoted from Gladys DeMaranville Vigers, *History of the Town of Lakeville, Massachusetts* (Lakeville, Mass.: Lakeville Historical Commission, 1983), 27, in Biron, "Teweelema."

26. "Massasoit Unveiling," *Old Colony Memorial*, 9 September 1921, PPLVF, Massasoit.

27. Albert Barker, "Newly-Found Relics Held in N.Y. Museum as Massasoit's," *Boston Sunday Herald*, 9 December 1923.

28. "Massasoit Unveiling," *Old Colony Memorial*, 9 September 1921, PPLVF, Massasoit; George Emerson, "Unveiling of the Massasoit Memorial," *News from Headquarters*, October 1921, 3, RMML.

29. Simmons, "From Manifest Destiny," 132. Jessie Little Doe Baird of the Wôpanâak Language Reclamation Program noted to us that the seventeenth-century leader's title (at the time of his death) was Muhsasôyut (Massasoit) and his proper name was Pâmôtakômut, rendered variously in the primary and secondary literature as Metacom, Metacomet, and Pometacomet. All are English-corrupted versions of the man's name, but Pometacomet is the closest proximate to the Wampanoag spelling. On the advice of Wampanoag language experts, we have chosen to use "Pometacomet" although it does not match the inscription on the monument erected to him in Plymouth in 1998 at the behest of the UAINE.

30. O'Brien, *Firsting and Lasting*, 160–62.

31. DeLucia, "Locating Kickemuit," 498. See also Simmons, "From Manifest Destiny."

32. Simmons, "From Manifest Destiny," 136; "Aged Indian Princess at Lakeville, Massachusetts, in Need," *News from Headquarters*, April 1927, 26, RMML. The Whitman, Massachusetts, chapter raised about $300 to be distributed to Charlotte in weekly installments. "Nunkatest Tribe No. 65 of Whitman, Mass., Provides for Descendant of Massasoit," *News from Headquarters*, June 1927, 15, RMML.

33. Schultz and Tougias, *King Philip's War*, 394n229.

34. Dubuque, "Fall River Indian Reservation," Internet Archive, 11 April 1907, https://archive.org/stream/fallriverindianroodubu/fallriverindianroodubu_djvu.txt.

35. Perry was apparently paid $2,000 in "poor relief" that would also have covered the expenses of moving. Dubuque, "Fall River Indian Reservation," Internet Archive, 11 April 1907, https://archive.org/stream/fallriverindianroodubu/fallriverindianroodubu_djvu.txt. The rejection of Fanny Perry's Indigenousness because she had received poor relief likely refers to the long-standing practice of Massachusetts to define Indians as not proper residents of any town, thus releasing towns from the responsibility and placing it with

the commonwealth (and defining them as extraneous to the social order). See O'Brien, *Dispossession by Degrees*.

36. For a contemporary Wampanoag perspective on this illegal seizure, see Moorehead, *Finding Balance*, 140–42.

37. "Redskin Revolt Rumbles in Claim for State Land," [likely the *Berkshire Eagle* from Pittsfield, Massachusetts], [1938?], photographic research file 3, "Massasoit," AAA, Roll 182.

38. George Brennan, "Pocasset Wampanoag Bridle at Perceived Land Grab," *Cape Cod Times*, 8 February 2010.

39. Horne, "Dallin's Gift," 508.

40. The number of Shoshone killed at the Bear River encampment ranges wildly from 100 to 400. The inconsistent numbers partially reflect the fact that some bodies were swept away in the river and were not included in official counts. For more on the massacre and its commemoration, see Barnes, "Struggle to Control the Past," 85–86; "In Remembrance of the Bear River Massacre," Lemhi-Shoshone, accessed 26 August 2016, http://www .lemhi-shoshone.com/bear-river-massacre.html; Schindler, "Bear River Massacre," 227–35; and "The Shoshones: At a Glance: Bear River Then and Now," We Shall Remain: Utah Indian Curriculum Project, 26 August 2016, http://utahindians.org/Curriculum/pdf /HSshoshone.pdf.

41. "Washakie and His Legacy," We Shall Remain: Utah Indian Curriculum Project, 26 August 2016, http://www.utahindians.org/Curriculum/pdf/7thshoshone.pdf.

42. Cyrus Dallin to William Spry, 16 February 1914, CCC, Series 2232, Roll 1.

43. Ted Conner, Scene Today, *Deseret News*, 27 August 1957, Vertical Files, USHS. Capitol correspondence records available today tell a slightly different story. Governor Spry forwarded Dallin's letter to Jeffrey Sjodahl, editor of the *Deseret News*, with a recommendation that the Utah State Peace Society purchase the statue on the state's behalf. Sjodahl responded that the organization had no funds to do so. Spry then brought the matter before the Capitol Commission, where it did not advance. In his response to Dallin, Spry ambiguously reported that while nothing was in the works for a commission, "the statue has not been dropped." Sjodahl to Spry, 18 March 1914; and Spry to Dallin, 4 April 1914, CCC, Series 1132, Roll 1.

44. Brothers J. Leo and Avard Fairbanks (painter and sculptor, respectively) were poised to receive the commission at the end of 1915. Avard and J. Leo Fairbanks quoted in J. Leo Fairbanks and Avard Fairbanks to William Spry, 4 August 1915, CCC, Series 1132, Roll 1.

45. Kammen, *Mystic Chords of Memory*, 301, 375, 396.

46. Alexander and Allen, *Mormons and Gentiles*, 174; " 'Massasoit' Original Is Presented to Utah," *Deseret News*, 22 March 1922, 8.

47. "Salt Laker Wins $3800 Contract for Statue Base," *Deseret News*, 29 November 1958, AAA, Roll 183. At some point this base was replaced with a more substantial structure.

48. "Sculptor Canes His Statue," *Idaho State Journal*, 18 May 1918, AAA, Roll 182; "Famed Sculptor, Native of Utah, to Attend Unveiling," newspaper clipping, ca. 25 July 1932, in Hoopes Scrapbook, CLDSCHL.

49. "Dallin's 'Massasoit' Is Unveiled by State with Impressive Ceremonies," *Deseret News*, 1 August 1922.

50. "Chief Massasoit Returns to the Utah State Capitol," *Utah State Capitol* (blog),

2 November 2009, http://utahcapitolvisitorservices.blogspot.com/2009/11/chief
-massasoit-returns-to-utah-state.html.

51. *Salt Lake Tribune*, 2 August 1922, AAA, Roll 179.

52. Horne, "Dallin's Gift," 509.

53. *Salt Lake Tribune*, 2 August 1922, AAA, Roll 179. In 2000, the state of Wyoming sent a statue of Washakie to the National Statuary Hall Collection in Washington, D.C.

54. "State Honors Utah Sculptor," *Ogden Standard-Examiner*, 4 August 1922.

55. "Pendentives and Cyclorama," Utah State Capitol, accessed 24 June 2016, https://utahstatecapitol.utah.gov/explore/capitol-art/pendentives-and-cyclorama; Gowens, "History," 13–14; Durham, *Desert between the Mountains*, 173; Reeve, *Religion*, 78; O'Neil and Layton, "Of Pride and Politics," 244–45.

56. George Emerson, "Unveiling of the Massasoit Memorial," *News from Headquarters*, October 1921, 3, RMML.

57. "Dedicate Statue," 15 September 1922, PPLVF, Massasoit.

58. Davis, *History of the Improved Order*, 408–9.

59. *News from Headquarters*, June 1921, 1, RMML.

60. *News from Headquarters*, April 1915, 4, RMML.

61. *News from Headquarters*, June 1921, 1, RMML.

62. "Dedicate Statue," 15 September 1922, 4, PPLVF, Massasoit.

63. "Dedicate Statue," 1.

64. "Dedicate Statue," 4.

65. "Dedicate Statue," 7.

66. Jerome K. Full, "Chief Massasoit Leaves Utah Capitol," *Salt Lake Tribune*, 6 July 1957. We could not confirm the inscription on this plaque. No photographs from the first installation show a plaque, yet this phrase appears repeatedly in newspaper coverage of the statue. We infer that "sachem" is an unfamiliar term because newspaper stories often described Massasoit as a "chieftain" or "Indian chief" for readers.

67. Culmsee, "Utah's Capitol."

68. Horne, "Dallin's Gift," 507–8.

69. Postcards addressed to Cyrus Dallin, "Near View of Capitol Dome and Massasoit," 28 March 1927, 25 May 1928, AAA, Roll 182.

70. Postcard produced by the Wasatch News Service. Date is illegible but the stamp is an eight-cent Eisenhower, in circulation 1971–74. Massasoit Vertical File, USHS.

71. *Salt Lake Tribune*, 1 February 1951, Massasoit Vertical File, USHS.

72. The sculptor who repaired the statue, Avard Fairbanks, surmised that the arm became detached "as much through vibration as through the decorations students hung upon it." Jack Goodman, "Plastic 'Surgeon' Splints Arm for Injured Capitol Brave," *Salt Lake Tribune*, 4 February 1953. See also *Salt Lake Tribune*, 1 February 1951, 6 February 1954, 2 February 1955, 1 February 1953; *Deseret News*, 2 February 1953; and *Deseret News*, 8 July 1957, B2, all in Massasoit Vertical File, USHS.

73. *Salt Lake Tribune*, 2 February 1953; and *Salt Lake Tribune*, 2 February 1955, Massasoit Vertical File, USHS.

74. Culmsee, "Utah's Capitol."

75. "In the Mail," *Salt Lake Tribune*, ca. 12 July 1948, Massasoit Vertical File, USHS. We assume, based on the stereotypes and tropes employed, that the letter writer was not Paiute. This letter writer echoed the quoted words of an "educated Ute" identified as Little-Eagle-with-Feathers-Missing Smith in a 1952 *Deseret News Magazine* story: "We

ought to picket that out-of-state party. He's unfair to local talent." Culmsee, "Utah's Capitol."

76. Quote attributed to Marguerite Sinclair of the Utah State Historical Society. "Notes on the Cuff Department," *Salt Lake Tribune*, 15 July 1948.

77. Culmsee, "Utah's Capitol."

78. Clarence Barker, "Great Sachem, He Likem Big Dome, No Makum Fuss," *Deseret News*, 7 January 1957; "Statues Sprint for Position in Rotunda of State Capitol," *Salt Lake Tribune*, 10 September 1957. For public outrage over the removal of the statue, as well as politicians' criticism of it, see Ted Connor, Scene Today, *Deseret News*, 25 February 1955, 10, 14 August 1957, Massasoit Vertical File, USHS.

79. "Chief Massasoit Leaves Utah Capitol," *Salt Lake Tribune*, 6 July 1957; "Capitol's Massasoit to be Cast in Bronze," *Deseret News*, 12 September 1956; "Statues Sprint for Position in Rotunda of State Capitol," *Salt Lake Tribune*, 10 September 1957.

80. "Massasoit Heads for New Camp," *Salt Lake Tribune*, 25 November 1958; "Statue of Massasoit Removed for Casting," *Deseret News*, 8 July 1957, B2; and "Chief Massasoit Leaves Utah Capitol," *Salt Lake Tribune*, 6 July 1957, Massasoit Vertical File, USHS.

81. Newell B. Turner, letter to the editor, *Salt Lake Tribune*, 18 August 1957. Also printed in Ted Conner, Scene Today, *Deseret News*, 17 August 1957; "The Public Forum," *Salt Lake Tribune*, 15 July 1957; and N. G. Morgan Sr., letter to the editor, *Deseret News*, 9 August 1957, all in Massasoit Vertical File, USHS.

82. Ted Conner, Scene Today, *Deseret News*, 15 February 1958. Examples of bigoted language and sentiment abound in Ted Conner, Scene Today. See 10 September, 19 December 1957, and 25 February 1958, Massasoit Vertical File, USHS.

83. Ted Conner, Scene Today, *Deseret News*, 20 February 1958, Massasoit Vertical File, USHS.

84. O'Neil and Layton, "Of Pride and Politics," 239; "Guide to the Scriptures: Lamanites," Church of Jesus Christ of Latter-Day Saints, accessed 28 August 2016, https://www.lds.org/scriptures/gs/lamanites?lang=eng.

85. Reeve, *Religion*, 66, 77.

86. David Rich Lewis, "Native Americans in Utah," Utah History Encyclopedia, accessed 23 June 2016, https://www.uen.org/utah_history_encyclopedia/n/NATIVE_AMERICANS.shtml; Ono, "Relocation and Employment," 28, 30, 33, 35.

87. Ted Conner, Scene Today, *Deseret News*, 11 September, 28 November 1957; and "Capitol Statuary," *Salt Lake Tribune*, 11 March 1958, Massasoit Vertical File, USHS.

88. "Salt Laker Wins $3,800 Contract for Statue Base," *Deseret News*, 11 November 1958; Clarence S. Barker, "State Sets Site for Massasoit South of Capitol," *Deseret News*, 16 June 1958; and "Massasoit Statue Lifted to New Base at Capitol," *Deseret News*, 9 January 1959, Massasoit Vertical File, USHS.

89. Editor, "Displaced Indian," *Salt Lake Tribune*, 26 August 1963.

90. "Massasoit Has Visitors—'Tribe' Not a War Party," *Deseret News*, 24 April 1965, B3. The Intermountain Indian School was a federally run boarding school serving mainly Navajo children from Arizona. It opened in 1950 and was changed to the Intermountain Inter-Tribal School in 1974. It closed in 1984. See "Outside the Homeland: The Intermountain Indian School," Box Elder Museum of Art, History, and Nature, accessed 22 June 2016, http://exhibits.boxeldermuseum.org/exhibits/show/intermountain-indian-school.

91. Worley, *J. C. Nichols*, 37.

92. Richard Longstreth quoted in Pearson and Pearson, *J. C. Nichols Chronicle*, 93.

93. In 1920 Nichols sent his architects to Spain, South America, and Mexico to collect ideas for building design. Worley, *J. C. Nichols*, 247–48; Worley, *Plaza, First and Always*, 43–45.

94. Janicke, *City of Art*, 25.

95. Worley, *J. C. Nichols*, 235; Worley, *Plaza, First and Always*, 73.

96. The *New York Times* reported that Miller Nichols was named the city's most influential businessman in a 1975 newspaper poll. Nichols exerted influence in politics and cultural institutions in the city. For example, the library at the University of Missouri at Kansas City is named after him, and he was deeply involved in other civic ventures. "Clone of History of Miller Nichols Library," University Libraries, 12 November 2011, http:// library.umkc.edu/about-history (article no longer available).

97. Nichols was familiar with Dallin's *The Scout* in Kansas City's Penn Park and may have known of the controversy over that statue's pedestal and staging. Miller Nichols to Forrest Fenn, 11 October 1977, MNC, Box 28, Folder 23, Art Objects—Massasoit.

98. "Nichols Donates Statue," *Kansas City Star*, 6 May 1979.

99. McFerrin email; Board of Parks and Recreation Commissioners, *Historic and Dedicatory Monuments*, 36.

100. Grinding stones, much like arrowheads, were collected by anthropologists and displayed as artifacts from another age, thus drawing on Americans' associations between Indians and outmoded technology. See, for example, the Overland Trail Museum, which displays items collected from along the trail connecting Kansas City to Denver and features grinding stones and arrowheads.

101. "Massasoit," The City of Fountains Foundation, 14 August 2016, http://www .kcfountains.com/single-post/2016/08/14/Massasoit.

102. Photocopied article included in folder with dedication ceremony photographs; see Ocko, "Chief Massasoit's Royal Family," 22–25.

103. Nichols to Fenn, 9 March 1979; and Fenn to Nichols, 29 March 1979, MNC, Box 28, Folder 23, Art Objects—Massasoit.

104. Nancy Sweeney to Miller Nichols, 20 April 1979; Robert Staples to Miller Nichols, "Thanksgiving" 1981; Miller Nichols to Robert Staples, 9 April 1982; and "Dedication Program," MNC, Box 28, Folder 23, Art Objects—Massasoit.

105. Bulletin released by Miller Nichols, 2 May 1979; and Miller Nichols to Scott Brown, 9 May 1979, MNC, Box 28, Folder 23, Art Objects—Massasoit.

106. Deloria, *Playing Indian*, 100; MNC, Box 28, Folder 23, Art Objects—Massasoit.

107. "Dedication Program," MNC, Box 28, Folder 23, Art Objects—Massasoit.

108. "Warbonnets," *Kansas City Times*, 29 March 1975, 12; postcards, Terapeak Online Sales Analytics, accessed 8 February 2018, https://www.terapeak.com/worth/warbonnet -indian-dancers-of-kansas-city-1971-unused-postcard/322010743180/ (site discontinued).

109. "Nichols Donates Statue," *Kansas City Star*, 6 May 1979.

110. MNC, Massasoit—JCN Art History. Woolf Brothers was an old and storied clothing store founded in Leavenworth after the Civil War. It moved to Kansas City in 1879 and closed its doors in 1992 due to changes in the industry. "Collection description," State Historical Society of Missouri Research Center, Kansas City, 16 November 2011, http://www.umkc.edu/whmckc/Collections/IKC0282.HTM (article no longer available).

111. C. DeClue, "What's Left Out," *Kansas City Star*, 27 July 1979. For more on the 1977 case *Mashpee Tribe v. New Seabury Corp. et al.*, see Campisi, *Mashpee Indians*.

112. Jeane Brashears to Miller Nichols, 23 November 1993; and Miller Nichols to Jeane Brashears, 29 November 1993, MNC, Box 28, Folder 23, Art Objects—Massasoit.

113. Mary Corwin to Miller Nichols, 4 December 1994, MNC, Box 28, Folder 23, Art Objects—Massasoit.

114. "Evergreen Plaza to be Torn Down for New Mall," *Chicago Tribune*, 19 March 2015, http://www.chicagotribune.com/suburbs/daily-southtown/news/ct-sta-evergreen-plaza-st-0319-20150319-story.html. The first enclosed mall in the country was built in Edina, Minnesota, in 1956. Phil Kadner, "A New Era as Historic Evergreen Plaza Is Demolished," *Chicago Tribune*, 6 October 2015, http://www.chicagotribune.com/suburbs/daily-southtown/opinion/ct-sta-kadner-evergreen-plaza-st-1007–20151006-story.html (article no longer available).

115. *Southend Reporter*, 7 April 1977, 6, https://www.newspapers.com/newspage/8538842.

116. Peso telephone communication.

117. Forrest Fenn reported to Nichols that one of five bronze copies of *Massasoit* had been shipped to a museum in Spokane. All that Fenn said of the transaction was, "It was given to them." Forrest Fenn to Miller Nichols, 29 April 1978, MNC, Box 28, Folder 23, Art Objects—Massasoit.

118. Wahl email, 24 March 2017.

119. Clipping attached to newspaper photo, *Spokane Chronicle*, 7 February 1978.

120. Davey email; Wheeler interview.

121. "Our History," Northwest Museum of Arts and Culture, accessed 26 March 2017, https://www.northwestmuseum.org/about/; Wahl email, 23 March 2017.

122. Art Acquisition Committee Meeting Minutes, 16 September 1976, 17 November 1977, MF.

123. Unnamed alum to Robert Kelshaw, 28 October 1982, MF.

124. Wright interview. One college sports blog from 2012 included a photograph of Massasoit wrapped in plastic for protection. See Kristin Bowser, "BYU Saran-Wraps Statues to Protect Them from Vandalism," The Spun, 11 September 2012, http://thespun.com/pac-12/utah/byu-saran-wraps-statues-to-protect-them-from-vandalism.

125. Christine Rappleye, "Those Mysterious Statues: A Campus Tour," *Daily Universe*, 24 October 1999, http://universe.byu.edu/1999/10/24/those-mysterious-statues-a-campus-tour/.

126. Serena Johnson, "The Indian Statue," *Daily Universe*, 17 December 2013, http://universe.byu.edu/2013/12/17/the-indian-statue11; "Dress Standards Campus Attire," Brigham Young University Student Honor Office, accessed 29 August 2016, http://www.byu.edu/student-honor-office/ces-honor-code/dress-and-grooming/campus-attire.

127. Jonathan Blackhurst, letter to the editor, *Daily Universe*, 15 October 1997, http://universe.byu.edu/1997/10/15/letter-to-the-editor-move-the-massasoit/.

128. Controversy about the appropriateness of Indian representation ripples out elsewhere as well, resulting in the moving of artwork. A heated debate erupted in 2013–17 in connection with the renovation of the Minnesota State Capitol that ultimately led to the relocation of two racist and stereotypical paintings offensive to Native people to less public locations and an uncertain future for several others. Moving the paintings came at

the behest of a subcommittee of experts that included two Native scholars empowered by the Preservation Commission to make recommendations to the Minnesota Historical Society (responsible for overseeing the collection of 148 artworks). The two paintings moved to a less public, third-floor location are *Father Hennepin Discovering St. Anthony* and *The Treaty of Traverse des Sioux*. Captions for the art and video clips outline the diverse perspectives around these controversial artworks. These emotional debates fit into the larger context of monuments to contested histories in the public. Briana Bierschbach, "The Restoration of the Minnesota Capitol Has Also Restored One of Its Original Purposes: To Showcase Art," MinnPost, 8 August 2017, https://www.minnpost.com /politics-policy/2017/08/restoration-minnesota-capitol-has-also-restored-one-its -original-purposes-sh. On the contours of the controversy, see Sheila Dickinson, "Battle Rages over Racist Paintings in the Minnesota State Capitol," City Pages, 9 December 2016, http://www.citypages.com/arts/battle-rages-over-racist-paintings-in-the-minnesota -state-capitol-8070152. For the paintings, see "Father Hennepin Discovering the Falls of St. Anthony," Minnesota State Capitol, accessed 4 January 2018, http://www.mnhs.org /capitol/learn/art/8960; and "The Treaty of Traverse des Sioux," Minnesota State Capitol, accessed 4 January 2018, http://www.mnhs.org/capitol/learn/art/8961.

129. "Restoration Project," Utah State Capitol, accessed 31 August 2016, https:// utahstatecapitol.utah.gov/explore/restoration-project.

130. "Massasoit Statue at the Utah State Capitol," *Utah State Capitol Visitor Services* (blog), 8 November 2009, http://utahcapitolvisitorservices.blogspot.com/2009/11 /massasoit-statue-at-utah-state-capitol.html.

131. Wheeler interview.

132. Rob Schmidt, "Stereotypical Massasoit Statue Returns," *Newspaper Rock* (blog), 5 November 2009, http://newspaperrock.bluecorncomics.com/2009/11/stereotypical -massasoit-statue-returns.htm.

133. Comments on Marc Haddock, "Statue of Indian Leader Returning to Capitol," *Deseret News*, 2 November 2009, http://www.deseretnews.com/user/comments /705341442/Statue-of-Indian-leader-returning-to-Capitol.html.

CHAPTER 3

1. Savage, *Monument Wars*; Benton-Short, "Politics."

2. Sturken, *Tourists of History*.

3. Basso, *Wisdom Sits in Places*.

4. The questions were intended to start conversations in addition to gathering qualitative data, so we deviated from the exact wording of the questions in some cases and followed up with questions in response to the answers we got. Most of our interviews lasted only a few minutes, though a few went on for some length. We made audio recordings of the willing respondents and transcribed the results. We collected interviews together in Kansas City and Plymouth; Blee conducted the Salt Lake City and Provo interviews on her own. After we located the Dayton statue, we asked Jessica Leslie Arnett to do follow-up research for us, including collecting interviews at the Dayton Art Institute.

5. Blee interviews, Salt Lake City.

6. Kirk Savage clarifies that not all monuments on the national mall inspire reflection and reckoning; the World War II monument is one notable exception. Savage, *Monument Wars*, 298–99.

7. Young, "Holocaust Memorials in America," 58.

8. Robert Schmidt, "Massasoit Statue in Utah," *Newspaper Rock* (blog), 1 December 2008, newspaperrock.bluecorncomics.com/2008/12/massasoit-statue-in-utah.html.

9. Blee interviews, Provo.

10. Cuch, *History*, xvii.

11. Rita Wright, director of the Springville Museum of Art and BYU alum, also mentioned it as a campus meeting point in Blee's 2014 interview with her.

12. Plaza Art Fair, accessed 9 September 2016, http://www.plazaartfair.com.

13. "International Works of Art," Country Club Plaza, accessed 9 September 2016, https://countryclubplaza.com/art-history/international-works-of-art.

14. Blee and O'Brien interviews, Kansas City.

15. Davey email.

16. "Building," The Dayton Art Institute, accessed 11 September 2016, http://www .daytonartinstitute.org/about-dai/history/building. Photos and video of the statue moved around the Great Hall and removed for a wedding are available at "Museum Rental," The Dayton Art Institute, accessed 22 March 2017, http://www.daytonartinstitute .org/about-dai/museum-rental; and "Weddings at the Dayton Art Institute," The Dayton Art Institute, accessed 22 March 2017, http://www.daytonartinstitute.org/weddingvideo /wedding-video. Arnett personal communication.

17. Arnett interviews, Dayton Art Institute.

18. Bruyneel, "Trouble with Amnesia," 249; DeLucia, *Memory Lands*.

19. "The Suppressed Speech of Wamsutta (Frank B.) James, Wampanoag: To Have Been Delivered at Plymouth, Massachusetts, 1970," United American Indians of New England, accessed 3 March 2016, http://www.uaine.org/suppressed_speech.htm.

20. Rubertone, "Engaging Monuments," 30.

21. "Agreement Between the Town of Plymouth and the United American Indians of New England," 3 March 2016, http://www.unaine.org/settext.htm.

22. Rubertone, "Engaging Monuments," 30, quoting Jill Lepore, *The Name of War: King Philip's War and the Origins of American Identity* (New York: Vintage, 1999).

23. Blee and O'Brien interviews, Plymouth.

24. Temkin, "Freeze-Frame," 132.

25. Pamphlet.

26. Fund-raising packet, courtesy of Richard Pickering.

27. "Who We Are," Plimoth Plantation, accessed 5 August 2016, http://www.plimoth .org/about/who-we-are.

28. Plimoth Plantation, accessed 1 September 2016, http://www.plimoth.org.

29. There are ways in which Plimoth Plantation is a signature post–World War II institution, though its interpretive stance has been revised quite a lot over the years. At that time, amateur archaeologist and Pilgrim aficionado Henry Hornblower II convinced his wealthy father, Ralph Hornblower, to donate $20,000 in preparation for creating a Pilgrim village. As the first director of education at Plimoth Plantation and expert on Plymouth history James Baker observed, the affirmation of national values came with victory in the war, and the Pilgrim story became a vehicle for espousing democratic values for international consumption to affirm U.S. international power. James Baker, *Thanksgiving*, 169.

30. Colonial Williamsburg was the brainchild of John D. Rockefeller Jr. Snow, *Performing the Pilgrims*, 24–25.

31. Quoted in James Baker, *Thanksgiving*, 168.

32. Baker, 169–70.

33. Snow, *Performing the Pilgrims*, 27–29; Baker, 5, 168. Located three miles down the coast from the original village next to the Eel River, the site of the English Village offers stunning views of Plymouth Harbor. The fifty-acre site came from the Hornblower family, who summered at Plymouth (but were neither from Plymouth nor Pilgrim descendants), and additional donations came in from those who claimed Pilgrim ancestors. The *Mayflower II* was removed to dry dock at Mystic Seaport in 2015 for a five-year restoration project, aimed for completion in time for Plymouth 400 in 2020. The *Mayflower II* is an important gateway for tourists to Plimoth Plantation, and its absence in Plymouth harbor has meant visitation to the plantation has taken a hit. *Annual Report*, a; Snow, *Performing the Pilgrims*, 29; James Baker, *Thanksgiving*, 5, 168. Currently, Plimoth Plantation includes the *Mayflower II* (1957), the English Village (1959), the Wampanoag Homesite (1973), the Hornblower Visitor Center (1987), the Craft Center (1992), the Maxwell and Nye Barns (1994), and the Plimoth Grist Mill (2014).

34. James Baker, *Thanksgiving*, 5 and throughout.

35. Snow, *Performing the Pilgrims*, 33–39, "working village," from p. 36.

36. Wampanoag leaders joined the plantation board of governors and offered advice on managing the program and remaking the Eel River Indian Summer Camp. James Baker, *Thanksgiving*, 6–7, 187–88.

37. Snow, *Performing the Pilgrims*, 98–101.

38. Snow, 214–15, 39–40. According to Richard Pickering, interpreters in the English Village have begun to transition to third person. Increasingly, visitors have become less comfortable posing questions to first-person interpreters and need to be actively engaged. Darius Coombs and Pickering interview.

39. Darius Coombs interview.

40. Darius Coombs and Pickering interview.

41. On the complex gender dynamics of emotional labor in public history and the role of the "creative autonomy" of interpreters at Historic Fort Snelling, see Tyson, *Wages of History*. On the emotional labor expended by women in law firms, see Jennifer L. Pierce, *Gender Trials*. On Native interpreters in living history museums, including visitors' insensitivity and the stereotypical notions they confront, see Peers, *Playing Ourselves*. On the public and private "faces" of Cherokee people in the tourism industry, see Beard-Moose, *Public Indians, Private Cherokees*. On the emotional toll of consultation around repatriation and preservation efforts of the Wampanoag, see Peters, "Consulting with the Bone Keepers."

42. "Wampanoag Homesite," Plimoth Plantation, accessed 5 August 2016, http://www.plimoth.org/what-see-do/wampanoag-homesite. The first issue of the magazine *Plimoth Life: Celebrating the Ways of the 17th Century* includes a boxed aside in an article on the Wampanoag Homesite, "Native Etiquette for the Homesite," with the instruction not to refer to their homes (*wetu* and nushweety8) as "huts." Coombs, "Ancient Technology."

43. Darius Coombs and Pickering interview.

44. Darius Coombs and Pickering interview.

45. Coombs, "Holistic History," 14.

46. "Record: Wampum Belt," 20.

47. "Celebrating 40 Years," 17–19.

48. "Celebrating 40 Years," 18.

49. *Annual Report*. Jean O'Brien participated in the conference.

50. Darius Coombs and Pickering interview.

51. *Annual Report*.

52. Darius Coombs interview.

53. Darius Coombs interview.

54. "Record: Wampum Belt," 20–21.

55. Goldstein, "Commemorating the Pilgrims."

56. "Celebrating 40 Years."

57. Darius Coombs and Pickering interview.

58. Coombs, "Holistic History," 14.

59. Coombs, 12.

60. Coombs, "Holistic History"; Darius Coombs interview.

61. Coombs, "Holistic History," 12.

62. Coombs, 13.

63. Coombs, 14.

64. "Plimoth Plantation."

65. "Plimoth Plantation."

66. "Plimoth Plantation."

67. "Plimoth Plantation."

68. "Plimoth Plantation."

69. The wording of this pitch brings to mind the opening of MTV's *The Real World*: "This is the true story of seven strangers, picked to live in a house, work together and have their lives taped, to find out what happens when people stop being polite and start getting real."

70. Colonial House, accessed 5 August 2016, http://www.pbs.org/wnet/colonialhouse/about.html.

71. *Colonial House*, episode 7.

72. "Behind the Scenes — The Training," Colonial House, accessed 5 May 2018, https://www.thirteen.org/wnet/colonialhouse/behind/training.html.

73. "Behind the Scenes — The Native American Story," Colonial House, accessed 5 May 2018, https://www.thirteen.org/wnet/colonialhouse/behind/native.html.

74. *Colonial House*, episode 7.

75. As of this writing, Perry was serving on the Aquinnah Tribal Council and was a senior cultural resource monitor with Aquinnah's Cultural and Historic Preservation Department and a former employee of the Wampanoag Indigenous Program at Plimoth Plantation.

76. Lodge, "Peopling *Colonial House*," 7.

77. "Colonial House," IMDb, accessed 8 September 2016, http://www.imdb.com/title/tt0403745/.

78. Compare this to the 361 viewers who collectively ranked *Frontier House* 8.6 out of 10, the 869 who ranked *Manor House* 8.5, or the 267 who gave *The 1900 House* an 8.1.

79. Brennan, "Setting the Scene," 1; Whalen, "Interview," 20.

80. Coombs, "Wampanoag Perspective," 26.

81. Coombs, 28.

82. Coombs, 28.

83. Coombs, 28.

84. Coombs, 25.

85. Coombs, 25.

CHAPTER 4

1. Sturken, *Tourists of History*, 12, 27.

2. For more on the construction of U.S. national innocence narratives, see Cothran, *Remembering the Modoc War*.

3. Khan, *Enlightening the World*, 160–62.

4. The committee intended to make 100,000 pocket pieces in the edition. *News from Headquarters*, July 1915, 3, RMML.

5. *News from Headquarters*, March 1915, 3, RMML.

6. *News from Headquarters*, March 1915, 3, RMML.

7. "Massasoit Memorial Committee, Reservation of Massachusetts, 1915," *Record of the Great Council of the United States*, Meeting Minutes (1915), 24–25, RMML.

8. Alexander Gilmore, "A Momentous Question," *News from Headquarters*, October 1916, 7, RMML.

9. Alexander Gilmore, "Massasoit Monument Fund," *News from Headquarters*, January 1916, 3, RMML.

10. "Massasoit Memorial Committee, Reservation of Massachusetts, 1915," *Record of the Great Council of the United States*, Meeting Minutes (1915), 24–25, RMML.

11. "Massasoit Monument," *Record of the Great Council of the United States*, Meeting Minutes (1916), 24, RMML.

12. Sturken, *Tourists of History*, 9, 12.

13. Sturken, 14–15.

14. Alexander Gilmore, "Massasoit Memorial Association," *Record of the Great Council of the United States*, March 1917, 7, RMML.

15. Alexander Gilmore, "Unveiling of the Massasoit Memorial," *News from Headquarters*, August 1921, 4, RMML.

16. Alexander Gilmore, "The Massasoit Memorial," *News from Headquarters*, June 1922, 4, RMML.

17. This agreement stipulated that Dallin deliver the statue, ready for unveiling, on or before 1 July 1921. "Memorandum of Agreement between the Massasoit Memorial Association, Incorporated, and Cyrus E. Dallin," 2 March 1921, AAA, Roll 178. Twenty days later, on 22 March 1921, the contract was revised. The wording of the "suitable" inscription on the bronze plate would now be determined by the Massasoit Memorial Association. Dallin was to supply the foundation for the boulder; if the Massasoit Memorial Association furnished the foundation, the payment to the artist would be reduced to $15,500. "Memorandum of Agreement between the Massasoit Memorial Association, Incorporated, and Cyrus E. Dallin," 22 March 1921, AAA, Roll 178. The Memorial Association raised enough money to purchase a concrete pedestal for the statue. *News from Headquarters*, March 1915, 3, RMML.

18. The stamp of the Gorham Manufacturing Company in Providence, Rhode Island, can be seen on *Massasoit*'s foot and on the Warren, Rhode Island, plaque.

19. Berenson, *Statue of Liberty*, 163–64.

20. Denson, *Monuments to Absence*, 78–81.

21. Denson, 81.

22. The timing of the tercentenary did not work as planned, but the Massachusetts Red Men nevertheless hosted an unveiling ceremony in 1921 and a separate Improved Order celebration the following year.

23. DeLucia, *Memory Lands*, 15–16. DeLucia cites the Edward Winslow passage we have drawn on here on that point.

24. Handsman, "Landscapes of Memory," 172–73; Rubertone, *Grave Undertakings*, 166–67; DeLucia, "Memory Frontier."

25. Coombs, "Wampanoag Foodways."

26. DeLucia, "Locating Kickemuit," quote p. 467.

27. Thoreau quoted in Seelye, *Memory's Nation*, 23, 78, 352; and Baker and Keith, *Plymouth through Time*, 3–4.

28. Seelye, *Memory's Nation*, 552.

29. Seelye, 446–48, 640; Briggs, *Picture Guide*, 8–9.

30. Handsman, "Landscapes of Memory," 178–80.

31. Handsman, 180; James Baker, *Images of America*, 49.

32. Quote from Brown, *Inventing New England*, 5. The guidebook was first published in the late 1870s and, by 1895, was sold for a quarter at the Pilgrim Bookstore. Handsman, "Landscapes of Memory," 182.

33. L. J. T. Biese, "The Pilgrim Tercentenary (1920)," report written for the Pilgrim Society, n.d., TPCP.

34. Seelye, *Memory's Nation*, 590; Briggs, *Picture Guide*, 9; James Baker, *Guide to Historic Plymouth*, 40.

35. Hebel, "Historical Bonding," 288.

36. In 1938, in the second "desecration" of the year, vandals covered the rock in bright red paint. "Vandalism Again Hits Plymouth Rock," *Norwalk Hour*, 9 May 1938. American Indian Movement activists also painted the rock red and buried it in 1970, suggesting a more political intent than the work of teenaged vandals. Doss, *Memorial Mania*, 361–62; Jacqueline Tempera, "Plymouth Rock Vandalized: Late-Night Intruders Paint 'LIES' on It," *Boston Globe*, 14 January 2014; Associated Press, "Vandals Put Swastika on Plymouth Rock," *Journal Times*, 14 August 1991. DeLucia notes that the William Turner Monument commemorating the battle at Turner's Falls in Massachusetts was emblazoned with "FREE LEONARD PELTIER" in October 1999. DeLucia, *Memory Lands*, 276.

37. Seelye, *Memory's Nation*, 631.

38. Seelye, *Memory's Nation*, 590; "Mayflower II" postcard available at tourist shops in Plymouth by Scenic Art, Inc., printing.

39. The Pilgrim Society organized the fund-raising efforts that successfully appealed to the town ($320,000), the state of Massachusetts ($275,000), and the federal government ($300,000). Handsman, "Landscapes of Memory," 183.

40. As David Glassberg noted of New England towns' self-consciously manufactured historical appearance, "These towns look much more colonial now than they did 150 years ago." Glassberg, *Sense of History*, 131.

41. Francis Holmes to Arthur Lord, 5 October 1920, TPCP; Seelye, *Memory's Nation*, 598.

42. Handsman, "Landscapes of Memory," 185; Hebel, "Historical Bonding," 282.

43. It is unclear whether "Chief Manabozho" was a Native performer, but his stage name was drawn from a larger pageant tradition. "Manabozho," one variant spelling of Nanobozho, a powerful and mischievous trickster figure in Anishinaabe stories, was the original title Henry Wadsworth Longfellow chose for the poem publishers retitled "The Song of Hiawatha," which in turn inspired the popular pageant performed by Ketegaunseebee Anishinaabe actors depicting "the vanishing Indian" trope. McNally, "Indian Passion Play," 105, 110; Bourgeois and Kidder, *Ojibwa Narratives*, 30–31; *Old*

Colony Memorial, 15 July, 9 September 1921, PPLVF, Massasoit; unsigned letter to Chief Manabozho, 23 September 1920, and Pawnee Bill to J. F. MacGrath, 4 August 1920, TPCP. Quote from Hebel, "Historical Bonding," 282.

44. Unsigned letter to Major G. W. Lillie, 9 August 1920, TPCP.

45. Arthur Lord to Francis Holmes, 21 September 1920; and L. J. T. Biese, "The Pilgrim Tercentenary (1920)," TPCP; Seelye, *Memory's Nation*, 594.

46. Goldstein, "Commemorating the Pilgrims," 25.

47. James Baker, *Thanksgiving*, 113. Baker points out that the other major Plymouth historical pageant of the time, Margaret M. Eager's *Old Plymouth Days and Ways* (1896–97), omitted Thanksgiving as well.

48. George Pierce Baker, "Electrical Facts"; Seelye, *Memory's Nation*, 597–98; Snow, *Performing the Pilgrims*, 17.

49. George Pierce Baker, "Electrical Facts." Quoted in Seelye, *Memory's Nation*, 600.

50. The Plymouth Electric Company building was the only exception to the demolition below Cole's Hill, and the Bradford Barnes fish dealership was all that remained from the 1921 Water Street razing. James Baker, *Guide to Historic Plymouth*, 50, 80; James Baker and Keith, *Plymouth through Time*, 45–46.

51. *News from Headquarters*, June 1921, 2, RMML.

52. George Emerson, "Unveiling of the Massasoit Memorial," *News from Headquarters*, October 1921, 3, RMML.

53. "Dedicate Statue," 15 September 1922, PPLVF, Massasoit.

54. Undated photocopy, photographic research file 3, "Massasoit," AAA, Roll 182.

55. Denson, *Monuments to Absence*, 69.

56. Pilgrim Hall Museum.

57. James Baker, *Historic Guide to Plymouth*, 67–68.

58. Pilgrim Hall Museum.

59. Thorsen and Dempsey, *One Small Candle*.

60. Peters interview; Paula Peters, "A lesser-known Atlantic Crossing," Plymouth 400, accessed 9 May 2018, http://plymouth400inc.org/lesser-known-atlantic-crossing; "'Our' Story: 400 Years of Wampanoag History," Plymouth 400, accessed 4 August 2016, https://www.plymouth400inc.org/OurStory. The exhibit is traveling rapidly through the region. The authors viewed the exhibit on display at the Weymouth Public Library in April 2017. DeLucia (*Memory Lands*, 273) notes that the tercentenary of the Deerfield Raid prompted a reimagining of that event and an alternative interpretation project.

61. "Exploring Thanksgiving History in Massachusetts," Plymouth 400, accessed 4 August 2016, http://www.plymouth400inc.org/exploring-thanksgiving-history-massachusetts.

62. The Plymouth 400 offices received no criticism about the exhibit, much to Peters's surprise. Peters interview.

63. Peters interview.

64. Peters interview.

65. "Excellent Wampanoag Exhibition," TripAdvisor, 8 April 2016, https://www.tripadvisor.com/ShowUserReviews-g41773-d102718-r362498350-Pilgrim_Hall_Museum-Plymouth_Massachusetts.html#CHECK_RATES_CONT.

66. Peters interview.

67. James Baker, *Guide to Historic Plymouth*, 34.

68. This is one of the targeted myths featured in Dunbar-Ortiz and Gilio-Whitaker, "*All the Real Indians*."

69. *Plymouth 2014–2015*. The 2016 marketing slogan for Plymouth was "History is just the beginning."

70. James Baker, *Thanksgiving*, 5.

71. "Calendar," Plimoth Plantation, accessed 5 August 2016, http://www.plimoth.org /calendar?trumbaEmbed=date%3D20161124.

72. Darius Coombs and Pickering interview.

73. The Town of Plymouth does not license tour guides, although Plymouth requires all persons who operate a business in Plymouth to procure a zoning application. Johnson email.

74. Victoria Bekiempis, "Should Tour Guides Be Licensed?," *Newsweek*, 27 November 2014, http://www.newsweek.com/should-tour-guides-be-licensed-286723. The city of Savannah responded by changing the tour guide registration process to eliminate the tour guide history test and other individual requirements. "Tour Guide Registration Process," Savannah, accessed 1 February 2018, http://www.savannahga.gov/index.aspx?NID=1493.

75. Jenney Museum, accessed 14 June 2017, http://www.jenneymuseum.org; Robert Knox, "Plimoth Plantation to Run Mill," *Boston Globe*, 30 December 2012, https://www .bostonglobe.com/metro/regionals/south/2012/12/30/plimoth-plantation-takes-over -running-jenney-grist-mill/tYX1YnAKacDjaePZOp4fSL/story.html.

76. The English asserted expansive claims to Indian lands based on the 1621 treaty they regarded as one of submission to them, including of the land. Jeremy Bangs follows this logic even while acknowledging Indians had different notions about land, asserting that "after the initial gift of land from Massasoit Osamequen, the policy of buying land started in 1633." Bangs, *Indian Deeds*, 5, 8–9, quote p. 15. In the first land document involving 8sâmeeqan that directly references land, he and his son pledge not to convey land without the permission of Plymouth. Bangs, 240.

77. Jenney Museum tour recording in the authors' possession.

78. One 2014 study surmised that about 10 percent of the reviews for hotels on the site were fake. Because the net gains from promotional reviewing are highest for independent businesses without brand recognition, the study concluded that smaller hotels had a higher incentive to fake more positive reviews. Mayzlin, Dover, and Chevalier, "Promotional Reviews," 2421–55; Judith A. Chevalier, "Can Online Reviews Be Trusted?," Yale Insights, 22 December 2014, http://insights.som.yale.edu/insights/can-online -reviews-be-trusted; David Meyer, "The FTC May Investigate TripAdvisor's Controversial Treatment of Negative Reviews," *Fortune*, 22 November 2017, http://fortune.com/2017/11 /22/tripadvisor-reviews-ftc/.

79. The only critique of the content of the tour (beyond one visitor who suspected a political agenda because of the Christian souvenirs sold in the museum gift shop) was that the guide did not ask *Mayflower* descendants on the tour about their own connections to historic sites. "Jenney Museum," TripAdvisor, http://www.tripadvisor.com/Attraction _Review-g41773-d208199-Reviews-or30-Jenney_Museum-Plymouth_Massachusetts .html#REVIEWS.

80. DeLucia (*Memory Lands*, 272, 313) notes the development of "critically informed walking tours" at Historic Deerfield in the context of shifting commemorative practices of the 1990s and 2000s as a form of "decolonizing cartography," and of "in-person

interpretive tours" that included sites associated with New England Indians sold into slavery on St. David's Island on Bermuda.

81. Jody Feinberg, "Tour Offers New Perspective on Plymouth's Past," *Patriot Ledger*, 24 June 2011, http://www.patriotledger.com/x2069921463/Tour-offers-new-perspective-on -Plymouth-s-past.

82. Handsman, "Landscapes of Memory," 169.

83. Turner, Native Plymouth Tour; Feinberg, "Tour Offers New Perspective."

84. Bruyneel, "Trouble with Amnesia," 251.

85. "Native Plymouth Tours," TripAdvisor, accessed 10 March 2016, http://www .tripadvisor.com/Attraction_Review-g41773-d2012842-Reviews-Native_Plymouth _Tours-Plymouth_Massachusetts.html.

86. Sturken, *Tourists of History*, 12.

87. Handsman, "Landscapes of Memory," 183.

88. The commemorative plates fired for tourists at the September 1921 *Massasoit* unveiling celebration depicted "the Indian and the Pilgrim clasping hands" and "the landing of the Pilgrims." George Emerson, "Unveiling of the Massasoit Memorial," *News from Headquarters*, October 1921, 3, RMML; photocopy of greeting card, undated (ca. 1920s–1930s), photographic research file 3, "Massasoit," AAA, Roll 182.

89. Handsman, "Landscapes of Memory," 183.

90. Riggs, *Ethnic Notions*. See a short film clip of *Ethnic Notions*, with Larry Levine interview, at "Ethnic Notions," California Newsreel, accessed 7 February 2018, http:// newsreel.org/video/ethnic-notions.

91. Sturken, *Tourists of History*, 12.

92. Olalquiaga, *Artificial Kingdom*, 74–76.

93. "Cyrus Edwin Dallin—Massasoit, Chief of the Wapanogas," Skinner, 11 September 2009, http://www.skinnerinc.com/auctions/2470/lots/436. The buyer's premium of 20 percent brought the actual price up to $7,700.

94. The piece was valued at $1,500–$2,500 and correctly labeled as a posthumous cast. It was identified from the previous auction by lot number and sale date. "1029: After Dallin, a Patinated Bronze 'Massasoit,'" Live Auctioneers, accessed 20 February 2016, John Moran Auctioneers auction, https://www.liveauctioneers.com/item/11806767_after-dallin-a -patinated-bronze-massasoit#.

95. "1029: After Dallin, a Patinated Bronze 'Massasoit,'" Live Auctioneers, accessed 20 February 2016, John Moran Auctioneers auction, https://www.liveauctioneers.com /item/11806767_after-dallin-a-patinated-bronze-massasoit#.

96. Gascoigne, in turn, gifted John F. Kennedy and British prime minister Harold Macmillan a porcelain figurine of a coral fish during their "Summit of Two" in 1961 to discuss the construction of the Berlin Wall. Kennedy chose his favored vacation spot as the location for a summit with the British prime minister. "Trip to Bermuda" photograph, accessed 20 February 2016, http://www.jfklibrary.org/Asset-Viewer/Archives/JFKWHP -1961-12-22-B.aspx (webpage no longer available).

97. "NCAI Video: Change the Mascot," National Congress of American Indians, 26 November 2013, http://www.ncai.org/news/articles/2013/11/26/ncai-video-change-the -mascot.

98. Ahrens, *Cyrus E. Dallin*, 25.

99. Denice Wheeler said that Dallin was not paid for the statue. Wheeler interview. The actual contract states: "Whereas the said Dallin has designed and owns the three foot four

inch model of the statuette 'Massasoit,' a copyright therefor having been duly issued to the said Dallin February 1, 1915. Entry: Class G, XXC, No. 48849. And whereas the said P. P. Caproni and Bro., Inc.; a corporation, desires to reproduce the same in plaster and to sell such reproductions; And whereas it has been agreed between the said Dallin and the said corporation, that the said corporation, its successors and assigns, shall have the license, right and authority to make reproductions in plaster of the above named three foot four inch statuette of 'Massasoit,' paying to the said Dallin, or his legal representatives, the sum of $5.50 as a royalty on each reproduction in plaster sold and furnishing to the said Dallin one plaster reproduction thereof free of charge; Whereas the said Dallin proposes to design a six foot size of the above named statuette of 'Massasoit'; And whereas the said P. P. Caproni and Bro., Inc., a corporation, desires to reproduce the same in plaster and to sell such reproductions; And whereas it has been agreed between the said Dallin and the said corporation, that the said corporation, its successors and assigns shall have the license, right and authority to make reproductions in plaster of the above named six foot size of the statue of 'Massasoit,' paying to the said Dallin, or his legal representatives, the sum of one hundred fifty dollars ($150) upon the delivery of the six foot model of the said statue, and thereafter the sum of $20. as a royalty for each plaster reproduction sold and furnishing to the said Dallin one plaster reproduction thereof free of charge." "Agreement between Cyrus E. Dallin and P. P. Caproni and Bro., Inc., February ___, 1915," AAA, Roll 178.

100. Caproni and Brother, *Caproni Casts*, 6.

101. Dallin's other Indian statues were much more popular among sellers. According to Gorham Manufacturing Company, the company sold many casts of *Appeal to the Great Spirit* and *The Scout*, but none of *Massasoit*. Dallin had received no royalties for the sale of *Massasoit* by 1920. Gorham Manufacturing Company to Cyrus Dallin, 28 January 1920, AAA, Roll 178.

102. The company founder died in 1928 and interest in plaster casts waned in the 1930s. Robert Shure, "The Stories and the People, Part 1: Caproni," Giust Gallery Blog, 8 August 2015, http://www.giustgallery.com/blogs/blog/55295747-the-stories-and-the-people -part-1-caproni; Caproni and Brother, *Catalogue of Reproductions*. Photocopy conveyed in George Gurner to Karin Goldstein, 5 February 1997, Pilgrim Hall Museum Archives, Plymouth.

103. "Cyrus Edwin Dallin (1861–1944): 'Massasoit,'" Christie's, lot notes, accessed 20 February 2016, http://www.christies.com/lotfinder/sculptures-statues-figures/cyrus -edwin-dallin-massasoit-5154319-details.aspx.

104. According to the Massasoit Memorial Association's accounting in September 1921, only one donation of twenty dollars or more was received from an individual. It is not clear whether this donor was sent an eleven-inch statue as part of the special offer. Alexander Gilmore, "The Massasoit Memorial," *News from Headquarters*, September 1921, 5, RMML.

105. Lintz email, 6 June 2016.

106. Wright interview. Denice Wheeler purchased one of these statues from the Springville Museum of Art in 1988; she recalled it was "expensive," at about $100. Wheeler interview.

107. World Folkfest, accessed 1 February 2018, http://www.worldfolkfest.dreamhosters .com.

108. The director was aware of individuals who endeavored to borrow the plaster original for reproductions (either for the market or public display), but she refused

to allow for additional casts because of the fragility of the original, problems with provenance, and her personal opinion that the museum store should not sell "those kinds of pieces" when the museum has the original Dallin work in its permanent collection. Wright interview.

109. "Lot 5: *Bronze Figure of Massasoit, Signed Dallin 20th C.*," invaluable, J. James Auctioneers and Appraisers auction, 8 November 2014, accessed 20 February 2016, http://www.invaluable.com/auction-lot/bronze-figure-of-massasoit,-signed-dallin-20th-c.-5-c-f6782fb289.

110. "Item 724. Massasoit Sculpture Signed Dallin," iCollector, Cowan's Auctions, Inc., 4 April 2009, accessed 20 February 2016, http://www.icollector.com/Massasoit-Sculpture-Signed-Dallin_i8477321; "275: 20th C. Cyrus Dallin Sculpture of Massasoit," Live Auctioneers, Kaminski Fine Art auction, February 2006, accessed 20 February 2016, https://www.liveauctioneers.com/item/1718139_20th-c-cyrus-dallin-sculpture-of-massasoit; "Lot 532: *After Cyrus Edwin Dallin, Bronze Massasoit Figure of Indian*," invaluable, Michaan's Auctions, 7 November 2015, http://www.invaluable.com/auction-lot/after-cyrus-edwin-dallin,-bronze-massasoit-figure-532-c-3504609a33 (not sold, estimated value $1,000–$1,500); Lot 2181, Michaan's Auctions, 10 December 2009 (not sold, estimated price $2,000–$3,000).

111. "Vintage Pure Bronze Statue Artwork," eBay, accessed 21 February 2016, http://www.ebay.com/itm/Vintage-Pure-bronze-statue-Artwork-by-Dallin-original-Rare-Massasoit-/161971912351?hash=item25b6473e9f:g:R5cAAOSwWTRWuAYZ (item no longer available).

112. Lintz email, 18 December 2014.

113. This statue was dated circa 1920 but is a copy of the statue in Plymouth rather than *Massasoit #1*. "Lot 77: *Cyrus Edwin Dallin (American 1861–1944)*," invaluable, Trinity International Auctions, 8 March 2014, accessed 20 February 2016, http://www.invaluable.com/auction-lot/cyrus-edwin-dallin-american-1861-1944-77-c-7664dbce79 (realized price $2,750); "Cyrus Edwin Dallin (American, 1861–1944): Massasoit, Chief of the Wapanogas," Skinner, accessed 20 February 2016, http://www.skinnerinc.com/auctions/2470/lots/436.

114. DeLucia, *Memory Lands*.

115. Stein, *Everybody's Autobiography*, 298; Galow, "Gertrude Stein's *Everybody's Autobiography*."

116. Sturken, *Tourists of History*, 22.

117. Sturken, 21–22, 25, quote p. 21.

118. "Dallin Museum Timeline," The Cyrus E. Dallin Art Museum, accessed 25 September 2016, http://dallin.org.

119. Dallin's descendants are also frustrated in their attempts to collect original and lifetime reproductions of the artist's work. Dallin's great-niece constantly stumbles upon poor-quality knock-offs at estate sales and auctions and on eBay. Wheeler interview.

120. The Mashpee Wampanoag Indian Museum features the 8sâmeeqan in its permanent display of past tribal leaders.

121. "Native Plymouth Tours," TripAdvisor, accessed 10 March 2016, http://www.tripadvisor.com/Attraction_Review-g41773-d2012842-Reviews-Native_Plymouth_Tours-Plymouth_Massachusetts.html.

122. "Epanow's Escape," Plymouth 400, accessed 5 May, 2018 http://www.plymouth400inc.org/epanow%E2%80%99s-escape.

123. Tyson, *Wages of History*.

124. The website bills as its signature events *Illuminate Thanksgiving 2021* and "*Our Story*," of which *Captured!* is the opening installment that "will travel regionally and expand each year leading up to 2020." "Signature Events," Plymouth 400, accessed 4 August 2016, http://www.plymouth400inc.org/signature-events.

EPILOGUE

1. Bruyneel, "Trouble with Amnesia," 236.

2. Katie Reilly, "Read President Obama's Speech at the Museum of African American History and Culture," *Time*, 24 September 2016, http://time.com/4506800/barack -obama-african-american-history-museum-transcript/.

3. Linda Coombs interview.

4. Linda Coombs interview.

5. Euan Kerr, "After Outcry, Sculpture Depicting Dakota Tragedy to Be Dismantled, Burned," MPR News, 1 June 2017, http://www.npr.org/2017/06/01/531081906/after -outcry-sculpture-depicting-dakota-tragedy-to-be-dismantled-burnedhttp://www.npr .org/2017/06/01/531081906/after-outcry-sculpture-depicting-dakota-tragedy-to-be -dismantled-burned.

6. Carolina A. Miranda, "Artist Sam Durant Was Pressured into Taking Down His 'Scaffold.' Why Doesn't He Feel Censored?" *Los Angeles Times*, 17 June 2017, http://www .latimes.com/entertainment/arts/la-et-cam-sam-durant-scaffold-interview-20170617 -htmlstory.html.

7. Sheila Dickinson, "'A Seed of Healing and Change': Native Americans Respond to Sam Durant's 'Scaffold'" *ARTNews*, 5 June, 2017, http://www.artnews.com/2017/06/05/a -seed-of-healing-and-change-native-americans-respond-to-sam-durants-scaffold/.

8. Carolina A. Miranda, "Artist Sam Durant Was Pressured into Taking Down His 'Scaffold.' Why Doesn't He Feel Censored?" *Los Angeles Times*, 17 June 2017, http://www .latimes.com/entertainment/arts/la-et-cam-sam-durant-scaffold-interview-20170617 -htmlstory.html.

9. Linda Coombs interview.

10. "'Our' Story: 400 Years of Wampanoag History," Plymouth 400, accessed 9 September 2017, http://www.plymouth400inc.org/OurStory.

11. Berlin, "Coming to Terms with Slavery," 6.

12. Jenny Jarvie, "New Orleans Removes a Statue of Confederate Gen. Robert E. Lee from Its Perch of 133 Years," *Los Angeles Times*, 19 May 2017, http://www.latimes.com /nation/la-na-new-orleans-general-lee-20170519-story.html.

13. Sheryl Gay Stolberg and Brian M. Rosenthal, "State of Emergency Declared in Charlottesville after Protests Turn Violent," *New York Times*, 12 August 2017; Hawes Spencer, "Constant Projectiles, and Sounds of Fists Pounding on Flesh," *New York Times*, 14 August 2017, A9.

14. Nicholas Fandos and Russell Goldman, "Baltimore Removes Confederate Statues; Mayor Cites Public Safety," *New York Times*, 16 August 2017; David A. Graham, "Arrests Begin Following Durham Confederate Statue Toppling," *Atlantic*, 15 August 2017; Lynn Bonner, "Why NC Gov. Roy Cooper Wants Confederate Statues Removed from State Grounds," *News and Observer*, 15 August 2017.

15. "Historians on the Confederate Monument Debate," American Historical

Association, accessed 6 September 2017, https://www.historians.org/news-and-advocacy/everything-has-a-history/historians-on-the-confederate-monument-debate. Quote from Jerome de Groot, "Monuments to the Past," *History Today*, 17 August 2017.

16. A poll conducted by NPR/PBS NewsHour found that 62 percent of adults agreed that statues honoring leaders of the Confederacy should *remain as a historical symbol*, while 27 percent agreed that statues should *be removed because they are offensive to some people*. Notably, the wording of the poll confused the distinction between history and memory and described the reason for removal as an offense felt by "some people." "Marist Poll," PBS NewsHour, accessed 28 January 2018, https://assets.documentcloud.org/documents/3933461/NPR-PBS NewsHour-Marist-Poll-Aug-17-2017.pdf; Campbell Robertson, Alan Blinder, and Richard Fausset, "In Monument Debate, Calls for an Overdue Reckoning on Race and Southern Identity," *New York Times*, 18 August 2017, https://www.nytimes.com/2017/08/18/us/confederate-monuments-southern-history.html?mwrsm=Facebook&_r=1.

17. Leah Donnella, "The Standing Rock Resistance Is Unprecedented (It's Also Centuries Old)," *Code Switch* (blog), NPR News, 22 November 2016 http://www.npr.org/sections/codeswitch/2016/11/22/502068751/the-standing-rock-resistance-is-unprecedented-it-s-also-centuries-old; Derek Hawkins, "Police Defend Use of Water Cannons on Dakota Access Protesters in Freezing Weather," *Washington Post*, 21 November 2016, https://www.washingtonpost.com/news/morning-mix/wp/2016/11/21/police-citing-ongoing-riot-use-water-cannons-on-dakota-access-protesters-in-freezing-weather/?utm_term=.1d24ab468501.

18. Bruyneel, "*Happy Days* of the White Settler Imaginary," 52.

19. Bruyneel, 53.

20. Kelman, *Misplaced Massacre*; Elliott, *Custerology*; Denson, *Monuments to Absence*. On the Potawatomi Trail of Death, see Potawatomi Trail of Death Association, accessed 19 September 2017, http://www.potawatomi-tda.org/; "Historic Highway Signs," Potawatomi Trail of Death Association, accessed 19 September 2017, http://www.potawatomi-tda.org/hwysigns/hwysigns.htm; and "Marshall County, Indiana," Potawatomi Trail of Death Association, accessed 19 September 2017, http://www.potawatomi-tda.org/indiana/chiefms.htm. Discomfort structures the memorialization of African slavery at places like Colonial Williamsburg and the Whitney Plantation in Louisiana, in lost cause narratives about the Civil War, and in civil rights monuments. See for example, Handler and Gable, *New History*; Seck, *Bouki Fait Gombo*; Upton, *What Can and Can't*; and Walkowitz and Knauer, *Contested Histories*.

21. Linda Coombs interview.

Bibliography

ARCHIVAL COLLECTIONS

Kansas City, Missouri
  State Historical Society of Kansas City / University of
      Missouri, Kansas City Archives
    Western Historical Manuscript Collection
      Miller Nichols Collection
Plymouth, Massachusetts
  Pilgrim Hall Museum Archives
    Tercentenary Planning Committee Papers
  Plymouth Public Library
    Vertical Files
Provo, Utah
  Brigham Young University Museum of Art Archives
    Massasoit File
      Art Acquisition Committee Meeting Minutes
        Massasoit Investigation File
  Arnold Lemmon Files
    Brigham Young University Police Investigation
        Summary, University Fine Arts Collection
    Massasoit Excerpts from Master Case File
Salt Lake City, Utah
  Church of Latter-Day Saints Church History Library
    Mary Isabelle Wilde Hoopes Scrapbook, MS 8312
  Utah State Historical Society
    Capitol Commission Correspondence
    Vertical Files
Waco, Texas
  Red Men Museum and Library
    News from Headquarters
    Record of the Great Council of the United States

Washington, D.C.
    Smithsonian Institution, Archives of American Art
        Cyrus E. Dallin Papers (Microfilm; finding aid: https://www.aaa
            .si.edu/collections/cyrus-edwin-dallin-papers-7307)

PUBLISHED PRIMARY SOURCES

Bradford, William. *Of Plymouth Plantation: The Pilgrims in America*. Edited and with an introduction by Harvey Wish. New York: Capricorn Books, 1962.

Bradford, William, and Edward Winslow. *Mourt's Relation or Journal of the Plantation at Plymouth: Early Encounters in North America*. Edited by Henry Martyn Dexter. Boston: J. K. Wiggin, 1865.

Wisecup, Kelly. *Good News from New England by Edward Winslow: A Scholarly Edition*. Amherst: University of Massachusetts Press, 2014.

INTERVIEWS AND CORRESPONDENCE

Ahlers, Julie. Email to Lisa Blee, 29 December 2016.

Arnett, Jessica Leslie. Personal communication with Jean O'Brien, 12 January 2017.

Coombs, Darius. Interview by Lisa Blee and Jean O'Brien. Honolulu, Hawai'i, 21 May 2016.

Coombs, Darius, and Richard Pickering. Interview by Lisa Blee and Jean O'Brien. Plimoth Plantation, Plymouth, Massachusetts, 29 April 2017.

Coombs, Linda. Interview by Lisa Blee and Jean O'Brien. Mashpee, Massachusetts, Public Library, 28 April 2017.

Davey, Jane, Collections Librarian, Northwest Museum of Arts and Culture. Email to Lisa Blee, 4 October 2011.

Interviews by Jessica Leslie Arnett. Dayton Art Institute, Dayton, Ohio, December 2016.

Interviews by Lisa Blee. Salt Lake City, Utah, 25 June 2014, and Provo, Utah, 26 June 2014.

Interviews by Lisa Blee and Jean O'Brien. Kansas City, Missouri, 7 June 2014, and Plymouth, Massachusetts, 13 and 14 September 2014.

Jenney Museum tour recording in the authors' possession. Plymouth, Massachusetts, 29 April 2017.

Johnson, Lisa, Administrative Assistant to the Plymouth Town Manager. Email to Lisa Blee, 11 December 2017.

Kurtz, Sally, Registrar at the Dayton Art Institute. Emails to Lisa Blee, 15 and 16 June 2016.

Lemmon, Arnold. Interview by Lisa Blee. Provo, Utah, 26 June 2014.

Lintz, David. Emails to Lisa Blee, 18 December 2014 and 6 June 2016.

Mahoney, Denise. Telephone conversation and emails with Lisa Blee, 17 February 2016.

McFerrin, Ann, Archivist, Kansas City Parks and Recreation. Email to Lisa Blee, 27 March 2017.

Peso, George. Telephone communication with Lisa Blee, 11 February 2016.

Peters, Paula. Interview by Lisa Blee and Jean O'Brien. Mashpee, Massachusetts, 28 April 2017.

Ryckbosch, Bart, Art Institute of Chicago. Telephone communication with Lisa Blee, 29 February 2016.

Turner, Tim. Native Plymouth Tour with Lisa Blee and Jean O'Brien, Plymouth, Massachusetts, 12 September 2014.

Wahl, Valerie, Museum Collection and Curator, Northwest Museum of Arts and Culture. Emails to Lisa Blee, 23 and 24 March 2017.

Wheeler, Denice. Interview by Lisa Blee. Evanston, Wyoming, 3 April 2015.

Wright, Rita. Interview by Lisa Blee. Springville Museum of Art, Springville, Utah, 26 June 2014.

VIDEOS

Colonial House. Episode 7. PBS Home Video. New York: Educational Broadcasting Corporation and Wall to Wall Television, Limited, 2004.

Riggs, Marlon, dir. *Ethnic Notions: A Brief History of Racial Stereotypes*. Oakland, Calif.: Signifyin', 1986. 56 min. Short film clip available on California Newsreel, newsreel.org.

One Small Candle. Pilgrim Hall Museum, written, produced, and directed by Karen Thorsen and Douglas K. Dempsey. Plymouth, Mass.: Pilgrim Hall Museum, 2009.

ONLINE NEWS SOURCES, NEWSPAPERS, MAGAZINES, AND NEWSLETTERS

ABC News
American Indian Magazine
ARTnews
Atlantic
Boston Globe
Boston Herald
Boston Sunday Herald
Cape Cod Times
capecodtoday: cape cod community news
Chicago Tribune
City Pages (Minneapolis, Minn.)
CNN
Daily Universe (Salt Lake City, Utah)
Deseret News (Salt Lake City, Utah)
Economist
Fortune
Goodwins Weekly
History Today
Idaho State Journal
Indian Country Today
Indianz
Journal Times (Racine, Wis.)
Kansas City Star
Kansas City Times
Los Angeles Times
Minneapolis Star Tribune

MinnPost
MPR News (Minnesota Public Radio)
NBC News
NDN News
News and Reporter
Newsweek
New York Post
New York Times
Norwalk (Conn.) Hour
Ogden (Utah) Standard-Examiner
Old Colony Memorial
Patriot Ledger (Quincy, Mass.)
Plimoth Life: Celebrative the Ways of the 17th Century
Portland (Maine) Press Herald
Pulse
Salt Lake Tribune
Seattle Post-Intelligencer
Southend Reporter (Chicago)
Spokane Chronicle
Springville (Utah) Herald
Time
Vox
Warren Times-Gazette (Bristol, R.I.)
Washington (D.C.) Examiner
Washington Post

The Affiliate: News about Smithsonian Affiliates. Washington, D.C.: Smithsonian Institution, 2014.

Ahrens, Kent. *Cyrus E. Dallin: His Small Bronzes and Plasters.* New York: Rockwell Museum, 1995.

Alexander, Thomas G., and James B. Allen. *Mormons and Gentiles: A History of Salt Lake City.* Boulder, Colo.: Pruett, 1984.

Annual Report. Plymouth, Mass.: Plimoth Plantation, 2015.

Baker, George Pierce. "Electrical Facts." In *The Pilgrim Spirit: Plymouth Tercentenary Pageant* (program). Boston: Marshall Jones, 1921.

―――. *The Pilgrim Spirit: Plymouth Tercentenary Pageant* (program). Boston: Marshall Jones, 1921.

Baker, James. *A Guide to Historic Plymouth.* Charleston, S.C.: History Press, 2008.

―――. *Images of America: Plymouth.* Charleston, S.C.: Arcadia, 2002.

―――. *Thanksgiving: The Biography of an American Holiday.* Lebanon: University of New Hampshire Press, 2009.

Baker, James, and Jonathan Keith. *Plymouth through Time.* London: Fonthill Media, 2013.

Baker, John. Introduction to *History of the Improved Order of Red Men and Degree of Pocahontas, 1765–1988,* by Robert E. Davis, xvii–xx. Waco, Tex.: Davis Brothers, 1990.

Baker, Virginia. *Massasoit's Town: Sowams in Pokanoket.* Original 1904 edition published in Warren, R.I. Reprinted with introduction and addenda by Edward Lodi. Middleborough, Mass.: Rock Village, 2016.

―――. *Sowams, The Home of Massasoit: Where Was It?* Boston: David Clapp and Sons, 1899.

Bangs, Jeremy. *Indian Deeds: Land Transactions in Plymouth Colony, 1620–1691.* Boston: New England Historical and Genealogical Society, 2002.

Barnes, John. "The Struggle to Control the Past: Commemoration, Memory, and the Bear River Massacre of 1863." *Public Historian* 30 (February 2008): 81–104.

Basso, Keith. *Wisdom Sits in Places: Landscape and Language among the Western Apache.* Albuquerque: University of New Mexico Press, 1996.

Batten, Bronwyn. "The Myall Creek Memorial: History, Identity, and Reconciliation." In *Places of Pain and Shame: Dealing with Difficult Heritage,* edited by William Logan and Keir Reeves, 82–96. New York: Routledge, 2009.

Beard-Moose, Christina Taylor. *Public Indians, Private Cherokees: Tourism and Tradition on Tribal Ground.* Tuscaloosa: University of Alabama Press, 2009.

Bederman, Gail. *Manliness and Civilization: A Cultural History of Gender and Race in the United States, 1880–1917.* Chicago: University of Chicago Press, 1995.

Benjamin, Walter. "The Work of Art in the Age of Mechanical Reproduction." In *Illuminations,* edited by Hannah Arendt and translated by Harry Zohn, 217–52. New York: Schocken Books, 1969.

Benton-Short, Lisa. "Politics, Public Space, and Memorials: The Brawl on the Mall." *Urban Geography* 27 (June 2006): 297–329.

Berenson, Edward. *The Statue of Liberty: A Transatlantic Story.* New Haven, Conn.: Yale University Press, 2012.

Bergstrom, Randolph. "Tough Telling." *Public Historian* 35, no. 3 (August 2013): 5–7.

Berlin, Ira. "Coming to Terms with Slavery in Twenty-First-Century America." In *Slavery and Public History: The Tough Stuff of American Memory*, edited by James Oliver Horton and Lois E. Horton, 1–18. Chapel Hill: University of North Carolina Press, 2006.

Bicknell, Thomas W., ed. *An Historical Address and Poem, Delivered at the Centennial Celebration of the Incorporation of the Town of Barrington, June 17, 1870, with an Historical Appendix*. Providence, R.I.: Providence Press, 1870.

Biron, Gerry. "Teweelema, Betty's Neck and Wampanoag Rye-Straw Basketry." *Historic Iroquois and Wabanaki Beadwork* (blog), 4 August 2013. http://iroquoisbeadwork.blogspot.com/2013/08/teweelema-bettys-neck-and-wampanoag-rye.html.

Bitgood, Stephen, and Harris H. Shettel. "An Overview of Visitors Studies." *Journal of Museum Education* 21, no. 3 (Fall 1996): 6–10.

Bittinger, Frederick W. *The Story of the Pilgrim Tercentenary Celebration at Plymouth in the Year 1921*. Plymouth, Mass.: Memorial Press, 1923.

Blight, David W. *Race and Reunion: The Civil War in American Memory*. Rev. ed. Cambridge, Mass.: Belknap Press, 2002.

Blount, Jennifer Lynn. "The Black Male Nude: A Study of John Singer Sargent's *Thomas McKeller Nude* within the Context of Nineteenth-Century Art and Culture." Master's thesis, University of Alabama, 2009.

Board of Parks and Recreation Commissioners. *Historic and Dedicatory Monuments in Kansas City*. Kansas City, Mo.: Kansas City Parks and Recreation Department, 1987.

Bogart, Michele H. *Public Sculpture and the Civic Ideal in New York City, 1890–1930*. Chicago: University of Chicago Press, 1989.

Borowsky, Larry. "Telling a Story in 100 Words: Effective Label Copy." Technical Leaflet #204. *History News* 62, no. 4 (2007): 1–8.

Bourgeois, Arthur, ed., and recorded with notes by Homer H. Kidder. *Ojibwa Narratives: Of Charles and Charlotte Kawbawgam and Jacques LePique, 1893–1895*. Marquette, Mich.: Marquette County Historical Society, 1994.

Bragdon, Kathleen J. *The Columbia Guide to American Indians of the Northeast*. New York: Columbia University Press, 2001.

Brennan, Nancy. "Setting the Scene for PBS's *Colonial House*." *Plimoth Life: Celebrating the Ways of the 17th Century* 3, no. 1 (2004): 1–3.

Briggs, Rose T., ed. *Picture Guide to Historic Plymouth*. Plymouth, Mass.: Pilgrim Society, 1963.

Brooks, Lisa. *Our Beloved Kin: A New History of King Philip's War*. New Haven, Conn.: Yale University Press, 2018.

Brown, Dona. *Inventing New England: Regional Tourism in the Nineteenth Century*. Washington, D.C.: Smithsonian Institution, 1995.

Brundage, W. Fitzhugh. *Where These Memories Grow: History, Memory, and Southern Identity*. Chapel Hill: University of North Carolina Press, 2000.

Bruyneel, Kevin. "*Happy Days* (of the White Settler Imaginary) Are Here Again." *Theory and Event* 20 (January 2017): 44–54.

———. "The Trouble with Amnesia: Collective Memory and Colonial Injustice in the United States." In *Political Creativity: Reconfiguring Institutional Order and Change*, edited by Gerald Berk, Dennis C. Galvan, and Victoria Hattam, 236–57. Philadelphia: University of Pennsylvania Press, 2013.

Buss, James. "Appealing to the Great Spirit." *Middle West Review* 2, no. 2 (Spring 2016): 143–67.

Campisi, Jack. *The Mashpee Indians: Tribe on Trial*. Syracuse, N.Y.: Syracuse University Press, 1991.

Caproni, P. P., and Brother. *Caproni Casts: American Indians and Other Sculptures by Cyrus Dallin*. Boston: P. P. Caproni and Brother, 1915.

———. *Catalogue of Reproductions of Sculpture Selected from the Masterpieces of the World*. Boston: P. P. Caproni and Brother, 1928.

"Celebrating 40 Years of the Wampanoag Indigenous Program: An Interview with Darius Coombs." *Plimoth Life: Celebrating the Ways of the 17th Century* 11, no. 1 (2012): 16–19.

Chang, EunJung. "Interactive Experiences and Contextual Learning in Museums." *Studies in Art Education* 47, no. 2 (Winter 2006): 170–86.

Clark, Carol. "Indians on the Mantel and in the Park." In *The American West in Bronze, 1850–1925*, edited by Thayer Tolles and Thomas Brent Smith, 24–55. New Haven, Conn.: Yale University Press, 2013.

Cohen, Matt. *The Networked Wilderness: Communicating in Early New England*. Minneapolis: University of Minnesota Press, 2010.

Conner, Janis, and Thayer Tolles. "Double Take: A Closer Look at American Bronze Sculpture." *Magazine Antiques* 170 (November 2006): 156–61.

Converse, John W. "The Indian's Capacity to Advance." *Quarterly Journal of the Society of American Indians* 3, no. 1 (January–March 1915): 16.

Coombs, Linda. "Ancient Technology: Building a Wampanoag Home of the 17th Century." *Plimoth Life: Celebrating the Ways of the 17th Century* 1, no. 1 (2002): 5–9.

———. "Holistic History: Including the Wampanoag." *Plimoth Life: Celebrating the Ways of the 17th Century* 1, no. 2 (2002): 12–16.

———. "Wampanoag Foodways in the 17th Century." *Plimoth Life* 4, no. 1 (2005): 13–19.

———. "A Wampanoag Perspective on *Colonial House*." *Plimoth Life: Celebrating the Ways of the 17th Century* 3, no. 1 (2004): 24–28.

Cothran, Boyd. *Remembering the Modoc War Redemptive Violence and the Making of American Innocence*. Chapel Hill: University of North Carolina Press, 2014.

Cuch, Forrest S., ed. *A History of Utah's American Indians*. Salt Lake City: Utah State Division of Indian Affairs and Utah State Division of History, 2003.

Culmsee, Carlton. "Utah's Capitol—A Foreign Indian's Tepee." *Deseret News Magazine*, 8 June 1952.

Davis, Robert E. *History of the Improved Order of Red Men and Degree of Pocahontas, 1765–1988*. Waco, Tex.: Davis Brothers, 1990.

Day, Virgie. "Misfeasance, Malfeasance and Theft Uncovered at Brigham Young University." *International Foundation for Art Research Reports* 9 (June 1988): 4.

———. "Sculpture Reproduction: A Chronicle of Dubious Practices at Brigham Young University." Unpublished manuscript, last modified 1997–98. Microsoft Word file.

Deloria, Philip J. *Indians in Unexpected Places*. Lawrence: University of Kansas Press, 2004.

———. *Playing Indian*. New Haven, Conn.: Yale University Press, 1999.

DeLucia, Christine M. "Locating Kickemuit: Springs, Stone Memorials, and Contested Placemaking in the Northeastern Borderlands." *Early American Studies: An Interdisciplinary Journal* 13, no. 2 (Spring 2015): 467–502.

———. "The Memory Frontier: Uncommon Pursuits of Past and Place in the Northeast after King Philip's War." *Journal of American History* 98 (March 2012): 975–97.

———. *Memory Lands: King Philip's War and the Place of Violence in the Northeast*. New Haven, Conn.: Yale University Press, 2018.

Denson, Andrew. *Monuments to Absence: Cherokee Removal and the Contest over Southern Memory*. Chapel Hill: University of North Carolina Press, 2017.

Doss, Erika. *Memorial Mania: Public Feeling in America*. Chicago: University of Chicago Press, 2010.

Dunbar-Ortiz, Roxanne, and Dina Gilio-Whitaker. *"All the Real Indians Died Off": And 20 Other Myths about Native Americans*. New York: Beacon, 2016.

Duncan, Carol B. "Aunt(y) Jemima in Spiritual Experience in Toronto: Spiritual Mother or Servile Woman?" *Small Axe* 5, no. 1 (March 2001): 97–122.

Durham, Michael S. *Desert between the Mountains: Mormons, Miners, Padres, Mountain Men, and the Opening of the Great Basin, 1772–1869*. Norman: University of Oklahoma Press, 1997.

Elliott, Michael A. *Custerology: The Enduring Legacy of the Indian Wars and George Armstrong Custer*. Chicago: University of Chicago Press, 2007.

Fairbrother, Trevor. *John Singer Sargent: The Sensualist*. Seattle: Seattle Art Museum, 2000.

Fessenden, Guy Mannering. *The History of Warren, R. I. from the Earliest Times with Particular Notices of Massasoit and his Family*. Providence, R.I.: H. H. Bron, 1845.

Foote, Kenneth. *Shadowed Ground: America's Landscapes of Violence and Tragedy*. Austin: University of Texas Press, 1997.

Francis, Rell G. "Cyrus E. Dallin and His Paul Revere Statue." *Utah Historical Quarterly* 44 (Winter 1976): 4–39.

———. *Cyrus E. Dallin, Let Justice Be Done*. Springville: Utah American Revolution Bicentennial Commission, 1976.

Frei, Cheryl Jimenez. "Towards Memory, Against Oblivion: A Comparative Perspective on Public Memory, Monuments, and Confronting a Painful Past in the United States and Argentina." In "Monuments, Memory, Politics, and Our Publics." Special virtual issue, *Public Historian*, September 2017. http://tph.ucpress.edu/content/special-virtual-issue-monuments-memory-politics-and-our-publics#_ftn46.

Fund-raising packet. Plymouth, Mass.: Plimoth Plantation Development Office, 2017.

Galow, Timothy W. "Gertrude Stein's *Everybody's Autobiography* and the Art of Contradictions." *Journal of Modern Literature* 32 (Fall 2008): 111–28.

Gibson, Susan G. *Burr's Hill: A 17th Century Wampanoag Burial Ground in Warren, RI*. Providence, R.I.: Haffenreffer Museum of Anthropology, Brown University, 1980.

Glassberg, David. *Sense of History: The Place of the Past in American Life*. Amherst: University of Massachusetts Press, 2001.

Goldstein, Karin. "Commemorating the Pilgrims in Plymouth Style." *Plimoth Life: Celebrating the Ways of the 17th Century* 10, no. 1 (2011): 22–25.

Gowens, Fred. "A History of Brigham Young's Indian Superintendency (1851–1857): Problems and Accomplishments." Master's thesis, Brigham Young University, 1963.

Grace, Catherine O'Neill, and Margaret M. Bruchac. *1621: A New Look at Thanksgiving*. With Plimoth Plantation. Washington, D.C.: National Geographic Society, 2001.

Handler, Richard, and Eric Gable. *The New History in an Old Museum*. Chapel Hill: University of North Carolina Press, 1997.

Handsman, Russell G. "Landscapes of Memory in Wampanoag Country." In *Archaeologies of Placemaking: Monuments, Memories, and Engagement in Native North America*, edited by Patricia E. Rubertone, 161–94. Walnut Creek, Calif.: Left Coast, 2008.

Hatt, Michael. "'Making a Man of Him': Masculinity and the Black Body in Mid-Nineteenth-Century American Sculpture." *Oxford Art Journal* 15, no. 1 (1992): 21–35.

Hebel, Udo J. "Historical Bonding with an Expiring Heritage: Revisiting the Plymouth Tercentenary Festivities of 1920–1921." In *Celebrating Ethnicity and Nation: American Festive Culture from the Revolution to the Early 20th Century*, edited by Jürgen Heideking, Geneviève Fabre, and Kai Dreisbach, 257–97. New York: Berghahn Books, 2011.

Hodge, Frederick Webb, ed. *Handbook of American Indians North of Mexico*. Part II. Bureau of American Ethnology Bulletin 30. Washington, D.C.: Smithsonian Institution, 1910.

Horne, Alice Merrill. "Dallin's Gift of Massasoit to Utah." *Relief Society Magazine* 9, no. 10 (October 1922): 505–9.

Horton, James Oliver, and Lois E. Horton, eds. *Slavery and Public History: The Tough Stuff of American Memory*. Chapel Hill: University of North Carolina Press, 2006.

Horwitz, Tony. *A Voyage Long and Strange: On the Trail of Vikings, Conquistadors, Lost Colonists, and Other Adventurers in Early America*. New York: Picador, 2008.

Houston, Robert B., Jr. *Two Colorado Odysseys: Chief Ouray Porter Nelson*. Bloomington, Ind.: iUniverse, 2005.

Hoxie, Frederick. *Parading through History: The Making of the Crow Nation in America, 1805–1935*. New York: Cambridge University Press, 1997.

Hughes, Anthony, and Erich Rannft, eds. *Sculpture and Its Reproductions*. London: Reaktion Books, 1997.

Humins, John H. "Squanto and Massasoit: A Struggle for Power." *New England Quarterly* 60 (March 1987): 54–70.

Hunter, J. Michael. "The Monument to Brigham Young and the Pioneers: One Hundred Years of Controversy." *Utah Historical Quarterly* 68, no. 4 (Fall 2000): 332–50.

Hutchinson, Elizabeth. *The Indian Craze: Primitivism, Modernism, and Transculturation in American Art, 1890–1915*. Durham, N.C.: Duke University Press, 2009.

Irwin-Zarecka, Iwona. *Frames of Remembrance: The Dynamics of Collective Memory*. New Brunswick, N.J.: Transaction, 1994.

Janicke, Tim J. *City of Art: Kansas City's Public Art*. Kansas City, Mo.: Kansas City Star Books, 2001.

Johnson, Wendell, and Rell Francis. *Frontier to Fame: Cyrus E. Dallin, Sculptor*. Self-published, 2005.

Kammen, Michael G. *Mystic Chords of Memory: The Transformation of Tradition in American Culture*. New York: Knopf, 1991.

Kearin, Madeline Borque. "The Many Lives of Chief Kisco: Strategies of Solidarity and Division in the Mythology of an American Monument." *Public Historian* 39 (August 2017): 40–61.

Kelman, Ari. *A Misplaced Massacre: Struggling over the Memory of Sand Creek*. Cambridge, Mass.: Harvard University Press, 2013.

Khan, Yasmin Sabina. *Enlightening the World: The Creation of the Statue of Liberty*. Ithaca, N.Y.: Cornell University Press, 2010.

Knapp, Alma. "The History of Cyrus Edwin Dallin, Eminent Utah Sculptor." Master's thesis, University of Utah, 1948.

Knapp, Oliver. *Chief Kisco and His Brothers*. Mt. Kisco, N.Y.: Mt. Kisco Historical Committee, 1980.

Kopelson, Heather Miyano. *Faithful Bodies: Performing Religion and Race in the Puritan Atlantic*. New York: New York University Press, 2014.

Leek, Tom. "A Circumspection of Ten Formulators of Early Utah Art History." Master's thesis, Brigham Young University, 1961.

Lipman, Andrew. *The Saltwater Frontier: Indians and the Contest for the American Coast.* New Haven, Conn.: Yale University Press, 2015.

Lodge, Liz. "Peopling *Colonial House.*" *Plimoth Life: Celebrating the Ways of the 17th Century* 3, no. 2 (2004): 4–7.

Lowenthal, Constance, ed. "Losses at Brigham Young University." Special issue, *International Foundation for Art Research Reports* 9, no. 6 (June 1988).

Mayzlin, Dina, Yaniv Dover, and Judith Chevalier. "Promotional Reviews: An Empirical Investigation of Online Review Manipulation." *American Economic Review* 104 (August 2014): 2421–55.

McElya, Micki. *Clinging to Mammy: The Faithful Slave in Twentieth-Century America.* Cambridge, Mass.: Harvard University Press, 2007.

McNally, Michael D. "The Indian Passion Play: Contesting the Real Indian in Song of Hiawatha Pageants, 1901–1965." *American Quarterly* 58, no. 58 (March 2006): 105–36.

Moorehead, Deborah Spears. *Finding Balance: The Genealogy of Massasoit's People and the Oral and Written History of the Seaconke Pokanoket Wampanoag Tribal Nation.* Edited by Joanne Cadenazzi. Greenfield, Mass.: Blue Hand Books, 2014.

O'Brien, Jean M. *Dispossession by Degrees: Indian Land and Identity in Natick, Massachusetts, 1650–1790.* New York: Cambridge University Press, 1997.

————. *Firsting and Lasting: Writing Indians out of Existence in New England.* Minneapolis: University of Minnesota Press, 2010.

O'Brien, Jean M., and Lisa M. Blee. "What Is a Monument to Massasoit Doing in Kansas City? The Memory Work of Monuments and Place in Public Displays of History." In "Unexpected Ethnohistories: In, of, and out of Place." Special section, pt. 1, *Ethnohistory* 61, no. 4 (Fall 2014): 635–53.

Ocko, Stephanie. "Chief Massasoit's Royal Family." *Early American Life* 9 (April 1978): 22–25.

Olalquiaga, Celeste. *The Artificial Kingdom: A Treasury of the Kitsch Experience.* New York: Pantheon Books, 1998.

O'Neil, Floyd A., and Stanford J. Layton. "Of Pride and Politics: Brigham Young as Indian Superintendent." *Utah Historical Quarterly* 46, no. 3 (Summer 1978): 236–50.

Ono, Azusa. "The Relocation and Employment Assistance Programs, 1948–1970: Federal Indian Policy and the Early Development of the Denver Indian Community." *Indigenous Nations Studies Journal* 5 (Spring 2004): 27–50.

Page, Walter Gilman. "A Descendant of Massasoit." *New England Magazine* 9 (January 1891): 642–44. https://babel.hathitrust.org/cgi/pt?id=coo.31924079637496;view=1up ;seq=653.

Pamphlet. Plymouth, Mass.: Plimoth Plantation, with the support of the Massachusetts Cultural Council and Smithsonian Institution Affiliations Program, 2017.

Pearson, Robert, and Brad Pearson. *The J. C. Nichols Chronicle: The Authorized Story of the Man, His Company, and His Legacy, 1880–1994.* Lawrence: University Press of Kansas, 1994.

Peers, Laura. *Playing Ourselves: Interpreting Native Histories at Historical Reconstructions.* New York: AltaMira Press, 2007.

Perez, Hiram. "The Rough Trade of U.S. Imperialism." *Journal of Homosexuality* 59, no. 7 (2012): 1081–86.

————. *A Taste for Brown Bodies: Gay Modernity and Cosmopolitan Desire.* New York: New York University Press, 2015.

Peters, Ramona L. "Consulting with the Bone Keepers: NAGPRA Consultations and Archaeological Monitoring in the Wampanoag Territory." In *Cross-Cultural Collaboration: Native People and Archaeology in the Northeastern United States,* edited by Jordan E. Kerber, 32–43. Lincoln: University of Nebraska Press, 2006.

Phillips, Ruth B. "Settler Monuments, Indigenous Memory: Dis-membering and Re-membering Canadian Art History." In *Monuments and Memory, Made and Unmade,* edited by Robert S. Nelson and Margaret Olin, 281–303. Chicago: University of Chicago Press, 2003.

Pierce, Ebenezer W. *Indian History, Biography and Genealogy: Pertaining to the Good Sachem Massasoit of the Wampanoag Tribe, and His Descendants.* North Abington, Mass.: Zerviah G. Mitchell, 1878.

Pierce, Jennifer L. *Gender Trials: Emotional Lives in Contemporary Law Firms.* Berkeley: University of California Press, 1995.

Pilgrim Hall Museum. Accessed 1 August 2016. http://pilgrimhallmuseum.org/index.html.

"Plimoth Plantation." TripAdvisor. Accessed 5 August 2016. https://www.tripadvisor .com/Attraction_Review-g41773-d196785-Reviews-Plimoth_Plantation-Plymouth _Massachusetts.html.

Plymouth 2014–2015: Dining, Shopping & Activities Guide. Plymouth, Mass.: Destination Plymouth, 2014. https://www.seeplymouth.com/.

"Record: Wampum Belt." *Plimoth Life* 14, no. 1 (2016): 20–21.

Reeve, W. Paul. *Religion of a Different Color: Race and the Mormon Struggle for Whiteness.* New York: Oxford University Press, 2015.

Rubertone, Patricia E. "Engaging Monuments, Memories, and Archaeology." In *Archaeologies of Placemaking: Monuments, Memories, and Engagement in Native North America,* edited by Patricia Rubertone, 13–34. Walnut Creek, Calif.: Left Coast, 2008.

———. *Grave Undertakings: An Archaeology of Roger Williams and the Narragansett Indians.* Washington, D.C.: Smithsonian Institution Press, 2001.

Salisbury, Neal. *Manitou and Providence: Indians, Europeans, and the Making of New England, 1500–1643.* New York: Oxford University Press, 1982.

Sargent, Mark. "The Encounter on Cole's Hill: Cyrus Dallin's 'Massasoit' and 'Bradford.'" *Journal of American Studies* 27, no. 3 (1993): 399–408.

Savage, Kirk. *Monument Wars: Washington, D.C., the National Mall, and the Transformation of the Memorial Landscape.* Berkeley: University of California Press, 2011.

———. "The Self-Made Monument: George Washington and the Fight to Erect a National Memorial." In *Critical Issues in Public Art: Content, Context, and Controversy,* edited by Harriet F. Senie and Sally Webster, 5–32. New York: HarperCollins, 1992.

———. *Standing Soldiers, Kneeling Slaves: Race, War, and Monument in Nineteenth-Century America.* Princeton, N.J.: Princeton University Press, 1997.

Schindler, Harold. "The Bear River Massacre: New Historical Evidence." In *Civil War Saints,* edited by Kenneth L. Alford, 227–35. Provo, Utah: Deseret Book, 2012. https:// rsc.byu.edu/archived/civil-war-saints/bear-river-massacre-new-historical-evidence.

Schultz, Eric B., and Michael J. Tougias. *King Philip's War: The History and Legacy of America's Forgotten Conflict.* Woodstock, Vt.: Countryman, 2000.

Seck, Ibrahima. *Bouki Fait Gombo: A History of the Slave Community of Habitation Haydel (Whitney Plantation) Louisiana, 1750–1860.* New Orleans: University of New Orleans Press, 2014.

Seelye, John. *Memory's Nation: The Place of Plymouth Rock*. Chapel Hill: University of North Carolina Press, 2000.

Senie, Harriet F., and Sally Webster, eds. *Critical Issues in Public Art: Content, Context, and Controversy*. New York: HarperCollins, 1992.

Shackel, Paul A., ed. *Myth, Memory, and the Making of the American Landscape*. Gainesville: University Press of Florida, 2001.

Shapiro, Michael Edward. *Bronze Casting and American Sculpture, 1850–1900*. Newark: University of Delaware Press, 1985.

Shoemaker, Nancy. *Native American Whalemen and the World: Indigenous Encounters and the Contingency of Race*. Chapel Hill: University of North Carolina Press, 2015.

Sienkewicz, Julia. "Beyond the Mohawk Warrior: Reinterpreting Benjamin West's Evocations of American Indians." *Interdisciplinary Studies in the Long Nineteenth Century* 9 (November 2009). Accessed 7 February 2018. https://www.19.bbk.ac.uk /articles/10.16995/ntn.515/.

Simmons, William S. "From Manifest Destiny to the Melting Pot: The Life and Times of Charlotte Mitchell, Wampanoag." In *Anthropology, History, and American Indians: Essays in Honor of William Curtis Sturtevant*, edited by William L. Merrill and Ives Goddard, 131–38. Washington, D.C.: Smithsonian Institution Press, 2002.

Snow, Stephen Eddy. *Performing the Pilgrims: A Study of Ethnohistorical Role-Playing at Plimoth Plantation*. Oxford: University of Mississippi Press, 1993.

Somerville City Directory. Boston, Mass.: W. A. Greenough, 1889.

Stein, Gertrude. *Everybody's Autobiography*. New York: Vintage, 1937.

Sturken, Marita. *Tourists of History: Memory, Kitsch, and Consumerism from Oklahoma City to Ground Zero*. Durham, N.C.: Duke University Press, 2007.

Tahmahkera, Dustin. *Tribal Television: Viewing Native People in Sitcoms*. Chapel Hill: University of North Carolina Press, 2014.

Temkin, Martha. "Freeze-Frame, September 17, 1862: A Preservation Battle at Antietam National Battlefield Park." In *Myth, Memory, and the Making of the American Landscape*, edited by Paul A. Shackel, 123–40. Gainesville: University of Florida Press, 2001.

Tolles, Thayer, ed. *American Sculpture in the Metropolitan Museum of Art*. 2 vols. New York: Metropolitan Museum of Art, 1999–2000.

Tyson, Amy M. *The Wages of History: Emotional Labor on Public History's Front Lines*. Amherst: University of Massachusetts Press, 2013.

Upton, Dell. *What Can and Can't Be Said: Race, Uplift, and Monument Building in the Contemporary South*. New Haven, Conn.: Yale University Press, 2015.

Walkowitz, Daniel J., and Lisa Maya Knauer, eds. *Contested Histories in Public Space: Memory, Race, and Nation*. Durham, N.C.: Duke University Press, 2009.

Warren, Wendy. *New England Bound: Slavery and Colonization in Early America*. New York: Liveright, 2016.

Weeks, Alvin Gardner. *Massasoit of the Wampanoags*. Fall River, Mass.: Privately printed, 1919.

Whalen, Lisa. "Interview." *Plimoth Life: Celebrating the Ways of the 17th Century* 3, no. 1 (2004): 20–21.

Whose Heritage? Public Symbols of the Confederacy. Montgomery, Ala.: Southern Poverty Law Center, April 21, 2016. Accessed 12 September 2017. https://www.splcenter.org /sites/default/files/whoseheritage_splc.pdf.

Wingate, Jennifer. "Over the Top: The Doughboy in World War I Memorials and Visual Culture." *American Art* 19, no. 2 (Summer 2005): 26–47.

———. *Sculpting Doughboys: Memory, Gender, and Taste in America's World War Memorials.* New York: Ashgate, 2013.

Wolfe, Patrick. "Settler Colonialism and the Elimination of the Native." *Journal of Genocide Research* 8 (December 2006): 387–409.

Worley, William S. *J. C. Nichols and the Shaping of Kansas City: Innovation in Planned Residential Communities.* Columbia: University of Missouri Press, 1990.

———. *The Plaza, First and Always.* Lanham, Md.: Taylor Trade, 1997.

Young, James E. "Holocaust Memorials in America: Public Art as Process." *Critical Issues in Public Art: Content, Context, and Controversy,* edited by Harriet F. Senie and Sally Webster, 57–70. New York: HarperCollins, 1992.

Index